Self-Study Processes

Self-Study Processes

A Guide for Postsecondary Institutions
SECOND EDITION

H. R. Kells

A handbook
for participants in self-study processes
and for all types of postsecondary
institutions at the institutional and
program level

A basic reference
for administrators on processes and
uses of self-study in institutional and
specialized accreditation

A reader-manual
for workshops on self-study and
accreditation conducted for and by
institutional and agency professionals

AMERICAN COUNCIL ON EDUCATION • **MACMILLAN PUBLISHING COMPANY**
NEW YORK

Collier Macmillan Publishers
LONDON

Copyright © 1983 American Council on Education and
Macmillan Publishing Company

The American Council on Education/Macmillan Series in Higher Education

Macmillan Publishing Company
A Division of Macmillan, Inc.
866 Third Avenue, New York, N.Y. 10022

Collier Macmillan Canada, Inc.

Library of Congress Catalog Card Number: 83–15848

Printed in the United States of America

printing number
1   2   3   4   5   6   7   8   9   10

Library of Congress Cataloging in Publication Data

Kells, H. R.
    Self-study processes.

    (The American Council on Education/Macmillan series in
higher education)
    Includes bibliographies.
    1. Universities and colleges—United States—Evaluation.
2. Universities and colleges—United States—Accreditation.
I. Title. II. Series.
LB2331.63.K376   1983   379.1'58'0973   83–15848
ISBN 0-02-916520-2

Contents

PART TWO   Conducting Self-Study Processes

Chapter 4   Preparation and Design   *29*

Chapter 5   Organizing for Self-Study   *51*

Chapter 6   Mechanics of the Self-Study Process   *61*

List of Figures

List of Tables

Introduction

The potential benefits of self-study processes conducted by colleges, universities, other postsecondary institutions, and constituent programs are often unrealized. Almost three decades have passed since some accrediting agencies began to require that, as part of the accreditation process, institutions examine themselves thoroughly before an evaluation team visit would be made. Nonetheless, most self-study processes remain as burdensome, descriptive, mechanical efforts, largely unrelated both to the real problems and to the major successes and opportunities of the institution or program in question. In short, the self-study processes conducted in postsecondary institutions have been isolated from any ongoing management process. Although recent participants have reported that some improvements stem from self-study efforts—that they are useful exercises—the incorporation of continuous self-study as part of a cyclical, systematic pattern of study, planning, development, and restudy is rarely attempted. Self-study is not yet seen as a central process of ongoing improvement and change in most American institutions.

The genesis of this book spans an entire decade. In 1969, I read my first self-study document and visited an institution to discuss it and other matters as a member of an evaluation team for an institutional accrediting agency. The unrealized potential of the process excited and frustrated me. These mixed emotions have propelled me through a decade of campus consultation, agency staff work, university teaching, training workshops, and research to improve these processes. The book evolved primarily from my work in the 1970s with over 300 institutions as they attempted to study themselves. Representatives of almost two-thirds of these institutions have taken part in three-day intensive residential workshops that I designed and conducted in four different regions of the country using the materials presented in this book. The book took form as these workshops were developed.

My purpose in this book is to present a method for improving institutions and programs. The method involves carefully designed and sensitively conducted processes of self-assessment—processes that can be welded into the basic framework of the institution to have an ongoing impact. The institution's internalization of ongoing self-assessment and change is the goal.

Self-study processes and the other aspects of accreditation with which self-study is often associated can be useful and change-oriented rather than a waste of valuable time, energy, and funds. People can become excited about them and about the possibilities for their programs and their institutions. The processes can be regenerative to people and to institutions.

I have tried to make the book as *useful* as possible. It is not intended as a document to be read, shelved, and perhaps reread occasionally. It is a book to be used by people—toted to self-study meetings, written in, and stuffed into mailboxes. This second edition contains major additions—a chapter on departmental or programmatic self-study and new diagrams, appendixes, and services—which were suggested by users of the book on campus and by association and accrediting agency officials. I welcome others' assessment of its usefulness and seek constructive suggestions about how to make future editions more useful to working professionals.

The book was prepared with several general uses in mind. First, it is designed to be a handbook for institutions and departments that want to conduct self-study processes whether or not they are part of accreditation activities. Internally motivated self-assessment, particularly as part of an ongoing study and planning cycle, would be the ideal situation for use of the book; it tells members of a self-study steering group what they need to know.

This book is intended also as a reader for a director, dean, chairperson, president, or chancellor who must authorize, understand, and evaluate self-study processes. Accreditation is not the only context in question. State licensing activities, departmental or program reviews, long-range planning processes, and other similar activities all ought to begin with carefully designed and useful self-study processes. The principles put forth in this volume apply fully to such undertakings.

Furthermore, this volume should be quite useful in the ongoing work of an institution. The principles espoused in the design and procedure segments of the book can be readily translated to such other institutional processes as planning, budgeting, and problem solving. The sections in the book on methods of analysis should be useful to institutional research offices, for the development of institutional research capacities at postsecondary institutions is a goal of self-study and accreditation. This book also attempts to translate into the working vocabulary of college and university professionals some of the valuable insights of the pioneers in organizational development who have toiled to date primarily in industry and government. It focuses on change processes that higher education professionals can make use of: how to employ visitors, how to make the most of the study efforts that too often remain unused on college campuses, how to make committees *work*, and how to function as a team in solving problems. Colleges and universities deserve a higher return than presently realized on the investment they make in committees, study groups, task forces, senates, and commissions, and in accreditation and planning processes. The principles presented in this book have helped many institutions eliminate wasted effort and duplication often characteristic of such processes, and increase the chance for useful change on the campus.

Finally, this volume has evolved in part from self-study training workshops for institution and agency representatives. It is a basic document for self-study and accreditation workshops and can be used that way by others—by and for staff members of state agencies *and* accreditation agency staff members. *Self-study Processes* can be (and in at least one region of the country has already been) used as a basic document for training evaluation team members, team chairpersons, and accrediting board members. It has been adopted to date for general use in four of the six institutional accreditation regions and by several specialized accrediting agencies. It is recommended by agency staff members in the other regions and by a growing proportion of the specialized agencies. However, this author will be satisfied only when the process discussed in this book need no longer be addressed by any accrediting agency.

Acknowledgments

I have been influenced by many people over the decade of travel and study that has produced the material for this book. The thousands of college faculty and staff members who shared their reactions and who opened their institutional and often their personal lives to me can never be fully thanked. My work on this book is a partial payment. A few people do deserve particular thanks, for without them none of what I have accomplished since 1969 would have been possible. First are Robert Kirkwood and Dorothy Heindel who, as the head and heart of the Middle States Commission on Higher Education, have displayed great hope for the processes of self-study and have daily encouraged those people seeking to improve institutions. A special debt is owed t o F. Taylor Jones, whose brilliant vision of the potential for self-study processes was clearly the cornerstone of what is put forth in this volume. To Kay Anderson, Jim Bemis, and Mac MacLeod, who had faith in the first edition as a handbook with nationwide applicability, I owe much. Many thanks are owed to the agencies which have helped to support my work in recent years—the Middle States Commission on Higher Education, the North Central Commisssion on Institutions of Higher Education, the Council on Postsecondary Accreditation, and the Rutgers University Research Council.

No words can adequately express the thanks I must give to my family—Eleanor, Laura, Yvonne, and Katie—who have sacrificed much in the past decade and who have often taken an active hand in the studies and workshops I have been privileged to experience. The same thanks are expressed to my caring friends, some of whom are or were graduate students at Rutgers, Harvard, and Nova and who have assisted and tolerated me. I am indebted to Robert Kirkwood, Eldon Park, Michael Reynolds, and Richard Richardson, who read and commented on the manuscript of the first edition, and to Hannah Hedrick, Jim Phillips, Mac MacLeod, and Allan Tucker, who reviewed the major additions to the second edition; and to Ann and Lou DeSantis, who prepared the diagrams. Finally, I owe much to the American Council on Education, which in several important ways has encouraged me over the last fifteen years.

Self-Study Processes

PART ONE

The Context for Self-Study

The same flexibility and adaptiveness that we seek for society as a whole are essential for the organizations within the society. A society made up of arteriosclerotic organizations cannot renew itself.

John W. Gardner, *Self-Renewal*

I cannot begin to guess at all the causes of our cultural sadness, not even the most important ones, but I can think of one thing that is wrong with us and eats away at us: we do not know enough about ourselves.

Lewis Thomas, in an address
at Douglass College, April 1978

1

The Organizational Context

Most of the faculty members and administrators I know at all kinds of postsecondary institutions are deeply interested in what they do—teaching, providing services, running a department or a school; most would not think of working in another type of organization. They are also frustrated and exhausted by the demands made upon them by the organization, by the nature of their work, and by what they see as external forces making unfair and inappropriate requests of them and the organization. Clearly some pressures are to be expected by educators. Learning, creativity, and research are complex, demanding, multifaceted processes only partially understood in their basic attributes. Other aspects of the malaise are probably attributable to the nature of the organization as opposed to the nature of the educational process.

The purpose of this chapter is to describe the organizational environment of postsecondary institutions in a useful way so that faculty members and administrators who are embarking on self-study processes can see their own institution and their role in it more clearly. It may be that by perceiving the complexities of our institutions in new ways, professionals may be able to set clearer personal goals and have a sharper view of the problems to be faced and possible courses of action. Any professional who seeks to participate in a self-study or other similar process for his or her program, department, or institution *must* have a context for such action. The professional should have a

command of what is known about that and comparable types of organization. It is particularly important that the potential participant in a self-study process understand those aspects of the organizational environment that may impede his or her work, but that can be nevertheless accommodated, and those aspects that may be helpful or, when understood, may permit more meaningful participation.

A Useful View of Management

It is fashionable for academics to deride any mention of managing a college or a school. This distaste is born both of a healthy respect for the complexity of the tasks they must attempt and, for many, of an almost complete lack of knowledge of the constituent parts of the management process. That is not to say that academics do not appreciate something well run—a bookstore, the physics department, a weekend workshop—but rather that they rarely attribute the success to proper planning in light of past performance and knowledge of the environment, to proper organization of the tasks and resources, to effective selection and training of the staff, to a leader or director with the ability to motivate the staff, and to the study of the achievement of the original goals and/or the quality of the product produced. Of course, to do so would be to acknowledge that the organization and its constituent parts can in some measure and under some circumstances *be managed.*

At the risk of offending the management and organization specialists, let us examine the concept of management in a way that enables us to translate the terms to be discussed into functions and steps we would recognize as, if not always imperative, at least generally desirable for a postsecondary program or a college.

In a 1969 article, R. Alec Mackenzie conceptualizes the traditional sequential functions of management as a kind of "management wheel." Mackenzie's article is accompanied by a large colorful pictorial representation, which hangs on the office wall or on the side of the filing cabinet of many students of management. But few uses have been made of this interesting article by faculty members from other than the management disciplines or by college administrators who find themselves in need of a useful conceptualization. Figure 1.1 is an adaptation of the Mackenzie wheel that permits us to relate visually the vital sequential subfunctions of management and to determine where self-study processes seem to fit in running a higher education institution.

A quick inspection of the management subfunctions as presented in figure 1.1 indicates the crucial relationship of research and study processes to planning. They precede planning in the sequence and are critical to its success. (More about this sequence is presented later in this volume.)

The most obvious aspects of the diagram in figure 1.1 are its circular, continuous nature and the interdependence of its subelements. An attempt to apply this conceptualization to any organization or organizational entity other than one just starting

would show that not only is the "wheel" endless, but that it also applies to each aspect of the organization—each unit, each task group, each activity conducted by each person! To complicate things further, in any organization a given activity or unit may be at a different point on the "wheel" at any given time. The picture becomes filled with dozens of different "wheels" turning at the same time.

Let us examine an example of the application to postsecondary education of the principles depicted in the management "wheel." The example concerns an individual: the assistant dean who must run an upcoming staff meeting. I have seen the principles successfully applied in many such cases. The dean would be well advised to consider applying each of the elements in the process.

Study and Quality Control. The dean should consider opinions about the usefulness of the last meeting: how well tasks were assigned and completed, what suggestions participants have about how to conduct the next meeting. This information should be gathered if it is not already available.

Planning. Then the meeting should be planned thoroughly. What is the reason for the meeting? What are its goals? What do we really want to accomplish? What methods or approaches are best suited to achieve those goals? Is staff work needed? Information? Position papers? Who should be asked to do these things? To present ideas? Should the meeting be held where it is usually held or would another site be better? Who should chair the session? Is equipment needed? Are there any costs? How should we evaluate the results? Formally?

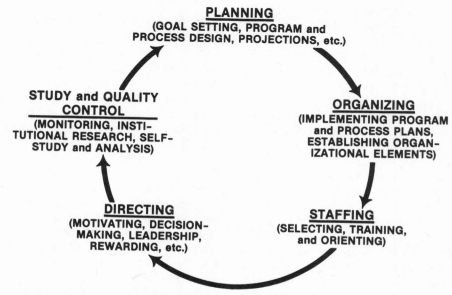

Figure 1.1. A simplified adaptation of Mackenzie's representation of management (1969).

Informally? Who will provide staff assistance? Should we have a meeting at all?

Organizing. Then the organizing phase should be undertaken. Space, equipment, and refreshments should be obtained. Staff assignments, chairperson and any resource persons, guests, and/or observers should be designated and their roles defined.

Staffing. Then roles should be filled and/or confirmed and any specific staffing, orienting, and briefing should take place.

Directing. Once the meeting starts, it is crucial that the leader or chairperson be qualified to lead the group to achieve the goals. If problems are to be solved, definite, strong group skills are required to lead the group to explore, to discuss, to summarize, and to reach consensus on solutions. The leader must be able to motivate, stimulate, and control the group. The leader must be able to report and further the analysis of the results.

Study and Quality Control. Then the assistant dean must arrange that opinions are gathered on the way the meeting was conducted and must design the schemes to follow up on assignments and/or to see that conclusions are implemented and recorded, and that results are assessed. Then the process must be initiated for the next meeting.

It does not require much imagination to translate the simple management principles to other simple functions at a college or school—to a grant-supported project; a summer program; a specific course. The application of the principles—remembering the steps, and making sure each step follows in the sequence—can improve the functioning of groups or individuals, the quality of decision making, and the attainment of project goals. However, one meets quite a few obstacles when one tries to apply these principles to a large, multifaceted educational program; to a college, school, or its equivalent. These obstacles crop up for a variety of important reasons.

Barriers to Effective Self-Study

Almost any dedicated academic will agree that schools and colleges cannot be run like shoe factories. The explanation of why this difference exists is of considerable importance to the issue at hand. I have found that few postsecondary administrators and faculty members understand the explanation in a useful way, and this lack of understanding stymies some of their efforts to run their institutions and certainly to study them

effectively. In my experience, patterns of study, approaches to problems, and even individual management style often improve noticeably when an administrator begins to grasp at least some of the complexities of the organizational environment. The good biologist or literary expert who has no understanding of organizations and no management skills or orientation is immediately baffled, and often has risen to his/her level of incompetence when promoted to a management position or asked to organize a major study or planning effort.

What are the special characteristics that vex the potential student of higher education institutions and the managers who attempt to harness institutional resources to achieve purposes and goals? First, some of the characteristics are not unique to colleges and universities. They are common in all nonprofit, service-oriented bureaucracies, particularly publicly supported government agencies and research organizations with a high percentage of professional staff members (Goodstein, 1978). These characteristics are as follows:

Goals: The goals of educational institutions are very complex. They are difficult to clarify. Consensus is often lacking about the goals, and unlike the usual noneducational profit-seeking organizations, there are few and generally poor measures of achievement of the goals.

Study and Useful Data: Relatively few educational institutions have well-developed methods for gathering, interrelating, and using data about the inputs, processes, and outcomes of the enterprise. Useful data are usually in short supply when they are needed. Institutional research functions at colleges are embryonic and limited (Kells and Kirkwood, 1978, 1979).

Governance: The way policies are formulated and decisions are made at postsecondary institutions is unique to these kinds of organizations. Decision making is shared and powers are delegated quite substantially. Decisions about the major production function—the teaching of students—are usually totally delegated to the lowest level of the organization with little if any review or supervision. The patterns of governance are mixed. That is, at any given time at a particular institution there exists a unique mixture of collegial (faculty meetings), bureaucratic (administrative functions), political (collective bargaining is an example), and anarchic governance models at work. For more on this potpourri, see the writings of Clark and Youn (1976), and Richardson (1974).

Organization: The program and service functions at colleges, unlike profit-making product-oriented institutions, are usually not sequential and therefore not highly interdependent. The subunits vie for attention and "ownership" of the clients. Cooperation is relatively low. Students follow unique paths through the programs, courses, and services; one step is not necessarily dependent on another. This reality tends to fragment the organization; the leaders and members of the subunits are consequently inexperienced at working together to solve problems.

Staffing: Higher education professionals are usually trained well in one or two specialties or to perform a particular function ("do research in biology"). However, they are also, often primarily, asked to perform in *other* areas for which they have little or no training. They are exceptionally good examples of "Peter Principled" professionals. Academic administrators, of course, are at a particular disadvantage. The good biologist may become a good teacher, but he/she may not be able to run a department or a school if little or no training is provided for the job.

Direction: Academics—particularly faculty members—bear another cross. They have learned to doubt, to question, and to pursue truth—at least answers—at almost any cost. Such training may result in excellent chemistry or history, but it can result in a human relations jungle for the program or institution. Management means getting things done through and with people; higher education administrators can have problems when faculty members are asked to function in groups, to plan together, to reach consensus, and to participate in such processes as self-study.

Solving complex tasks—the kind we find all the time at colleges and universities—requires flexibility, trust, warmth, and risk-taking, which are often in short supply in these organizations. There is a strong tendency in service-oriented bureaucracies to perceive conflict or dysfunction as interpersonal in nature and as undesirable. Conflict is usually therefore denied and compromise, voting, or coin-flipping, which are techniques for reducing adversary conditions, are used. Differences or criticism are rarely seen as problems to be solved. In light of this belief, leaders tend to delegate less and to control information and decision making more than leaders do in profit- or product-oriented institutions (Goodstein, 1978).

Academics often have greater loyalty to their disciplines than they do to their employing institution. They seek rewards from a number of sources external to the institution, which usually cannot match the psychological, monetary, status, and other rewards that can stem from outside involvements; Indeed, postsecondary reward structures are often meager.

Planning: Until recently, academic managers have placed very little stock in planning processes. When such processes have been conducted, their design and execution have often been poor. Neither have they led to a systematic, cyclical, useful

evaluation of the institutions' programs (Kells, 1977; Richardson, 1977).

Functioning of Groups: For some of the reasons already detailed above, most groups or committees at postsecondary institutions function very badly. The leadership of committees is often designated for the wrong reasons and most leaders have no training in the skills they need to work well with groups. Committee functioning is often typified by poor use of time, no "pretask" planning, poor or no choice of communication pattern, inadequate staff support, poor decision processes, and poor problem identification, clarification, and solution. The best resources in the group often remain unused; solutions arrived at may not be the best answers. Members are often used inappropriately, vested interests can easily prevail, and a climate necessary for action on the solutions chosen is rarely created.

Few of these characteristics (subjected to analysis in chapter 4 of this book) are compatible with what the pioneers of organization development theory and practice call "healthy" organizations. Effective, healthy organizations regularly diagnose problems, seek solutions, and employ change strategies (Lewin, 1947; Lindquist, 1978; Huse, 1975; Beckhard and Harris, 1977; Berquist and Shoemaker, 1975). Useful, systematic consideration of the achievement of goals, studies of the functioning of organizational subsystems, open, continuous communication, and systematic ongoing self-analysis and planning are all very difficult in the face of the characteristics described above.

Postsecondary institutions, with some exceptions, do not exhibit vital management. They tend to be reactive instead of proactive. Change comes slowly. The direction function may be strong at a particular institution, but such high motivational ability eventually is swamped by the backlash from poor study and control and planning functions (see figure 1.1). Planning or organizing capacities may be excellent, but notoriously poor personnel (staffing) functions often undo the best-laid plans.

The "antimanagement" characteristics of academia provide stumbling blocks to formulating and completing a useful self-study process and to initiating and sustaining ongoing, internally motivated cycles of such activity. Steps that may be taken to overcome some of the barriers are presented in this book starting with chapter 3. Those readers who wish to achieve a basic understanding of modern management, including the bearing of human relations techniques on basic management concepts should read Hersey and Blanchard (1977). This book, particularly the first half, is required reading for anyone without training in basic management techniques who is about to embark on a self-study process. It would make a good companion piece to this handbook and to basic works on management principles for administrators at all postsecondary institutions.

References

Beckhard, R., and Harris, R. T. *Organizational Transitions: Managing Complex Change.* Reading, MA: Addison-Wesley, 1977.

Berquist, William, and Shoemaker, William. "System-Based Planning for Institutional Change." In *New Directions for Higher Education: Strategies for Significant Survival*, no. 12. Edited by C. T. Stewart and T. R. Harvey. San Francisco: Jossey-Bass, 1975.

Clark, Burton R., and Youn, T. I. K. *Academic Power in the United States.* ERIC/Higher Education Report No. 3. Washington, DC: American Association for Higher Education, 1976.

Goodstein, Leonard D. "Organization Development in Bureaucracies: Some Caveats and Cautions." In *The Cutting Edge: Current Theory and Practice in Organization Development.* Edited by W. Warner Burke. La Jolla, CA: University Associates, 1978.

Hersey, Paul, and Blanchard, Kenneth. *Management of Organizational Behavior.* 3rd ed. Englewood Cliffs, NJ: Prentice Hall, 1977 (paperback).

Huse, Edgar F. *Organization Development and Change.* St. Paul, MN: West Publishing Co., 1975.

Kells, H. R. "Academic Planning: An Analysis of Case Experiences in the Collegiate Setting." *Planning for Higher Education*, October 1977, pp. 2-9.

Kells, H. R., and Kirkwood, Robert. "Analysis of a Major Body of Institutional Research Studies Conducted in the Northeast 1972-1977." Paper presented at the meeting of the Northeast Association for Institutional Research, 12 October 1978, at State College, PA (ERIC HE #010540).

Kells, H. R., and Kirkwood, Robert. "Institutional Self-Evaluation Processes." *Educational Record*, Winter 1979, pp. 25-45.

Lewin, Kurt. "Frontiers in Group Dynamics: Concept, Method, and Reality in Social Science; Social Equilibria and Social Change." *Human Relations*, June 1947, pp. 5-41.

Lindquist, Jack. *Strategies for Change.* Berkeley, CA: Pacific Soundings Press, 1978. (Now available only from the Council of Independent Colleges, One Dupont Circle, Washington, DC 20036.)

Mackenzie, R. Alec. "The Management Process in 3-D." *Harvard Business Review*, November/December 1969, pp. 80-87.

Richardson, Richard C., Jr., "Governance Theory: A Comparison of Approaches." *Journal of Higher Education*, May 1974, pp. 344-54.

Richardson, Richard C., Jr.; Gardner, Don E.; and Pierce, Ann. "The Need for Institutional Planning." ERIC/Higher Education *Research Currents*, pp. 3-6. Washington, DC: American Association for Higher Education, September 1977.

2

Relationship of Self-Study to Accreditation

If postsecondary institutions were more like non-educational, profit-seeking, product-oriented businesses, they would conduct useful self-study processes continuously or they would perish. But colleges and universities provide services whose nature and outcomes are only partially understood for a public and in an environment that until recently has not pressed the institution to perform efficiently or effectively. The professionals at colleges and the nature of their work defy many of the usual management approaches; and, in general, their leaders either have not been interested in or have been diverted or lured away from developing useful self-study processes. Under such circumstances, pressure from outside the institution has been required to stimulate even a modicum of institutional or program self-evaluation.

Although today enough external forces exist to prod most institutions to know themselves better, the concept of institutional self-study in the post-secondary world has been advanced primarily because of peer pressure through the accreditation process. While this association may not always yield the ideal circumstances to foster thorough, frank, improvement-oriented study processes (Kells, 1976), without it American postsecondary institutions would not have experienced the pressure needed to produce periodic self-study exercises, successful or otherwise.

It would be a welcome circumstance if most readers seeking information from this book were pre-

paring to participate in a process not generated by an impending accreditation review, for it would indicate that more postsecondary institutions were initiating or repeating the process without the onus of the accreditation review as the motivation to do so. This circumstance would be desirable because an internally motivated, ongoing process of study, followed by planning and then by the rest of the management sequence, conducted college- or programwide, is much more useful to the institution than an externally stimulated accreditation review that might generate anxiety and defensiveness.

But we must face reality. The majority of major self-study processes *are* related to accreditation processes. The people involved in these reviews must have a thorough working knowledge of such processes.

The Roots of Self-Regulation

The sources of power and authority in American postsecondary education are different from those in most other countries. In contrast with ministerial or other nationally controlled systems, American education is controlled at the institutional level. Specifically, its power is entrusted to corporate boards of trustees chartered by the state in which they reside to carry out the educational mission of the institution. These boards delegate power and responsibility for some tasks to their executive staff. While this tradition has produced a large, diverse, fairly flexible, responsive "system" of postsecondary institutions (at least compared to those of other countries), little consistency exists among American institutions with respect to the important issues of admissions standards, quality of the student body, and specific levels of program expectation or performance (Clark and Youn, 1976). While there has been a sizeable increase in the extent of state coordination and control in recent years, particularly with respect to licensing of private institutions and program approval or review for those with public support, the bulk of the evaluation and control function for American postsecondary education is *self*-regulation—peer professional and institutional pressure to meet generally accepted standards and to improve through self-assessment and periodic peer review. This process, originating in the long-established, extensive practice of voluntarism in this country (Harcleroad, 1980) and required by the aforementioned authority structure, is expressed in the educational system at several levels and in several ways.

Self-regulation is manifest, of course, when individual professionals assess their own efforts periodically and make adjustments where and when needed. It is buttressed by peer collaborative efforts through professional societies, by the creation of licensing and certifying tests for individuals, and by the creation of standards of good practice to guide programs to prepare professionals and for entire postsecondary institutions. To some extent this picture has been enhanced by recent concerns about consumer protection (El-Khawas, 1983). Additional efforts to define ethical conduct and desirable principles for various administrative functions and problem areas have been initiated by national educational associations such as the American Council on Education (see appendix B). But the cornerstone of the American self-regulation system is voluntary accreditation.

Accreditation: Knowledge About It

To find that students, parents, and the rest of the public are confused about the meaning of the word accreditation and lack knowledge of the procedures and uses is not surprising. But there is much evidence that accreditation is misunderstood by a large percentage of the members of the academic community as well. To find that most faculty members and many administrators at colleges and universities lack not only perspective and acquaintance with the subtleties but also basic knowledge and fundamental understanding about accreditation is disturbing. My visits to over 300 institutions since

1970 confirm these statements. Since a knowledgeable accreditation agency staff member or a convincingly useful experience is encountered each year by only a small percentage of the academic community, the myths, confused notions, and third-hand stories about accreditation prevail.

Informing even a small percentage of the over one million postsecondary academic professionals in this country about anything is difficult enough. Accreditation agency staff members are few. Their status and ability to motivate and explain vary greatly. Accreditation is not a popular or sympathetic subject to academics who view all external agencies—even those run by their peers—with suspicion. Until recently, even the written materials about accreditation have been meager and not very helpful. Useful handbooks did not evolve in most agencies until after 1970. The featuring in the *Chronicle of Higher Education* of current lists of agencies and news about accreditation is a recent development; but only a fraction of the audience at postsecondary institutions reads it. Finally, accreditation purposes and procedures have changed greatly over the last ten years. Under the best conditions for communication, the lag in understanding will persist, leaving the bad impressions of the 1960s uncorrected (Koerner, 1971). This gap in understanding is one of the major problems facing postsecondary accreditation today. A recent study of knowledge of and motivation for accreditation confirms this need (Parrish, 1983).

The accreditation community has begun to respond to the need for improved communication. Readable, useful pieces have been written in the last few years about the purposes and uses of accreditation (Selden and Porter, 1977), about the myths that plague the process (Kirkwood, 1973), and about the facts concerning parts of the process (Kells, 1979; Kells and Kirkwood, 1979). New books such as *Understanding Accreditation* (Young et al., 1983) and *The Accreditors* (Kells, 1983) should help the situation greatly. The Council on Postsecondary Accreditation (COPA), formed in the mid-seventies to coordinate and represent all voluntary, nongovernmental accrediting in the United States, recognizes and describes accrediting agencies (COPA, 1980) and has sponsored a series of studies, essays, and bibliographies (Van Antwerp, 1974; Kells and Robertson, 1980); and it holds conferences on pressing issues in the field. The work has begun, but much remains to be done.

Definition of Accreditation

A useful working definition of accreditation is as follows: Accreditation is a voluntary process conducted by peers via nongovernmental agencies to accomplish at least two things—to attempt on a periodic basis to hold one another accountable to achieve stated, appropriate institutional or program goals; and to assess the extent to which the institution or program meets established standards. The major purposes of the process are to foster improvement and to identify institutions and programs that seem to be achieving stated goals and that seem to meet the agreed-upon standards.

Several complexities and subtleties in this definition must be noted. The process is voluntary only to the extent that an institution or program is not influenced by the high percentage of their kind that already have been accredited or by the possibility that, without accreditation, eligibility to apply for federal funds might be denied—an aspect added to the process by Congress in the 1960s. The linking of federal funding eligibility with accreditation has caused some people to refer to the accreditation process as quasi-governmental.

The attention to goal achievement has evolved in recent years and is greater in institutional accreditation than it is in specialized or program accreditation. Similarly, the focus on agency standards, which are expressions of current good practice in a field, is much sharper in specialized accreditation than it is in institutional accreditation.

Finally, accreditation relates to institutions and programs, *not* courses, and *not* people and credits. This confusion about accreditation "coverage" is the source of the most common misunderstanding about the process. In response to the press of paperwork and the difficulty of assessing individuals and courses, civil service personnel, state certifying boards, admissions officers, assistant deans, and registrars, among others, have used accreditation listings of institutions and programs as though these certified the quality of a given student or a particular course. Students have been barred from sitting for a civil service examination (formulated ostensibly to test their ability and knowledge!) because they did not graduate from an accredited program or college. Colleges have been denied access to funds that would help them develop because they lacked accredited status, and students have been denied transfer credits because they were earned at an unaccredited institution. Many able students have been injured by the misuse of the results of an otherwise useful or potentially useful process. Until appropriate methods are developed for assessing student competence and the "value" of courses, such abuse of institutional and program "credentials" will continue. (For a more extensive discussion, see Kells, 1976.)

Accreditation: Types, Procedures, and Uses

The world of accrediting is divided into two parts—*institutional* accreditation and *specialized* (or program) accreditation. Institutional accreditation deals with the entire institution and is conducted by elected commissions, small professional staffs, and volunteer consultants and evaluation team members via nine regional commissions in six accrediting regions and via four national agencies. Over 95 percent of the nonprofit institutions and a small but growing percentage of the profit-seeking degree-granting institutions in the six regions work with the regional accrediting commissions. The four national institutional agencies deal largely with non-degree-granting, profit-seeking institutions.

More than forty specialized accrediting agencies are recognized by the Council on Postsecondary Accreditation and even more than these are recognized by the U.S. Office of Education. They work with constituent programs or clusters of programs within postsecondary institutions. Not every institution with a program for which an accrediting agency exists seeks accreditation from that agency. But institutions do have relationships with more than one agency (some institutions work with quite a few). A complete list of all the accredited institutions and programs in the country (Harris, 1982) is produced every year. In addition, the individual agencies maintain a list of accredited institutions or programs. The terms employed, standards utilized, and similarities and differences among them have been studied (Peterson, 1978), as has the complete pattern of multiple accreditation relationships of postsecondary institutions (Kells and Parrish, 1979).

In table 2.1, the major contrasting characteris-

TABLE 2.1. Characteristics of Two Types of Accreditation

INSTITUTIONAL	SPECIALIZED
Deals with entire institution.	Deals with programs.
Organized regionally or nationally.	Organized nationally.
Relies somewhat on general, qualitative standards.	Relies heavily on standards—some of which may be quantitative.
Heavily emphasizes ascertaining whether institution appears to be achieving its goals and is functioning in a way that will permit it to continue to do so.	Focuses somewhat on goal achievement; more on ascertaining which programs meet standards of good practice in the field.
Relies heavily on institutional self-study.	Relies increasingly on self-study.

tics of the two general types of accreditation are listed.

Both types of accreditation use elected peer commissions to develop policies, standards, and procedures, and to make accreditation decisions. All employ very small professional staffs and all rely primarily on volunteer evaluation teams to consult with and to visit institutions. The volunteers may or may not receive training for the work. All of the agencies have appeal processes for use by the institutions if they disagree with a major accrediting decision. All follow a general code of good practice in accrediting (Harris, 1982).

Consistent with the list of contrasts presented above, all the accrediting agencies follow the same general *steps in the accreditation process*. They are as follows:

1. The institution or program describes and studies itself in a self-study process.
2. An evaluation team of peers visits the institution or program and examines it in light of the documents that result from the self-study process and in light of the stated standards of the agency. It makes a report to the institution and to the agency.
3. The institution or program responds formally to the report of the team.
4. The accrediting commission of the agency decides whether to grant, deny, or reaffirm accreditation in light of the self-study document, the team report, and the institution's response.

As one might expect, with more than fifty agencies operating in the accrediting field, the extent to which each step is emphasized and the specific details concerning exactly how each is carried out— even what it is called—vary greatly. Even the purposes vary somewhat. Institutional accrediting agencies espouse institutional improvement and its achievement through the establishment of ongoing capacities for institutional self-study and research. They naturally place considerable emphasis on step 1—the self-study; and they speak of a step five— which would consist of continuous study by the institution of the results of the self-study process and the institutionalization of greater study and planning capacities. They have introduced a five-year reporting step between the normal ten-year cycles or required study and visits in order to foster continuing study, planning, and improvement. Some have recently sharpened and strengthened their standards. Specialized agencies, in contrast, espouse the certification of programs that are examples of "good practice." Therefore, they focus on review of programs

in light of their standards and place great emphasis on the team visit. Their standards generally are expressions of consensus among the top professionals in the field. While little evidence exists as yet that the application of these standards will result in good professional practice (Friedrich, 1980), the leaders of some fields are involved in critically important studies in an attempt to validate their standards and to make them more outcome-oriented. An important beginning has been made in the field of ministry (Schuller, 1973, 1975–76). Studies are also beginning in the fields of law, business, and allied health.

The accreditation definition provided earlier refers to two major purposes of accreditation—institutional and program improvement and identification of institutions and programs meeting good practice standards. But the process and the *uses of accreditation* extend beyond these. These uses, according to Selden and Porter (1977), may be paraphrased as follows:

Internal Uses

1. Identifying an institution or program as having met established standards
2. Assisting institutions in the determination of acceptability of transfer credit
3. Encouraging the involvement of faculty and staff in study and planning
4. Stimulating self-improvement and thereby generally enhancing quality

External Uses

1. Assisting potential students to select institutions
2. Helping in the identification of institutions and programs for the investment of funds
3. Providing one basis for the determination of eligibility for federal funds
4. Serving as an instrument for the enforcement of social policy.

Professional Uses

1. Acting as one source of criteria for professional certification and licensure
2. Serving as a lever to gain increased support for a program or programs

Societal Uses

1. Protecting postsecondary institutions from harmful external or internal pressures

2. Serving as an integral part of the governance of postsecondary education

Some of the uses of accreditation at times may not correspond well with the basic nature of the process. An example, as explained earlier, is its use to transfer credit. Some uses have made the realization of accreditation's basic purposes more difficult. Some people believe that the requirement that institutions be accredited in order to apply for federal funds, and furthermore the use of accrediting to enforce social policy, are examples of this misuse. At times the uses may be expressions of raw political leverage unrelated to program quality or reasonable needs in light of circumstances. That is, accreditation can be erroneously cited to promote or discourage change in a given setting. But such is the reality of people-oriented processes and too often of our daily institutional lives.

Institutional Accreditation: Definition and History

Many users of this book will be involved with institutional accreditation processes. It is important for those people to understand and to remember a more specific working definition, for it will help them design and conduct their self-study processes.

The working definition of an accredited institution is as follows:

An accredited institution

1. Has clearly stated, appropriate purposes and goals;
2. Appears to be achieving them in large part;
3. Studies goal achievement, processes, and problems continuously and attempts to use the results to improve the institution;
4. Appears to meet the accrediting agency's qualitative standards in large part; and
5. Appears to have the human, fiscal, and physical resources to continue meeting those standards for a reasonable period of time.

Although the emphasis on items 2 through 5 will vary somewhat from region to region, this definition is generally applicable nationwide. More important, the elements in the definition can be used as general criteria for making decisions about self-study design and for writing the self-study report. These five elements ought to be the primary guides for evaluation teams, consultants, institutional leaders, and accrediting agency commission members and staff members. All would function better and be even more consistent in their actions if they kept the work-

ing definition at their fingertips. A definition such as this should be on the first page of every accreditation handbook and every list of standards of every regional agency.

Some of the history of regional accreditation should be understood by those involved in it today.

In the 1880s, regional efforts began for the purposes of improving educational articulation and introducing agreements on terms, admissions, and the like.

In the 1920s, accreditation was an elitist, exclusive process undertaken by liberal arts colleges only. It involved no self-study, no periodic review, and no team visits. The standards used were arbitrary, and partially quantitative.

In the 1950s, self-study was introduced, as was periodic review. The types of institutions participating became more varied and the shift began toward qualitative assessment of goal achievement.

In recent years, attention to self-study and to services to institutions and goal achievement has increased. Flexible approaches to self-study have been introduced. Diversity among accredited institutions has increased, as has cooperation with specialized agencies.

Essentially, accreditation in the last two decades has shifted from being a primarily exclusive ("separate the wheat from the chaff") to a primarily inclusive process. Membership in the accredited group is no longer elitist, but egalitarian. The focus is no longer quantitative, but qualitative. Neither is the primary focus any longer on the agency; now it is on the institution. The stated intentions have evolved from having the agency periodically involved to stimulating continuous study and change at institutions, and from an inspection orientation to the identification and solution of problems before any visit occurs. Accrediting agency reactions have generally shifted from being prescriptive in nature to being supportively probing. They continue to evolve.

Specialized Accreditation: History and Recent Developments

Perhaps the most useful introduction to the large and complicated world of specialized accreditation was written by Robert Glidden, a former agency executive and early member of the Board of the Council on Postsecondary Accreditation (Glidden, 1983). Glidden's chapter is part of a long-needed reference work, a collection of essays entitled *Understanding Accreditation* (Young et al., 1983). In it the author explains that the first specialized accreditation actions taken by the American Medical Association actually predated regional accrediting activities and is believed to be the earliest use of accreditation as a means of quality improvement. It was initiated out of the concerns of a profession rather than of educational institutions. The tension thus created between professions and institutions has continued in various ways as specialized accreditation has grown to include well over fifty professional and disciplinary fields, subfields, or areas of study.

As indicated earlier, specialized accrediting agencies generally concern themselves with units within educational institutions, but some work with freestanding professional schools. While the agencies vary greatly in size, workload, and organizational affiliation, some being sponsored by professional associations and some by groups of institutions, all operate nationally. The membership and orientation of the agency staff, accrediting teams, and accrediting boards vary somewhat by type of agency; those related to associations of institutions employ more educators and involve themselves somewhat more with institutional concerns than those agencies with a professional orientation (Glidden, 1983). But the process of accreditation employed by all specialized agencies is the same.

Self-study assumed its position in the schedule of steps to be completed by aspirants to initial and reaffirmation status only in the last decade. Indeed, only since 1981 has COPA strictly enforced its criterion that all agencies require a meaningful, periodic self-study process of the programs seeking status. The relative newness of serious self-study requirements for many of the specialized agencies and the necessary emphasis on the standards of the agency are the major distinguishing characteristics of the specialized accreditation self-study processes. These characteristics and several others are explored in depth in chapter 7. They must be carefully accounted for in the design of such study efforts.

According to Glidden (1983) the issues of concern being addressed by specialized agencies, their COPA Assembly, and the institutions which choose to work with the agencies are (1) the proliferation of such agencies; (2) the issue of "voluntariness," including the tie of such accreditation to licensure for professional practice; (3) the costs of the accrediting process; (4) the nature of standards, including prescriptiveness and validity; (5) the nature of team visits—size, training of members, and the like; (6) the nature of decision making; and (7) interagency cooperation. Most of these areas are receiving serious study by COPA's Assembly of Specialized Accrediting Agencies, and some interesting refinements and explorations are being made by specific agencies. The future should see continued improvement in this large and generally impressive self-regulatory effort.

Future Possibilities

The institutional accreditation process, and the specialized accreditation process as well, continue to change and develop, particularly at a time when institutions are under great pressure from many sources. Institutional and agency leaders are demanding that the processes continue to become more responsive, more helpful, and less onerous and costly. Accreditation is being examined and questioned as never before. The years immediately ahead should see the process evolve further or falter badly.

The accrediting processes described in this chapter are important aspects of the governance of postsecondary institutions. They influence the development of institutions, often very positively. However, because they can be executed only through the efforts of people (accreditation and self-study are "people processes") and are often misunderstood, they face obstacles or become obstacles themselves.

Accreditation processes vary greatly in the extent to which they live up to their stated goals, and any given agency in its interaction with a particular institution or program can perform well. On the other hand, for a host of reasons—some of which stem from the institution in question—accreditation can fail to achieve its purposes. Some of the most obvious of these reasons should be kept in mind.

Many academics expect the accreditation process to end in failure. They expect it will be a bad experience. The process has indeed resulted in some failures. Some team members have performed badly in some instances, and tales about bad experiences die hard. Some professionals expect an "inspection," rather than a dialog among postsecondary educators after a period of self-study. These professionals brace for the inspection, do little else, and thereby create the circumstances under which nothing else can occur.

The faculty and administrators of some institutions refuse to believe that the motivation and the focus of accreditation should be *internal* and not related to the agency. If the motivation is primarily a reaction to an outside agency, little useful activity can result. The need for good leadership on this matter is imperative. Where it is absent, the conditions deteriorate. In addition, institutional anxiety or reluctance to engage in a useful study and review can cause a wasteful "spit and polish" mentality, a poor, descriptive self-study process and document, and a defensive response to the agency.

The accrediting process staggers under other millstones. The onus of federal fund eligibility can create panic at new institutions and at those often most in need of frank self-assessment because they are on the brink of bankruptcy. The process may also be "used" unfairly in a dispute on campus. Ascribing "thou shalt not" prescriptions to a process that—at least for institutional accreditation and some specialized accrediting—no longer uses them can suppress new and often creative ideas.

Finally, accreditation, particularly the institutional type, sometimes suffers because of state-by-state differences in licensing procedures and concomitant reliance on the accrediting agency to fill what many feel should be the role of the state—enforcing basic minimal standards, assuring basic fiscal stability, and implementing social policy such as consumer protection and responses to certain federal initiatives. The regionals also differ a bit in the way they proceed with new institutions, in the flexibility they permit in self-study procedures, and in the ways they assist and keep proper peer pressure on institutions needing help or requiring a stimulus to improvement.

The accrediting process has great potential for helping institutions and programs. Like any other major social process, however, it has irregularities and difficult dimensions. In the future, it should focus clearly on more service to institutions, on less duplication of effort, on the validation of any standards employed, and on the clear communication of its message—its intentions, its legitimate uses, and its function in stimulating and assisting institutional and program self-study. Recent results of a COPA self-study should help agencies to move confidently in these directions (COPA, 1981).

References

AACSB (American Assembly of Collegiate Schools of Business). "Accreditation Research Report: Report of Phase I." *AACSB Bulletin*, no. 2 (1980), pp. 1–46.

Clark, Burton R., and Youn, T. I. K. *Academic Power in the United States*. (See refs. for chapter 1.)

Council on Postsecondary Accreditation. "Board Adopts Self-Study Advisory Panel Recommendations." *Accreditation*, no. 3 (1981), p. 7.

Council on Postsecondary Accreditation. *A Guide to Recognized Accrediting Agencies 1980–82*. Washington, DC: Council on Postsecondary Accreditation, 1980.

El-Khawas, Elaine. "Self-Regulation and Accreditation," in *Understanding Accreditation*, edited by K. Young et al. San Francisco: Jossey-Bass, 1983.

Friedrich, L. W. "Assessing Validity and Reliability of Standards." Paper presented at the meeting of the Council of Specialized Accrediting Agencies, 5 September 1980, Indianapolis, IN.

Glidden, Robert. "Specialized Accreditation: The Agency Perspective." In *Understanding Accreditation*, edited by K. Young et. al. San Francisco: Jossey-Bass, 1983.

Harcleroad, Fred. "Accreditation: History, Process and Problems," ERIC/AAHE Higher Education Research Report, no. 6. Washington, DC, 1980.

Harris, Sherry S., ed. *Accredited Institutions of Postsecondary Education, 82–83*. Washington, DC: Published for the Council on Postsecondary Accreditation by American Council on Education, 1982.

Kells, H. R. "The People of Institutional Accreditation: A Study of the Characteristics of Evaluation Teams and Related Aspects of the Accrediting Process." *Journal of Higher Education*, March/April 1979, pp. 178–98.

Kells, H. R. "The Reform of Regional Accreditation Agencies." *Educational Record*, Winter 1976, pp. 24–28.

Kells, H. R. *The Accreditors: A Characterization of Institutional Accrediting Boards*. Washington, DC: Council on Postsecondary Accreditation, 1983.

Kells, H. R., and Kirkwood, Robert. "Institutional Self-Evaluation Processes." *Educational Record*, Winter 1979, pp. 25–45.

Kells, H. R., and Parrish, Richard. *Multiple Accreditation Relationships of Postsecondary Institutions in the United States*. Washington, DC: Council on Postsecondary Accreditation, 1979.

Kells, H. R., and Robertson, Mary P. "Accreditation in Postsecondary Accreditation: A Current Bibliography." *North Central Association Quarterly*, Spring 1980, pp. 411–426.

Kirkwood, Robert. "Myths of Accreditation." *Educational Record*, Summer 1973, pp. 211–15.

Koerner, James. "Preserving the Status Quo: Academia's Hidden Cartel." *Change*, March/April 1971, pp. 50–54.

Parrish, Richard. *A Study of Faculty Member and Administrator Knowledge and Motivation Concerning Institutional and Specialized Accreditation*. Ed.D. Dissertation, Rutgers University, 1983.

Petersen, Dorothy. "Accrediting Standards and Guidelines: A Profile." *Educational Record*, Fall 1978, pp. 305–13.

Schuller, David, et al. "The Assessment of Readiness for the Practice of Professional Ministry: Rationale and Research Method." *Theological Education*, Fall 1973, pp. 48–65.

Schuller, David, et al. *Readiness for Ministry*. Vols. 1 and 2. Vandalia, OH: American Association of Theological Schools, 1975–76. (P.O. Box 396, Vandalia, OH 45377).

Selden, William K., and Porter, Harry V. "Accreditation: Its Purposes and Uses." Washington, DC: Council on Postsecondary Accreditation, 1977.

Van Antwerp, Eugene. "Postsecondary Accreditation: A Sometimes Annotated Bibliography." Federation of Regional Accrediting Commissions of Higher Education. Washington, DC: Council on Postsecondary Accreditation, 1974.

Young, K., et al., eds. *Understanding Accreditation*. San Francisco: Jossey-Bass, 1983.

3

The Concept
of Self-Study

In chapters 1 and 2, the organizational environment and the relationship of self-study processes to accreditation were examined as a prelude to covering the more practical, "how to" aspects of self-study. An additional aspect must be explored and mastered, however, if one is to design and conduct an effective self study. One must understand the purposes, goals, desired attributes, and expected outcomes of self-study processes. In this chapter, these elements will be examined, as will the current thinking about examining the effectiveness of organizations, and about the conduct of self-study processes in post-secondary institutions.

Purposes of Self-Study

The purposes of self-study processes can be divided into two categories—those having to do with the life of the institution or its programs; and those having to do with any use of the self-study results in an accreditation process.

The purposes that are related to the institution are as follows:

- *Self-study processes are intended to help institutions and programs improve.* By clarifying goals, by identifying problems, by studying goal achievement, by reviewing programs, procedures, and resources, and by identifying and

introducing needed changes during and as a result of self-study processes, institutions and programs can become more effective. For institutions with serious problems, such study processes can influence their very survival.
- *Self-study processes should result in the further incorporation into the life of the institution or program of ongoing, useful, institutional research and self-analysis.* The capacity of the institution for studied change should be enhanced by these processes. The development of such capacity should be the legacy of self-study.
- *Self-study processes should precede and should be the firm foundation for all planning efforts.* Plans should be based upon a clear sense of strengths and weaknesses. Honest self-analysis provides the confidence for an institution to project newly clarified goals and the means to achieve them.

Other aspects of the institution-related purposes are worthy of notice. First, *involvement in self-study processes is an effective orientation for recently hired staff members, particularly chief executive officers.* Participation in the process—even limited participation, such as reviewing draft reports and attendance at hearings at which data or new ideas are discussed—can be a very useful introduction to the campus.

Self-study processes, if properly designed and

enthusiastically led, can also provide the psychological cement of which "organization development" experts speak. One of the chief payoffs to any institution from self-study is staff members' meaningful participation in clarifying and solving problems. Such involvement often yields a more positive identification with the organization for those who do participate. Those who help frame solutions to problems usually become committed to carrying out the steps required. In short, *through effective self-study the gap that often exists between personal and organizational goals is narrowed.*

The third correlative institution-related purpose of self-study is the enhancement of institutional openness. Self-study can improve openness of communication patterns, trust, and listening and heighten effective group functioning to face and solve problems, results which organization development advocates see as signs of organizational "health" (Huse, 1975; Beckhard and Harris, 1977). The healthy organization has the potential to be flexible and change-oriented—to survive. Such qualities are directly related to how people feel about themselves as part of the community of the organization. If they are treated as valued, trusted members of the community and if their best efforts can be elicited to achieve organizational and personal goals, then the effectiveness of the organization will be enhanced. Properly designed and executed self-study processes can further these conditions.

Another purpose of self-study is the identification of important, vigorous, and committed new leaders who often emerge from its processes. This writer has been involved with over 250 self-study processes. In many of these instances new faculty and administrative leaders have blossomed from the "laboratory" that a thorough self-study can provide. Self-study processes are an important device for staff development. The institution that uses them wisely can benefit substantially.

Finally, self-study processes have two institution-related purposes of a less people-centered character. *The leverage self-study provides can stimulate the often long neglected review of policies, practices, procedures, and records.* These reviews, though important to the organization, are usually left on the "to do" list for months or years as the press of regular business or the irregular near catastrophes occupy our attention. *Self-study processes can also yield very useful fund-raising ideas and the basic documents upon which such efforts can be based.*

In those instances when self-study is related to an accreditation review, several important purposes of the study are related more to the accrediting process, its participants, and its audiences than to the institution or program that conducts it. The first purpose, which is especially important in program accreditation, is *the opportunity the self-study provides for thoroughly assessing the extent to which the institution or program meets accreditation standards.* The accrediting agency can thereby inform the public of those institutions that appear to meet the standards of good practice in the field.

The other major purpose of a self-study related to an accreditation process is to *provide useful written materials for the evaluation team that visits the campus after the self-study period.* In the past, this purpose tended to dominate self-study process; the sole reason of most on-campus work during accreditation was to produce a report for use by the team. This exercise was, and in many cases still is, wasteful, duplicative, and costly; unfortunately, it can be multiplied many times if the institution has multiple accreditation relationships (Kells and Parrish, 1979). Recently, progress has been made in countering this practice. Many accrediting agencies have begun to emphasize self-study processes useful to the institution that *also yield* useful reports for the team. Some progress is being made to understand and remove the waste associated with overly descriptive and otherwise duplicative exercises.

Relationship to Recent Concepts of Organizational Effectiveness

An important purpose of self-study—a process organized and conducted with a particular institution and its circumstances in mind, by the staff of that institution—is improving institutional effectiveness. The concept of organizational effectiveness is a very complex one about which there is voluminous literature but little agreement. According to one experienced observer, two models for describing effectiveness dominate: (1) One model is based upon assessing the achievement of goals; (2) the other considers the organization's capabilities for dynamic, flexible functioning or its capacity to survive (Campbell, 1977). These models are not mutually exclusive, nor are they inconsistent with the basic intentions of self-study processes. The linear systems model, which relates organizational inputs, goals, and processes to outputs—often called the goal achievement model—surely must overlap the more process-oriented model, which examines the organization's ability to function, to react, to compete, and to survive. If observers were not inclined to examine an entity's functioning, as well as its goal achievement, they would be giving kudos to many organizations that appear to be achieving their goals—be they profits or more nebulous services—but that are staggering along very near the cliff's edge. Our abilities to measure well all organizational outputs is meager, and many vital processes within an organization are difficult to relate directly to goal achievement. Therefore both models would seem to be required to analyze effectiveness.

The two general theories of organizational effectiveness are not difficult to relate to postsecondary institutions or their constituent programs. The last decade has seen many colleges falter that seemed to observers to be amply achieving their major institutional and programmatic goals. Some of these institutions have encountered—after examination—serious problems with morale, program definition, and administrative functioning. Not a few have seemed to lose their major markets relatively quickly and their financial stability and even have had to close their doors. Therefore, when examining the effectiveness of our institutions, we must assess the major operating problems, as well as goal achievement.

The view of self-study as a means for improving effectiveness is in tune with the current literature on organizational development, which indicates that effective organizations regularly diagnose problems, seek solutions, and employ strategies to introduce, manage, and sustain change. However, as has been pointed out by Wildavsky (1972), the political difficulties of internalizing a commitment to constant self-evaluation in any organization are often great. Staff members' perceptions of the purposes for self-evaluation, of the structure for such study, and of others' perceptions of the activity are difficult to align properly in an organization. Wildavsky indicates that under some circumstances it may not be possible to adopt the posture of a self-evaluating organization to any extent. Such a circumstance can occur in postsecondary education. A politicized college as well as one run by a powerful autocrat in which the professionals feel they must watch every word and every step are not climates in which open, trusting, improvement-oriented self-study can flourish. Those people who are most uncomfortable with any kind of change will certainly tend to oppose such processes, the people who propose them, and the entities that would tend to support and enrich them over time.

While the literature about assessing organizational effectiveness and the general experience with self-evaluation are compatible with postsecondary self-study processes, some aspects are sobering. Clearly, the goals for such processes had best be clear and the climate appropriate.

Desired Attributes—The Intentions of Self-Study Processes

In light of the self-study purposes previously indicated and the literature on organizational

effectiveness the following attributes are desirable in a self-study of an institution or a program.

1. *The process should be internally motivated.* If the study is merely a response to an outside agency, few of the goals for self-study will be achieved and the participants will resent the time and effort involved in carrying out the tasks. If the process can be seen as a way to improve the institution or the program, it is likely to be effective.
2. *The top leadership must be committed to the process.* They must express this commitment several ways, formally and informally, in writing and orally, to demonstrate that they believe the process can be useful.
3. *The design of the self-study must be appropriate to the circumstances of the institution.*
4. *The process should contain an informed attempt to clarify organizational goals and to assess achievement of the goals (to study "outcomes") for purposes of improvement.*
5. *There should be representative, appropriate, and useful participation by members of the various segments of the academic community.*
6. *The process must be well led.* Effective group process, problem clarification and solving, staff work, and group leadership must be used.
7. *The ability of the organization to function effectively should be studied and enhanced.* Problems should be assessed and solved.
8. *Some improvement should occur both during and as a result of the process.*
9. *A readable report, potentially useful to several audiences, should result from the process.*
10. *A better system of ongoing institutional research, self-analysis, and self-improvement should be a major product of the process.*

A recent retrospective analysis of self-study processes employed in the 1970s during institutional accreditation procedures indicated clearly that the first three items on the above list of desired attributes were positively related to perceived satisfaction with the process. The study also pointed out that perceived satisfaction was not related to any particular institutional characteristic (type, size, sponsorship, degree level, etc.), nor was it related to any specific way of approaching the process (structure, cost, absolute participation levels, etc.). Apparently, with the right design, motivation, and leadership, *any* organization can have a useful self-study process (Kells and Kirkwood, 1979).

Steps 4 through 10 on the list of desired attributes proceed from the literature on organizational development and from the purposes of accreditation. Steps 1 through 7 may be seen as the *process goals of self-study*. Steps 8 through 10 may be seen as the *outcome goals of self-study*.

Adapting to Institutional Circumstances: The Need for Design

The design of the self-study—its scope, its depth, the sequence of activities, the particular goals for the process, the nature of participation, its relationship to current problems and to other vital processes under way, recently completed, about to be completed, or about to be undertaken—is critical to its success (Kells, 1972; Kells and Kirkwood, 1979). Although the study is sometimes thwarted by factors within and beyond the control of those designing such a process (Kells, 1976), it is surely doomed to fail if certain basic decisions within the control of the designers are not made.

Until recently, most self-study processes were designed, consciously or by default, to be comprehensive in nature. That is, all aspects of the institution or program, including control, purposes, goals, programs, problems, resources, and outcomes (goal achievement), were described and perhaps to some extent studied. Until the early 1970s, the comprehensive form, though acknowledged by some to be just one of several possible approaches, was generally seen as the only viable approach to use if accreditation was involved (Dressel, 1971). The regional institutional accreditation agencies began to examine alternative approaches to self-study processes in the early 1970s (Kells, 1972). The availability of optional approaches endorsed by regional accrediting agencies and usually approved for use by these agencies has since spread to most of the regions of the country. These changing attitudes resulted in the use of other than comprehensive self-studies in about one-third of the instances during the period 1972–77 in the Middle States region (Kells and Kirkwood, 1979).

Whether one is working with an accrediting agency or not, the circumstances of an institution or program must be thoroughly considered in order to design a process which will enable the goals for self-study to be achieved, and contrary to the opinion held by many, *even if a totally comprehensive process is to be employed, design is still required.* The specific steps in the design process are presented in chapter 4. The *concept*, however, must be perceived clearly if one is to use the details effectively. Basically, if all institutions or programs were of similar age, size, complexity, and stage of development; if all had similar needs and problems; if all had similar, clearly stated, and useful goals; and if all had a useful planning process, data system, and institutional research program; then all could approach

self-study the same way and all or most would achieve the goals for self-study. But, of course, they differ markedly in many of the ways indicated above and in some other important ways—external climate and psychological, historical, and political factors. Thus, some institutions and programs have a need for comprehensive study and some do not. Some must emphasize certain aspects of their own current agenda quite to the exclusion of other factors and approaches, for most have a list of "must fix" problems and "must do" activities. All of this is totally compatible with and necessary for processes in which a thorough review of a set of accreditation standards must be conducted.

The General Procedures for Self-Study

Through one type of design or another it should be possible to achieve all or most of the ten desired attributes of self-study listed earlier in this chapter. In most designs, a basic procedural construct is present that seeks answers to the following *questions:*

1. What are the institution's *goals*? Are they clear, appropriate, and useful? Is there a consensus on and understanding of them?
2. Are the *programs and services* consistent with the goals? Are they designed to achieve them? Do they seem to be working well? *What are the problems? How can they be solved?*
3. Are *resources* (human, fiscal, and physical) available to carry out the programs and services? Will they continue to be available?
4. Are the *goals being achieved?* How can evidence systematically gathered about the extent *of achievement be used to improve the institution?*

And, for institutions or programs which are dealing with an outside accrediting or other agency,

5. Does the institution or program satisfy the standards of the agency? If not, what, if anything, should be done about it? How?

The *steps* usually taken to help answer the questions stated above are as follows:

1. *Preparation and Design*
   Establish:
       Leadership
       Internal motivation
       The specific list of local needs
   Design the study
2. *Organization of the Study Process*
   Define tasks and roles
   Establish a means for guiding the study

Select people; orient and train them

Obtain resources, including adequate staff assistance

Establish work groups

Define the sequence of events

Establish coordination and communication mechanisms

3. *Mechanics of the Study Process*

Work with goals

Study input, environment, program, and process

Review agency standards

Collect facts and opinions

Undertake goal achievement studies

Discuss results and prepare a useful report

Use the results; implement changes

4. *Use of Peers*

Use consultants, if needed

Use any team visit

Work will with any outside agencies

5. *Legacy: Cycles of Study and Planning*

Use self-study as a basis for planning

Increase ongoing institutional research

These five steps are the necessary, sequential elements that must be present in *any* self-study process if the purposes and goals (the ten attributes) are to be realized by an institution or a given program. These steps have been established through analysis of successful self-study processes (Kells and Kirkwood, 1979) and they continue to be confirmed as essential to the process by the graduates of self-study workshops conducted by this author. They form the outline for the remainder of this book.

These five procedural steps are analogous to the sequential functions of management presented in chapter 1: any process should be managed. We must *manage* self-study processes. Essentially, step 1 corresponds to the "planning" in the management process; step 2 is, of course, the "organizing" and "staffing" step; step 3 is the "directing" step; steps 4 and 5 are the "study and control" steps—and the process should recycle from that point.

General Models

This chapter on the concepts of self-study should present some general models which the reader can consider together with the design of an institutional or program self-study process. Several kinds of models will be used. First, one ought to have a useful conception, ideally in the form of a diagrammatic representation, of the *system* to be studied—the college, the department, the program, or other unit—and of *the two major elements* in any study of effectiveness—the extent to which goals are achieved, and the functioning of the system ("problem solving"). In figure 3.1 such a general model

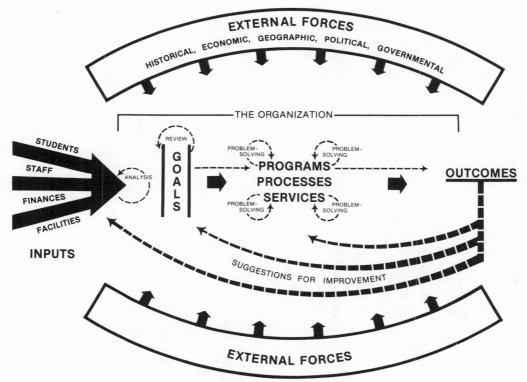

Figure 3.1. The general linear systems model depicting the organization, its environment, and the study elements (broken lines).

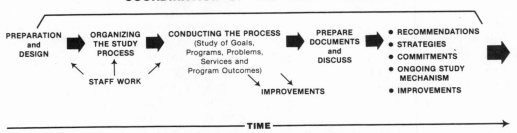

Figure 3.2 General flow model for a self-study process.

is presented. The organization (college or program) is represented by the elements of input, goals (stated intentions), programs, etc., and outcomes (results). External forces are depicted. The general focuses for study are presented by dotted lines. These are the review of goals; the relationships of intentions to results (often called "outcomes," or goal achievement studies); the analysis of inputs; the analyses of functioning (with identification, clarification, and solving of problems); and the suggestions for improvement of any of the elements as a result of the process.

The second general type of model, *a flow model for a self-study process* itself, is presented in figure 3.2, discussed at length in the remainder of this book, and depicted in much greater detail in chapter 4, figure 4.1. The steps mentioned earlier in this chapter are generally depicted in figure 3.2 and the major elements in the flow model correspond in large the remaining chapters in the book.

The third general kind of model, and unfortunately the one that has received most of the attention to date, is a much more restricted one. It presents various versions or *representations of the third element in the general flow model: "conducting the process."* For the most part, these models represent various degrees of comprehensiveness of study effort. They gained popularity in the early 1970s because institutional accrediting agencies began to approve them under certain circumstances for postsecondary institutions (Kells, 1972).

They are as follows:

1. The comprehensive approach
2. The comprehensive approach with special emphases
3. The selected-topics approach
4. The current special-study approach
5. The regular institutional research approach

THE COMPREHENSIVE SELF-STUDY APPROACH: The comprehensive approach is the most common type; every major aspect of program—governing and supporting structures, resources and services, and educational outcomes—is appraised in relation to an

institution's self-defined and rescrutinized goals and in light of the agency's standards. Problems are assessed and solved, and outcome information is analyzed to improve the program. A comprehensive self-study is usually the desirable one unless an institution has recently conducted a thorough and comprehensive self-evaluation or has a regular program of internal institutional research that would render this approach repetitious or otherwise unprofitable. See figure 3.3.*

COMPREHENSIVE APPROACH WITH SPECIAL EMPHASIS: This approach is a variant of the basic comprehensive self-study. It is useful for institutions or programs wishing to give special attention to selected areas or issues within the context of the analysis of their overall goals and performance. This form involves a general review of goals, program, and supporting elements and outcomes, followed by an in-depth examination of those aspects of primary significance to an institution at that time. An institution might find it useful, for example, to study specially its charter and trustees, its faculty and teaching practices, and/or the system of assessing the outcomes (goal achievement) of its total operation. An institution's ability to select this variant is based largely on the availability of useful materials on and knowledge of the overall functioning and performance of the institution. See figure 3.4.

THE SELECTED-TOPICS APPROACH: In this approach, the concentration is on certain areas, units, or aspects of an institution, or program when the basic performance and functioning can be readily verified through available information and when intensive study of selected functions or aspects of its work promises to illuminate the whole.

This approach is most useful with accrediting

*These diagrams were developed by the author in the early 1970s while a member of the staff of the Middle States Comission on Higher Education. The written descriptions were developed by the Middle States staff members and are adapted here from the commissions's current *Handbook on Self-Study*. Recently, several other accrediting agencies have adopted these models and descriptions. The diagrams are revised from an earlier report (Kells, 1972).

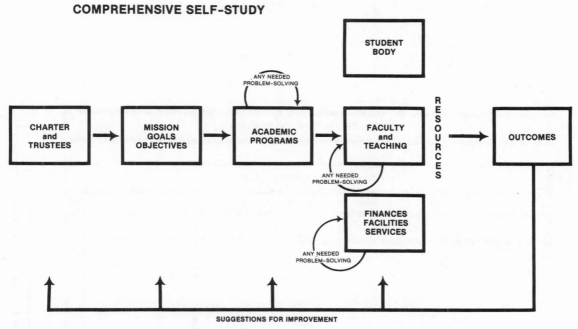

Figure 3.3. Comprehensive self-study of an institution.

agencies when the institution presents, early in the process, a detailed plan for study and then develops a relatively brief introductory paper setting forth the institution's or program's goals, describing its organization, program, resources, and goal achievement or outcomes information, and providing such quantitative data as are necessary. This preparation sets the stage for an in-depth review of the chosen areas or topics and permits a view of the special topics and a view of the institution as a whole. See figure 3.5.

A typical user of the selected-topics approach might be a state college with a fairly active institutional research program, a recently completed

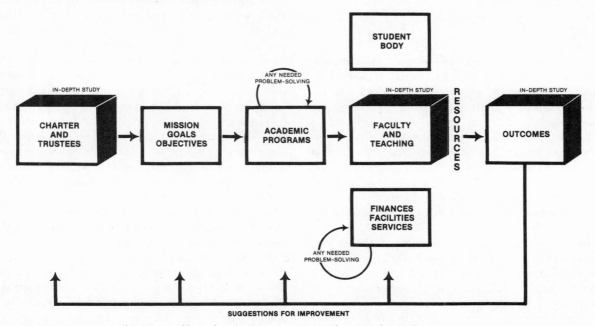

Figure 3.4. Comprehensive self-study of an institution with special emphases.

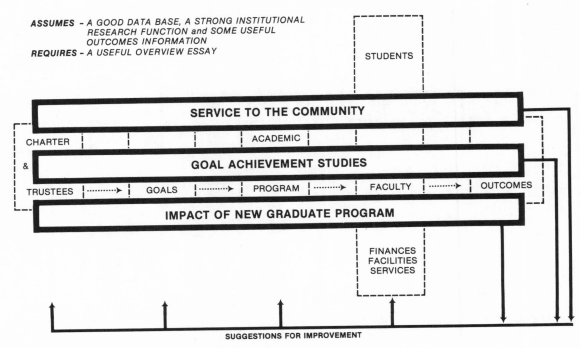

Figure 3.5. The selected-topics approach to self-study.

review of the undergraduate teaching programs, and generally clear and useful goals. In light of these attributes, study designers decide to focus on three topics in need of substantial study—graduate programs, community service programs, and the establishment of an ongoing capacity for goal achievement (outcome) studies. Accompanied by materials already available, and with a thorough essay describing other programs and services, the results of those there needed studies could suffice for a regional accreditation review.

CURRENT SPECIAL-STUDY APPROACH: An institution studying or about to study all or part of its educational program or about to conduct a long-range educational planning or similar process may benefit much more if the special-study approach is used instead of a more conventional form of self-study. See figure 3.6. If the current study is a planning process, adequate information on the present functioning of the institution and on program outcomes is required at the start. If it is not available, a brief but useful study process must be the prelude to planning.

The premise of this model, of course, is that study, followed by planning, then more study, and so on, should be a continuous and improving cycle at any college or in any program. Useful changes can occur at any step in the cycle. For accreditation purposes, this model provides the opportunity for an institu-

tion fully involved in a participatory planning process (particularly if it has started the planning process with an adequate self-study) to present itself for useful review by peers without initiating an unnecessary, separate study process.

REGULAR INSTITUTIONAL RESEARCH APPROACH: For accreditation purposes, this model involves the accrediting agency's acceptance of the product of an institution's regular research program in fulfillment of the self-study requirement, without further documentation other than an introductory statement. Such a procedure is considered only when institutional research covering the general range and outcomes of an institution's programs is a significant part of its established procedures. See figure 3.7.

The regular institutional research approach is a theoretical construct; it represents the idea that sequences of successful specially conducted self-study processes can eventually obviate the need for such processes if ongoing study capacity is enhanced enough. This approach is the ideal, since the study, planning cycle, and the management wheel discussed in chapter 1 would be functioning well in every area of the institution.

In figure 3.8 are presented alternate depictions of the first three of the five comprehensiveness models. They are arrayed so that the extent of effort required in each study area (corresponding generally to accreditation standards categories for most regional

CURRENT SPECIAL STUDY APPROACH

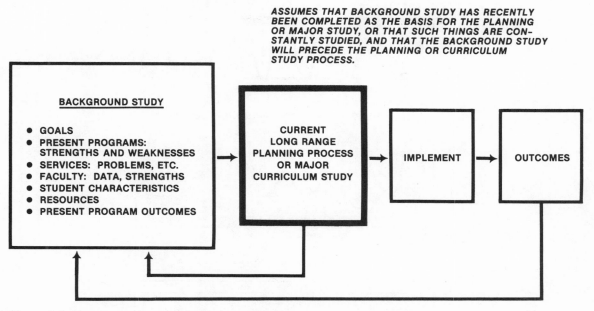

ASSUMES THAT BACKGROUND STUDY HAS RECENTLY BEEN COMPLETED AS THE BASIS FOR THE PLANNING OR MAJOR STUDY, OR THAT SUCH THINGS ARE CONSTANTLY STUDIED, AND THAT THE BACKGROUND STUDY WILL PRECEDE THE PLANNING OR CURRICULUM STUDY PROCESS.

BACKGROUND STUDY

- GOALS
- PRESENT PROGRAMS: STRENGTHS AND WEAKNESSES
- SERVICES: PROBLEMS, ETC.
- FACULTY: DATA, STRENGTHS
- STUDENT CHARACTERISTICS
- RESOURCES
- PRESENT PROGRAM OUTCOMES

CURRENT LONG RANGE PLANNING PROCESS OR MAJOR CURRICULUM STUDY

IMPLEMENT

OUTCOMES

Figure 3.6. The current special-study approach.

NO NEW SELF–STUDY INITIATIVE IS REQUIRED BECAUSE THE ONGOING STUDY PROCESSES ARE SUFFICIENT.

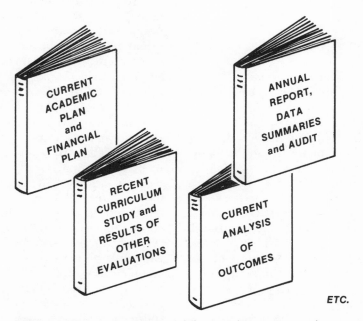

CURRENT ACADEMIC PLAN and FINANCIAL PLAN

RECENT CURRICULUM STUDY and RESULTS OF OTHER EVALUATIONS

ANNUAL REPORT, DATA SUMMARIES and AUDIT

CURRENT ANALYSIS OF OUTCOMES

ETC.

Figure 3.7. A representation of the regular institutional research approach.

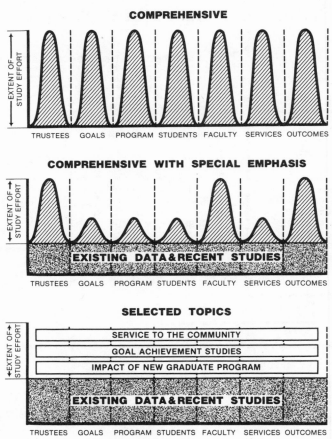

Figure 3.8. Alternate depiction of types of self-study processes.

or specialized agencies) is depicted for each of the models.

Some Research Results

In a recent study, 208 institutional self-study processes conducted in the 1970s were studied retrospectively in an accreditation region in which institutions had the opportunity to negotiate the use of one of the five models (Kells and Kirkwood, 1979). Among many other interesting results, the incidence of use of the models was determined.

The investigators postulated that if models other than those involving comprehensive self-study were heavily used, the ongoing study capacity of these institutions could be characterized as substantial. If the reverse were shown, then such capacities could only be described as meager or at least embryonic. As can be seen in table 3.1, more external impetus would be involved with the more comprehensive studies. That is, when approached by an outside agency to present comprehensive evidence about functioning and outcomes, the institutions that have little ongoing study must initiate study on a broad scale.

The institutions with strong ongoing study capacity can respond to internal, more locally determined needs. The extent of new effort required is proportional to the comprehensiveness of the study. The extent of focus on the institution's current problems is, theoretically at least, inversely proportional to comprehensiveness.

The data in table 3.2 on self-study approaches chosen indicate that few institutions were able to tap the results of an ongoing, active, broadly based institutional research capacity to respond to basic questions about program functioning, goal achievement, educational effectiveness, strengths and weaknesses of processes, and the like. In short, they did not have a choice; they *had* to study comprehensively. The authors concluded that continuous, broadly conceived, fairly complete programs of institutional research and self-study are still not widely present in American higher education institutions. Similarly, complete programs of useful, ongoing studies of goal achievement—that is, outcomes studies—are also not well developed. Both are still in rather rudimentary stages. These results were confirmed by Day (1980).

Research into the self-study process is continuing.

TABLE 3.1. Attributes of the Forms of Self-Study Processes

	External Impetus	Comprehensiveness	Extent of New Effort Expended	Focus on Institution's Current Problems	Adequacy of Ongoing Institutional Research
	HIGH	HIGH	HIGH	LOW	LOW
FORM 1 (Comprehensive) FORM 2 (Comprehensive with Special Emphases) FORM 3 (Selected-Topics Approach) FORM 4 (Current Special-Study Approach) FORM 5 (Regular Institutional Research Approach)	↕	↕	↕	↕	↕
	LOW	LOW	LOW	HIGH	HIGH

Source: Adapted from H. R. Kells and Robert Kirkwood, "Institutional Self-Evaluation Processes," *Educational Record*, Winter 1979, p. 35.

Specialized accreditation agencies are beginning to examine the characteristics of good professional practice in certain fields. This will set the stage for studies to test the applicability of study processes which use these materials. Studies concerning factors which influence the effectiveness of self-study processes have been continued as part of doctoral study by several investigators (Casserly, Day, Harris).

Summary and a Useful Exercise

In this chapter we have reviewed the purposes and uses of self-study processes, the ten desired attributes or goals of such processes, and the relationship of self-study to models for assessing organizational effectiveness. We have enumerated the five major steps required in self-study processes and thereby set the agenda for the chapters to come. Finally, we have explored general models for self-study and discussed their use to date.

Before moving on to the mechanics of conducting a self-study process, it is important that readers attempt to apply some of the material explored in

TABLE 3.2. Percentage of Institutions Using Various Forms of Self-Study
(N = 208; 1971–1977; MSA Region)

Form of Self-Study	Percentage of Institutions
Comprehensive approach	49
Comprehensive approach with special emphases	18
Selected topics approach	28
Current special-study approach	5
Regular institutional research approach	0

this chapter. The following exercise is very useful to reinforce the concepts.

It is suggested that readers gather and review the evidence concerning the last institutional or program self-study process conducted at their institutions or in their programs—or both. They should look over the documents and query any faculty members and administrators who were involved in the most recent studies. The basis of the queries should be the ten desired attributes of self-study processes and some related issues—all of which are included in the retrospective analysis checklist that follows. The results should enlighten readers and may help greatly as they prepare for further self-studies.

References

AACSB. "Accreditation Research Report: Report of Phase I" (Chap. 2).

Beckhard and Harris. *Organizational Transitions* (Chap. 1).

Campbell, John P. "On the Nature of Organizational Effectiveness." In *New Perspectives on Organizational Effectiveness*, edited by Paul S. Goodman and Johannes M. Pennings, pp. 13–55. San Francisco: Jossey-Bass, 1977.

Casserly, Mary. "Self-Study and Planned Change in Academic Libraries." Doctoral Dissertation, Rutgers University, 1983.

Day, Philip. "A Retrospective Analysis of Community College Participation in Non-Traditional Forms of Institutional Self-Study." Doctoral Dissertation, University of Massachusetts, 1980.

Dressel, Paul L. "Accreditation and Institutional Self-Study." *The North Central Association Quarterly*, Fall 1971, pp. 277–87.

Harris, Edwin. "A Multi-Case Study of the Self-Study Component of the Regional Accreditation Process: Identifying Influential Factors." Doctoral Dissertation, Syracuse University (in progress).

Huse. *Organization Development* (Chap. 1).

Kells, H. R. "Institutional Accreditation: New Forms of Self-Study." *Educational Record*, Spring 1972, pp. 143–48.

Kells, H. R. "The Reform of Regional Accreditation Agencies" (Chap. 2).

Kells and Kirkwood. "Institutional Self-Evaluation Processes" (Chap. 2).

Kells and Parrish. *Multiple Accreditation Relationships* (Chap. 2).

Schuller, David, et al. "The Assessment of Readiness for the Practice of Professional Ministry: Rationale and Research Method" (Chap. 2).

Wildavsky, Aaron. "The Self-Evaluating Organization." *Public Administration Review*, September/October 1972, pp. 509–20.

CHECK LIST

For Retrospective Analysis of Self-Study Processes

1. Was the process clearly internally motivated? Or was it predominantly a response to an outside agency? _____
_____

2. Were the top leaders of the college or program committed to the process and supportive of it? _____
Did they believe it would be *useful* to the institution? _____

3. Was the process *designed* at all in light of the circumstances of the institution or program? _____
Was it a rote following of standards or questions by one accrediting agency? _____

4. Were *goals clarified* in the process? _____
Were *goal achievement (outcome) studies* conducted to gather information for improvement purposes? _____
Examples _____
_____
_____

5. Was the *participation* in the process representative and useful? _____
Evidence _____
_____

6. Was the process *well led?* _____ In what ways? _____ In what ways did the leadership fail at the work group and steering group levels? _____
_____
_____

7. Was the *functioning* of the programmatic aspects and services of the institution and/or program studied well? _____
Good examples _____
_____
Were *strengths and opportunities for improvement* noted? _____
What major ones were noted? _____
_____
_____
Were *any problems solved* or programs and services strenthened? _____
_____

8. Did change occur *during* the process? _____
As a result of it? _____
Examples _____
_____

9. Was the *report* that resulted from the process useful and readable? _____ Could it be read in one sitting by a busy professional? _____

10. What was the legacy of the study in terms of *ongoing capacity for institutional study, analysis, and self-improvement?* _____
_____
What does the forgoing tell you about the last self-study experience? Are there major items which *must* receive attention in the next study?
_____
_____
_____

PART TWO

Conducting Self-Study Processes

PREPARATION
AND DESIGN
(CHAPTER 4)

ORGANIZING FOR
SELF-STUDY
(CHAPTER 5)

MECHANICS OF
THE STUDY PROCESS
(CHAPTERS 6, 7, 8, AND 9)

ENHANCING THE
STUDY/PLANNING
CYCLE
(CHAPTER 10)

The process must be managed—planned, organized, staffed, directed, studied, and controlled.

4

Preparation and Design

Part 2 of this book is made up of three chapters that parallel the steps of the management process. The major message of part 2 is that to be useful, self-study processes must be planned, organized, directed, and studied. They must be managed.

The first part of the self-study process—preparation and design—is probably the most crucial to eventual success. It is also the part that, in my experience, is the most neglected. In essence, it represents the "pretask" planning for the process. If it is done well, the potential for a useful process is created. If it is neglected or poorly done, the process will falter and the chance that the self-study goals will be achieved is meager.

The essential elements of the preparation and design phase of the self-study process are as follows:

- Creation and utilization of a prestudy planning group
- The establishment or confirmation of needed leadership
- The fostering of internal motivation
- Establishment of the agenda of local needs
- Design of the study process
- Planning for change and continuing study
- Approval of the design

Each element will be discussed in sequence in this chapter. Several case examples will be presented, and, finally, some checklists are offered for use in planning institutional and program self-studies.

The Prestudy Planning Group

The first step in starting a self-study is to form a group to plan the process. The group, which usually becomes the steering group, has a most important function—*to plan the process before it is begun.* This simple step, unfortunately, is too often overlooked. Frequently, a coordinator is appointed and then a steering group, which doles out "areas to be covered" to a group of subcommittees. Thus, the flag is dropped and the race is on or the wait for subcommittee reports begins. The crucial questions of leadership, motivation, specific institutional or program needs, group processes, sequence of activities, and any appropriate process design are rarely handled before the start. At times, these issues are neglected because they are not raised. Sometimes they are not covered because the hope is that the design will emerge from the groups' deliberations. These issues, however, should be dealt with *before* the process begins in order that the human and other resources of the institution or program can be marshaled to achieve the goals of the process. Dealing with them properly does make a difference.

Please notice that there has been no mention here of comprehensiveness or any particular model or type of study. *All self-study processes, even those which are comprehensive in nature, require extensive preparation and design.*

Whether or not the prestudy planning group should be composed of representatives of all constituencies depends on local circumstances. What the group *must* contain are those professional staff members with the best sense of: the institution's or program's real needs; the political climate; the nature and availability of data; perceived major strengths, problems, and opportunities; the psychological climate—the willingness of the staff to participate in a given effort; and the nature of the informal leadership on the campus or in the program. For an institutional study such a group would probably contain a key member of the academic administrative staff, a key member of the administrative services staff, a senior faculty member or two, and possibly an institutional research staff member. It may or may not include a trustee, a student, or the institutional, department, or program head.

For a departmental or program self-study the group would be quite small, perhaps as few as two people, and should either be composed of senior faculty members or the unit head and faculty member(s). It may, of course, be a larger group, perhaps four or five people when the program staff is quite large, and the group may or may not include a student, a member of the support staff, or someone from outside the unit, perhaps from a related program. It should be chaired by the member who commands the most respect, who can rise above any factional differences, and who is the best group leader—more about that later in this chapter.

The chief executive officer of the institution, department, or program should bring the group into existence. The group should be charged to consider the possibilities that exist for a useful self-study process. They and the steering group that succeeds them should start their activities by thoroughly reviewing an available handbook on self-study processes. Two or three members of the group should attend a self-study workshop that includes study design exercises, in which they can use case materials from other institutions, and during which they can discuss the experiences of others in similar circumstances. The work of the prestudy group can usually be accomplished in two or three sessions over two weeks to a month.

The agenda for the prestudy planning group is essentially the material which constitutes the rest of this chapter.

Establishing Necessary Leadership

A recent major retrospective analysis of successful and unsuccessful processes (Kells and Kirkwood, 1979) indicated that strong, positive leadership was one of only three factors—internal motivation and an appropriate design were the other two—which correlate strongly and positively with perceived usefulness of self-study processes. The analysis showed quite clearly that those institutions in which the leader—the chief executive officer—was enthusiastic about the self-study and those in which it was indicated as a high-priority activity were generally the ones in which respondents reported improvement and other useful results of the process.

The first task for the prestudy planning group is to ascertain the nature and the extent of the commitment of the top leader or leaders to the process which the group will plan. If the president or director is positive and supportive, and intends that the process have high priority with adequate staff and other support, he or she should be asked to publish that message throughout the institution. The leader should be asked to plan to reinforce that message in several ways during the study at the various major levels of the institution—from board of trustees to student and alumni organizations. The members of the academic community must receive the message if they are to make personal decisions about the extent and nature of their own participation in and commitment to the process.

It is possible that the planning group might perceive that the leader either is not supportive of the process or feels that a pro forma response to an accrediting agency or to the dean's request is called for. In such a case, the group should cease all activity until this critical issue is dealt with. Leaders who apparently believe that self-study requires no special attention are taking a common position, given the lack of understanding about useful study processes and/or accreditation. But, to go ahead hoping that the leader will become interested in the unique plans and activities the group will formulate is to risk alienating participants in such activities when the leader is unresponsive or even unfriendly to group activities that he or she sees as competing with the real agenda.

Several options are available to a planning group facing such a situation.

1. Members, especially the most influential, could carefully present to the leader the arguments for placing high priority on the self-study process as a useful, needed activity to maintain or advance the institution's programs. They should attempt to show how the self-study can be merged fruitfully with the leader's agenda.
2. The group might ask the leader to authorize the visit of either an accrediting agency staff member or a self-study consultant who can discuss the possibilities for using the self-study process to accomplish the leader's favored tasks or solve his or her problems. The group should be careful to select an outsider who has substantial ex-

perience in self-study design or organization development.

3. The leader might be asked to review one or more of the articles from the self-study literature that emphasize the useful, improvement-oriented aspects of the process. (A handbook such as this one could also be used.)

If the leader refuses to bring the process into the mainstream of institutional priorities, the group has no choice but to proceed cautiously, focusing on problem assessment and solution as the climate permits. Close contact with the leader and careful handling of the issues during the process might lead to a convergence of the planning group's self-study purposes and the expressed needs of the leader. At the minimum, it might eliminate any feeling by the leader that the process should be suppressed.

More than ten years of experience in working with this problem have convinced me that an important set of roles exists in a self-study process for the chief executive officer. They are as follows:

- helping to shape internal motivation
- setting a high priority on the study
- responding positively to new behaviors which may be generated during the study
- supporting the coordinator, after selecting the *right* one
- rewarding participation in the process
- providing support for the study
- not fearing change; perhaps even helping to design the strategies for change
- promoting ongoing study and planning processes
- *using* the results of the study.

Certainly the role of the leader should *not* include rewriting the self-study report, isolating or forgetting the study process, or other defensive behavior. Sadly, this kind of reaction is relatively common. It can be obviated if the planning group puts the leader in touch with one or more of a growing group of chief executives who have had a good experience. Such executives have found that self-study processes can be a solid starting point for the next planning cycle and can yield an agenda for constructive change. They have found that self-study can provide a way for previously unaware campus citizens to discover the stark realities, economic and other, and thus to adopt new behaviors; and that self-study is an opportunity to identify and test some new campus leaders—people to whom one can delegate responsibilities and from whom one can expect results. Finally, some chief executives have been presented with marketable new ideas as a result of self-assessment efforts.

Promoting Internal Motivation

The second factor determined by the recent retrospective study as critical to success is the degree to which participants (from leader to worker) perceive the process as springing from and being responsive to institutional needs rather than to an outside agency. To instill such a perception among participants and other community members, the prestudy planning group must again start with the leader. In any discussions with the leader, group members should seek to ensure that the leader will exhort the community to conduct and participate in the process *for the sake of the institution* and to *forget any outside agency or factor*. The analysis of successful study processes shows that any required response to an outside agency either takes care of itself or can easily be handled administratively *if* the participants believe the process can be useful and if it is shaped to meet local needs.

Beyond the leader's commitment to improving the institution or program by self-study, there is a "continuum of persuasion" that must be guided by the prestudy group. The group must organize a short orientation and persuasion campaign to tell as many of the potential participants as possible why they should participate and what it could mean for the institution.

Here the methods of transmitting this message to the community are probably obvious—an "upbeat" report at faculty meetings or staff conferences; a well-written report in the house newspaper or a special newsletter on the study process. A good speaker from the outside at the right time to the right audience or a special one-day, miniworkshop led by the planning group and well supported by the leader at a usual staff retreat or orientation for the year's work can be very effective means of informing and persuading. If an outsider can appear who has conducted an internally motivated self-study, the impact of his or her message can be substantial.

Continuous persuasion and informal, enthusiastic leadership by the members of the planning group are required to sustain internal motivation. Such enthusiasm, of course, must be reinforced by *results* during the process, but a large slug of persuasion is needed at the start of the process.

Establishing the Agenda

Each successful self-study process, even successive ones at the same institution, should be different in significant ways. The circumstances and needs of an institution or program change over time. Its study and planning capacity mature slowly even under ideal conditions. Therefore, the specific institution-

or program-related study goals (as opposed to the general intentions described in chapter 3) should be developed by the prestudy planning group. For instance, part of the study agenda for a college with a new president may be the thorough orientation of that new leader. A study of a program that has not reviewed its career-oriented curriculum in ten years or more probably ought to place more than usual emphasis on market studies, the work needs of professionals in the field, and a thorough review of what similar departments have been developing. The struggling institution may set survival as the essence of its study process. What one does in each of these study contexts and the approach in each context may vary greatly. A given purpose or agenda requires specific procedures to accomplish it. Just hoping that a self-study will "renew the program" or an institution will not be enough to assure that such renewal will in fact occur.

The prestudy planning group must engage in discussions in a particular setting and with an experienced group leader, so that a useful appraisal of the major conditions of the college or the program will result. Do not mistake this step for the detailed study process that will follow. It is a "first cut," an informed listening to those who can speak generally and usefully about the conditions and the stage of development of the college or unit in question. The group may wish either to augment or to confirm its impressions by using some of the techniques described by Fordyce and Weil (1971). One such technique is the "family group diagnostic meeting," at which, with proper preparation, key campus citizens are asked to help list and describe major needs, opportunities, and problems. The "organizational mirror" or "fishbowl" techniques are other possibilities for eliciting information about the life of the institution or program. By these techniques, study team or planning group members note the comments of properly oriented "clients" of the institution (students, employers of graduates, users of the institution's services) about the quality of service they receive and their suggestions for approaching the study and for improvement. These techniques can be very helpful in building a self-study agenda if they are sensitively led and if the tone can be kept positive and improvement-oriented.

There are, of course, other techniques which can be employed to get a "fix" on the agenda of primary needs, problems, and opportunities at a college or in a department or program. Some institutions have used faculty retreats or the beginning-of-the-year orientation day quite successfully to gather information and to involve a broad range of individuals in the early stages of a study process. Discussion groups following a preretreat or early-in-the-day, anonymous questionnaire have been very useful in the formulation of lists of things which "need study," "definitely don't need study," "don't seem to work well," "constitute strengths," and the like. The self-study planning group can then take these data, augment them with selected conversations and with study of previous reports and other documents, and use them to formulate the primary purposes of the study process and the agenda of issues to receive any special attention.

A self-study agenda for an institution or a program may well end up being comprehensive, with no special emphases. Nevertheless, it is an agenda, and is needed. Even such studies must be designed.

Designing the Study Process

The prestudy planning team now has almost all the ammunition it needs to design the self-study process. It has the list of generally desirable attributes for any self-study process (see the checklist at the end of chapter 3). It has the general models for self-study to guide members in accommodating the desired scope of the study (chapter 3); and it has produced a general agenda of needs—the special things that this particular self-study process should attempt to accomplish.

Specific Design Models

One piece of information which may be useful at this point is the translation of each of the general models of self-study depicted in chapter 3 into practical, sequential diagrammatic representations which contain the elements of a useful self-study process. The beginning of this translation and perhaps the most important depiction in this book is presented in figure 4.1. It is the diagram of an entire self-study process which includes all of the major elements recommended and in the generally appropriate sequence. The first three clusters of items in the flow diagram ("prepare and design," "organize the study," and "coordinate the study process") correspond to chapters 4, 5, and 6 in this book. The sections in the diagram to the right of "coordinate the study process" are covered in chapters 8 through 10.

What actually happens in the design stage is the determination of the substance, the sequence, the structure, the human dimensions, and the expectations of the process—which is then organized in the next segment of the study process and actually conducted in the following one. The structure depicted in the central portion of the diagram in figure 4.1 is just one possible sequence. Many others are possible.

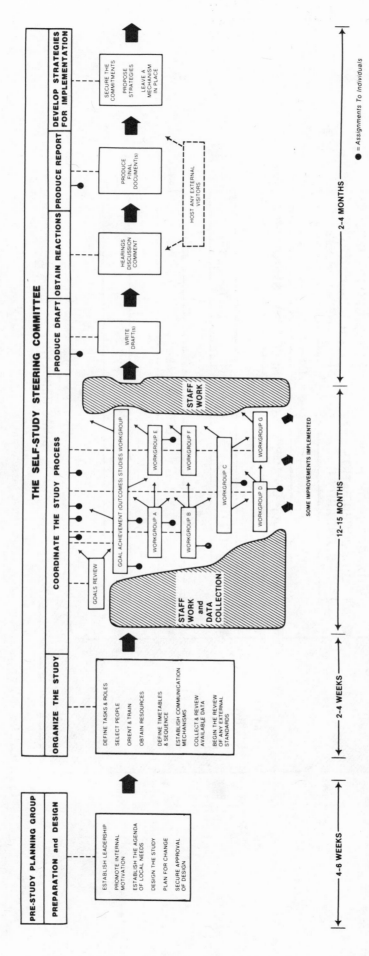

Figure 4.1. Flow diagram of an entire self-study process.

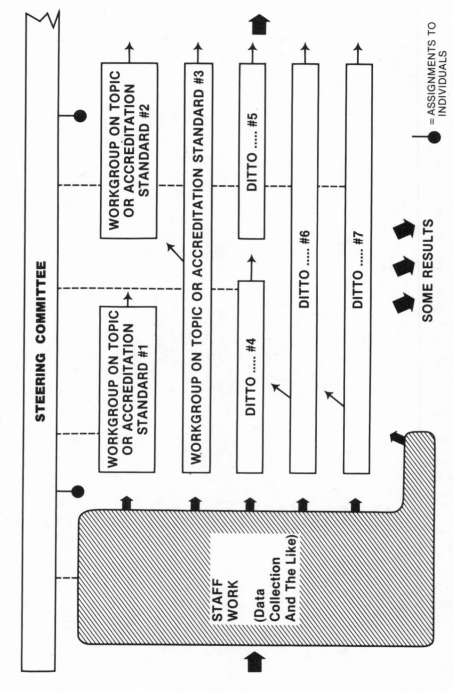

Figure 4.2. Flow diagram of work groups in a comprehensive self-study.

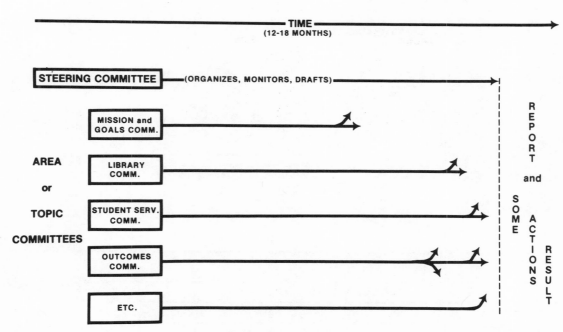

Figure 4.3. Traditional self-study committee organization and work flow. *Source:* H. R. Kells, "An Alternative Model for Self-Study in Higher Education," *North Central Association Quarterly (NCAQ)*, Vol. 52, Fall 1977, p. 342.

In figures 4.2, 4.4, and 4.5, the general models organized according to the idea of comprehensiveness and presented in the previous chapter are translated into the form found in the central portion of the flow diagram. In figure 4.2 the work groups are depicted for a comprehensive self-study process *with the numbers 1-7 corresponding either to major units and functional areas of the college (or program) or to accrediting standards of any agency involved.*

One should notice that even though the plan for the work-group part of the study process depicted in figure 4.2 is for a comprehensive self-study, the designers have realized that the elements of sequence and proportion are important; some tasks logically must happen before others, and some are much larger or more complex than others, requiring more time to complete. Some must wait for the results of other work and some can be accomplished, indeed, accomplished much better in several weeks of intensive meetings than in a semester or a year of work. And, of course, two other critical design dimensions, less obvious than the aforementioned, are just as important for comprehensive self-studies as for other types. First, the process can be designed so that results happen *during* the process rather than just at the end, so that psychological "lift," certainly a reinforcement of effort, can benefit the rest of the process. Second, a sequence of events, rather than totally concurrent work-group effort, permits better use of the most talented people. In other words, one can employ a person talented to lead, enhance, and

otherwise stimulate the efforts of two or even three different groups during the same period of time.

None of the extremely valuable ideas just described are present in the traditional and (unfortunately) overwhelmingly popular self-study work-group scheme depicted in figure 4.3. For over twenty years self-study efforts have been organized this way. I call it the "divide up the troops into groups and drop the flag" scheme. Besides the fact that preparation of all kinds is generally neglected, the absence of the design concepts mentioned above yield invariably an uneventful, often lengthy and tiring scheme with but modest results at the end of the process—often a year too late to be of maximum benefit. Such schemes are generally discouraging ventures for faculty members whose willingness to participate in subsequent efforts understandably decreases with time.

The translation of the other major models from chapter 3 into flow diagrams of work-groups structure and sequence can be seen in figures 4.4 and 4.5. In figure 4.4 the "Comprehensive Self-Study with Special Emphases" (C.S.S.E.) model is put forth in three different ways. In variation 1, two distinct phases are employed. In the first, the various elements, units, or functions of the college or program (or the standards of any accrediting agency) are briefly reviewed by a natural work group (offices, departments, standing committees) with staff help, in order to assess functioning or compliance with expectations or outside standards. Remember, this general model assumes that some areas of the college or program in question don't require intensive study. In

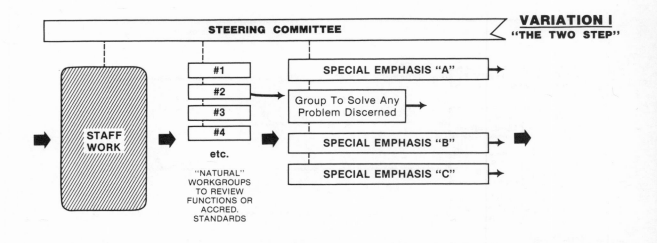

VARIATION I
"THE TWO STEP"

STEERING COMMITTEE

STAFF WORK

#1
#2
#3
#4
etc.

"NATURAL" WORKGROUPS TO REVIEW FUNCTIONS OR ACCRED. STANDARDS

SPECIAL EMPHASIS "A"

Group To Solve Any Problem Discerned

SPECIAL EMPHASIS "B"

SPECIAL EMPHASIS "C"

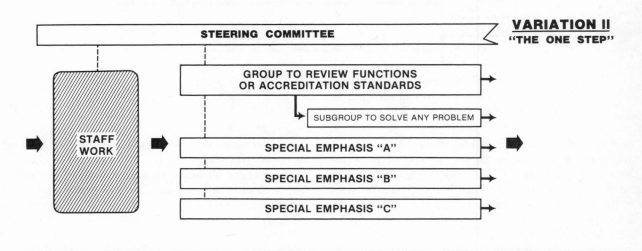

VARIATION II
"THE ONE STEP"

STEERING COMMITTEE

STAFF WORK

GROUP TO REVIEW FUNCTIONS OR ACCREDITATION STANDARDS

SUBGROUP TO SOLVE ANY PROBLEM

SPECIAL EMPHASIS "A"

SPECIAL EMPHASIS "B"

SPECIAL EMPHASIS "C"

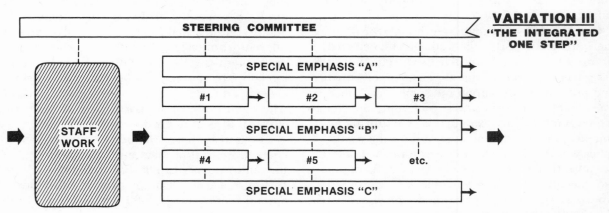

VARIATION III
"THE INTEGRATED ONE STEP"

STEERING COMMITTEE

STAFF WORK

SPECIAL EMPHASIS "A"

#1   #2   #3

SPECIAL EMPHASIS "B"

#4   #5   etc.

SPECIAL EMPHASIS "C"

#1–#5 = "NATURAL" WORKGROUPS TO REVIEW FUNCTIONS OR ACCREDITATION STANDARDS

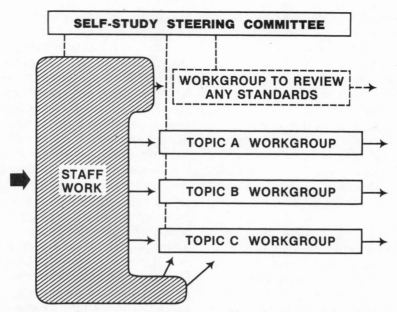

Figure 4.5. Flow diagram for work-group segment of selected-topics self-study process.

phase two, any problems turned up in phase one are pursued by specially constituted work groups, and the special emphases (functions or problems) selected in the design phase are pursued by major task forces also specially constituted to do the job. I refer to this variation as the "Two-Step" C.S.S.E.

In variation 2 of the C.S.S.E., the "One-Step," the two activities mentioned in the description of the two-step model are accomplished simultaneously after sufficient staff preparation. The abbreviated review of the major aspects of the educational unit (or of the standards of any accrediting or other agency) are completed by one task group which initiates any needed problem-solving task groups. The special-emphasis task groups operate at the same time.

In variation 3, "The Integrated One-Step," separate, short-term groups conduct the abbreviated functional or standards review *while* the special-emphasis task forces are conducting their studies. A case example in which this model was employed is presented later in this chapter.

Finally, in figure 4.5 is presented the flow diagram for the work-group segment of the selected-topics approach to self-study, which is described in more detail in chapter 3. The reader should remember that these are greatly oversimplified diagrams. Representing the sequence of activities as they really occur would be most difficult and the diagram would be confusing. For instance, the various links between the steering group and work groups are not represented. The extended and vital staff work needed *during most of the process* (not just before the groups start) is not depicted, nor are the interactions between groups, the common use of survey techniques,

or the sharing of data. The use of consultants during the work-group process or the sorties made by work groups or their representatives to discuss problems or program efforts at other institutions are not depicted. The use of program or collegewide retreats during the process in order to gain new perspectives and to lay the groundwork for change is not shown. (Some of these activities, however, are presented in the case examples provided in the last part of this chapter.) Finally, it would be difficult to depict a most important notion, namely, that *design goes on*—changes are made throughout the process.

Using Design Questions

Now the planning group must prepare the actual design—specific focuses, procedures, sequences, human resources, and expected outcomes of the process. The following questions should help in composing the elements and selecting a model.

1. What is the status of *institutional research* at the institution, and what is the status of the data base on students, staff, programs, resources, and goal achievement (outcomes)? Should the self-study process result in improved capacities for ongoing study in these areas? Which areas?
2. What is the status of *master planning* at the institution? How recently has a thorough planning process been conducted? When is the next cycle to be conducted? What studies would enhance the next planning process?

3. What is the status of the statement of *goals* for the institution, its subunits, and/or the program in question? Are they clearly stated, complete, and current? Is there reasonably useful consensus on these goals? Are they commonly understood and used as the basis of program and institutional management? What work remains to be done in this area?

4. Have there been *recent, useful study processes* at the institution? What written evidence is available that resulted from such processes? How can the current study process build on and complement what was done in these studies?

5. What has been the rate of *turnover* in institution or program leaders and/or staff members? What are the orientation needs of any new members of the community? How can the study process meet these needs?

6. What is the level of *morale* at the institution or in the program? What *historical and/or political factors* must be considered? What implications will these factors have for the level of participation in the study, and in the timing or sequence of its separate elements?

7. Is there a *consensus* among the formal and informal leaders at the institution *concerning the major problems* that the institution or program faces?

8. How "tired" is the staff, *psychologically*, in terms of their *readiness* to undertake a major participatory venture in self-analysis? What are the implications of their readiness for the design?

9. What *other accreditation relationships* and state-related or other activities or responsibilities does the institution or program have or must it complete in the near future? Is it possible to combine the processes and perhaps synergistically to produce better results from all such processes?

10. What accommodations must be made to the *size and complexities* of the institution or program?

The answers to these questions, when accompanying the agenda and the general goals for any study, provide the raw material out of which the design for the self-study process should emerge.

Some Design Examples

CASE ONE: Suburban Community College

The setting.   Suburban Community College has been in existence for thirty years. It was one of the earliest and it is perceived as being one of the most

successful, traditional tripartite (transfer programs, career programs, and community service) public community colleges in its region. In the early years (a time of frantic growth for Suburban), the region which it serves—the town of Suburbia and the larger county area—was still relatively sleepy, mostly rural, and fairly conservative in tone. The county benefited from Suburban's presence and as the college grew from its early size of about 1,500 students to its present size of over 4,000 students, the average age of the student body crept upward, the percentage of part-time students and the use of off-campus sites increased. A pressure to increase community service and noncredit courses and to add a second major group of specific career programs was felt. In the last decade, the county grew and "greened." The population became diverse as people moved out from the larger cities and as industry opened plants in the Suburban sending district. This pattern of growth and change is a familiar one.

Under the leadership of a strong president, now at Suburban some fifteen years, the college rose to most of its challenges, but unevenly, of course—at least as many perceived it. And serious stocktaking had not occurred in the last decade. Although planning and growth had happened at Suburban, they had been largely incremental in nature. The faculty at Suburban had organized for purposes of collective bargaining seven years ago, and some felt that the builder president had perhaps overstayed his term. As the dean and his assistant began to plan for the upcoming regional accreditation review, they sensed the need for a thorough, fairly useful review of Suburban's situation. However, they feared that the faculty would balk at the invitation to participate (citing the president's likely domination and proprietary interest in the results), that the president would indeed want reaffirmation of the value of his tenure in office, and that real problems (and there were several) would not be discussed, much less solved.

Prestudy Activity.   The dean of Suburban decided to meet with the president to discuss the situation. He asked that he be given the opportunity to propose how to go about the self-study and the accreditation review, arguing that it would be good for him personally to do so and that the leverage of the process could be used to accomplish a few things he thought needed doing. The president agreed, although it was clear that he did not feel much studying was needed "to get reaccredited." He had been through it before, indeed had chaired evaluation teams to other colleges, and thought it "all fairly pro forma." It was agreed that the dean and his assistant would attend a self-study workshop conducted by the regional accrediting agency.

The workshop proved to be helpful, for other colleges faced problems similar to those of Suburban. Approaches were discussed and the need for design was emphasized. Several design cases were explored. The Suburban College duo returned from the workshop convinced that a protracted design stage was needed at their institution during which a steering/planning group could be brought to sense Suburban's needs, acknowledge the need for participative study, convince the president to accept the process, and devise the steps needed to conduct the whole thing.

The dean, with the president's approval, selected a ten-member planning group broadly representative of all aspects of the Suburban community, gave them materials from the workshop he had attended, and asked them to design the self-study process. To orient them he and a consultant conducted a one-day workshop for them on campus using "hands-on" materials from the previous workshop. The group, after reviewing concepts of self-study, was asked to formulate lists of "strengths," "problems," and "things needing or not needing study" at Suburban. The president was asked to sit in during the end of the day to "lend his support." He respected the consultant, so he agreed to do it. What he saw happening impressed him, and the constructive participative tone removed some of his apprehensions about the process.

The planning group made several decisions over the ensuing three months—that they needed a great deal of staff help, that *they* would run the process, that Suburban had several major problems which they wanted addressed, and that they would help convince their colleagues to participate.

The Design. The planning group decided that with two or three changes in their membership, they would become the steering group for a process which is represented diagrammatically in figure 4.6. It is their own version of what has previously been described as Comprehensive With Special Emphasis, variation 3, "The Integrated One-Step." Their adaptations included (1) a protracted design stage with plenty of training and orientation activities in order to arrange internal motivation and commitments from the president and the various faculty and staff factions; (2) a very heavy reliance on staff work (they decided that their committee should not spend time describing things and collecting data, but that rather others should do it for them—see chapter 5 for an example of their staff work expectations); (3) a decision to conduct collegewide surveys about goals, functioning, and

problems very early in the study in order to promote "ownership" of the process, and to get valuable participation and ideas; and (4) a recommendation that the mission and goals of Suburban be reviewed first, and reviewed thoroughly, in order to spur further commitment to the process.

The Suburban case is a very typical design situation and the approach they chose is a very useful one. It was, of course, designed for *their* specific circumstances; but several aspects of it are generally applicable, such as the reliance on heavy staff work to assist committees, the on-campus workshops, and the early use of surveys and data collection.

CASE TWO: State College

The setting. State College is a medium-sized, multipurpose (teacher education, liberal arts, and some other career programs) institution located in a small town. It is regionally accredited in a region where the accrediting commission emphasizes both self-improvement and adherence to the accreditation standards. The college also has three programs that are accredited by specialized agencies. There is a small but active institutional research program at State College, which was enhanced during a planning process completed three years ago. The enrollments have been stable at the college recently but early indications of some slippage are appearing. The enrollments in some programs have not held up well and the State Board's executive staff has begun to think about cutbacks and regional program planning within the state.

Prestudy planning. The president of State College asked the academic vice-president to think about the college's current needs and to consider ways that the upcoming regional accreditation review could be used to assist the college. The academic vice-president formed an eight-person planning group of three key chairpersons, three senior faculty members, and the institutional research officer and his associate vice-president. The group met four times over six weeks. At the second meeting they met with the staff representative of the regional accrediting commission. They discussed options and read handbooks on self-study. At the third meeting, they discussed recent institutional research reports, memos from the state board, and the last master plan projections. At the fourth meeting—an all-day retreat—they formulated a design and asked that the academic vice-president present it to the president, to the council of chairpersons and deans, and then to the regional commission for agreement.

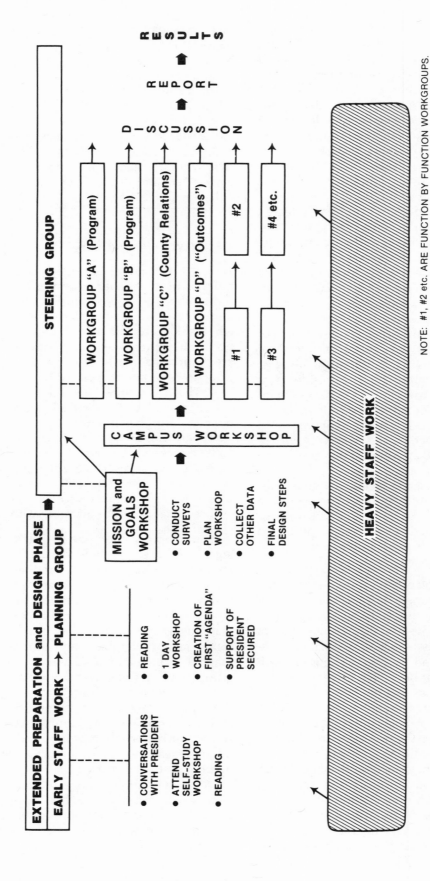

Figure 4.6. Diagrammatic representation of the self-study design for Suburban Community College.

The design. The prestudy planning group at State College decided that a fairly comprehensive review was needed. The self-study model that came closest to accommodating the college's needs was the Comprehensive with Special Emphasis. They felt the college must review, area by area, the progress made to implement the plan formulated several years earlier. They also felt that each area should assess its strengths and problems (the written regional accrediting standards would be a start) and then strengthen itself in light of the challenges ahead. The planning group added two special twists to the agenda. First, the college should place a special, heavy emphasis on program reviews. To that end, a program review task force would be formed and led by the academic vice-president. For one year, this group would study each program, host consultants, and formulate required action. Second, for two of the three specialized accreditation relationships, self-studies would be coordinated with the larger effort and a concurrent or joint team visit from the three agencies would be requested—to save time and money and to foster one view of the institution and its needs.

The mechanics of the study would be organized in what planning group members called a "rolling structure": With the exception of the program review task force and the two specialized program self-study groups, the tasks required under the comprehensive institutional review would occur in sequence—with two- to three-month efforts specially organized for each area in question. Groups to study goals, students, student services, facilities, institution, business affairs, academic services, and the like were formed, but the activities of each were scheduled in such a way that a steering group could move needed human and other resources from group to group. Work completed in some areas could then also be the needed starting point for other efforts. One or two groups worked simultaneously, and one group—the outcomes task force—was planned for longer tenure. It was to begin immediately and work closely with the goals group, the institutional research office, and the program review task force. It would function as long as required.

The culmination of the study would be a document that presented the perceived strengths, problems, and changes initiated or proposed in each area of the college. This document would accompany the report of the program review task force and the two specialized program reviews. Several workshops to discuss these reports would be organized under the top leadership of the college. The accreditation team visit would then be held. All the results of these efforts would be used as the starting point for the next planning effort, to commence immediately, the goal for which would be the creation of the plan for the next five years at State College that required some difficult decisions on program cutbacks, changes, and emphasis (see figure 4.7.)

Analysis. The situation at State College is a difficult but typical one. Clearly, the agenda of the college and the state must prevail over that of any outside agency. In light of the political ramifications of the study content, the potential benefits of inside and outside collaboration and of the concept of study-*then*-plan must be tapped, if possible. It is probable that a more useful, comprehensive study could be conducted if the need for serious program review were not present. But in this study-planning cycle, State College must mix its study patterns and attempt to focus on the program review. The nature of *that* review must also be carefully designed—with an appropriate emphasis on market studies, goal clarification and review, faculty and course strengths and weaknesses, well-orchestrated visits of outside reviewers, and close review of research, service, and other outcomes of the program being studied. The skill needed to manage such a review is substantial and will be a key factor in determining whether the potentially useful design will work. The other key factor—under the stressful circumstances of declining enrollment at State College—is the segmentation of the process. People can be used more effectively, and they probably will participate more willingly, if the process is divided into study phases, then planning and decision phases. They also will be able to focus better if each phase is carefully divided into discrete, manageable pieces, for few people can function in a total "systems" sense.

CASE THREE: A Private College Struggling to Survive

The story of the self-study process described here is an important one. It really happened and may be considered in more detail by reading the primary report of the case (Kells, 1977). It is the story of Mercy College in Dobbs Ferry, New York, and it is adapted here with the permission of the institution.

The setting. In the spring of 1976, Mercy College found itself at the end of a five-year period of frantic activity. Under the strong leadership of a new, marketing-oriented president, the college had explored and developed several new student markets and branch campuses. It had survived and was growing. It had just completed a useful master

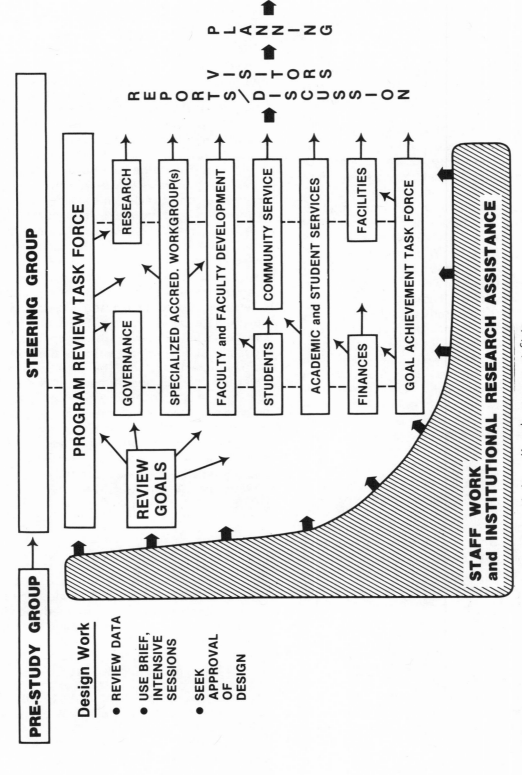

Figure 4.7. Diagrammatic representation of the self-study process at State College.

plan and it had recently reviewed its mission statement and specific college goals. It was now time to begin a self-study process in preparation for a regional accreditation review in eighteen months.

The prestudy planning. The president realized that the college now had to take stock, but was concerned that a traditional, descriptive, comprehensive review might not be helpful nor possible. He asked the dean of the college to head a planning group to design a useful self-study. The dean invited a self-study consultant to participate in the first meetings and to address the faculty about the plans the group would develop. The group was formed with three senior, hardworking faculty members and three administrative staff people as the members. At the first meeting with the consultant, the following situation was described.

- Most group members were aware that the college had changed but not *how* it had changed —particularly with respect to the traditional liberal arts objectives, the student body, and the image others had of the college.
- All felt that the college must know much more about the new student body and the recent graduates.
- Most were concerned about the way in which the college now functioned with respect to services and governance.
- A consensus among members was that the master plan was generally useful, but might need some polishing.
- All reported that the institutional research capacity of the college was nil.
- It was obvious that the college staff was small and *very* tired.

Design decisions—The planning group, which would become the steering group for the study, made the following decisions:

1. The master plan would be used and improved.
2. Mercy's needs would be emphasized in the study.
3. The self-study would emphatically be used to develop some institutional research capacity.
4. The effort would use the recent apparent outcomes of the college's programs in order to improve Mercy.
5. The study would identify and solve some problems.
6. A comprehensive study was neither needed nor possible.
7. The staff would be used appropriately, intensively, and in carefully sequenced activities.
8. Outsiders would be used intelligently.

9. Use would be made of natural work groups— the departments—to do some of the work.
10. The study would be an educational venture. Others would share in the study results, too.

The prestudy planning group of Mercy realized that an extremely busy faculty, with a relatively small percentage of full-time professionals, could not afford to waste time in long-term committee efforts. The planning committee was ready to work hard and wanted to involve the departments actively as work groups. They also wanted some open, well-attended workshops that could produce results for the college.

The committee formulated the scheme depicted in figure 4.8, under which an interrelated sequence of intensive activities was planned to accomplish the design decisions. The committee first took steps to gather needed data and to become aware of the perceived problems. They asked the consultant to propose ways to gather information about goal achievement and the functioning of programs and services. The group reviewed the drafted procedures and instruments, chose four or five, and assigned them to be polished and run on the campus by individual offices and student groups. Included was a cohort attrition study, faculty and senior student surveys, and a commercially available functioning inventory. The committee also asked the department chairpersons to convene department meetings during September and October of 1976. The departments were asked to provide data that would be hard to gather in other ways and that had not been available in recent years. They were also asked to answer the following questions about strengths and problems at the departmental and college level.

1. What are the educational goals of your department?
2. What are the three most important educational problems faced by your department?
3. What are the solutions to the educational problems which are suggested by your department? (Solutions within the department as well as external solutions should be thoroughly considered.)
4. What are the three most important problems faced by the college? (Please review the data submitted for your review by the Self-Study Steering Committee.)
5. What are the solutions proposed by your department to college problems?
6. What are the college's greatest strengths?
7. What are the greatest opportunities for the college? (For growth, improvement, development, and the like.)

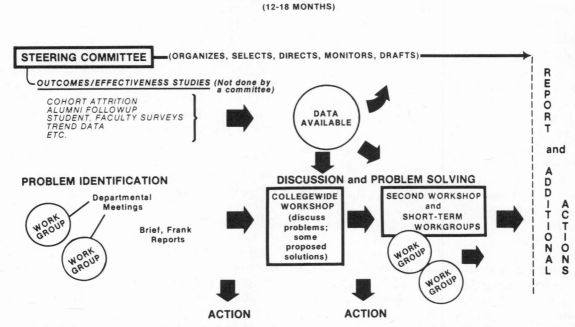

Figure 4.8. The design of the Mercy College self-study process. *Source:* H. R. Kells, "An Alternative Model for Self-Study in Higher Education," *NCAQ*, Vol. 52, Fall 1977, p. 343.

The departments were given about ninety days to respond, at the end of which time all departments but one had responded. The average response was five pages; none exceeded the ten-page limit.

Finally, the planning group proposed that, when the data were available, a collegewide workshop be held to discuss the results, recommend responses, and authorize several short- or longer-term work groups to solve problems not readily solvable during the self-study. An invitational workshop for the academic communities of Mercy and of other colleges was planned for the end of the process. The written summary of the full design was submitted to the staff of the regional accrediting commission, which approved the report.

Analysis.   The Mercy self-study went largely as planned. The positive leadership and internal motivation propelled the process. Delays were encountered in collecting the data and conducting the surveys, so schedules were adjusted. The studies and the problem identification steps were quite useful. Some problems common to all departments were identified. The college responded immediately to those problems which were more quickly solvable. College leadership changed staffing and organization and provided modest but needed administrative assistance to several overloaded department chairpersons who had borne the brunt of recent program expansion. They strengthened diagnostic testing and remedial activ-

ities for part of the student population. The departmental responses to the self-study process were frank and illuminating and prompted many of the changes. The momentum for change was created by the simultaneous, participatory identification of common concerns by most of the twelve departments. Action became possible on problems which were previously only partially recognized. Indeed, such action became politically impossible to neglect.

The first faculty workshop was a success. It focused on two of the problems identified in the first phase of the study. The faculty participated readily in this event, and some volunteered for subsequent work groups, since they were relieved of the burden of yearlong self-study committee work. These work groups were to attack the larger problems not addressed in the self-study. The quality of the workshop experience was high. Participants were pleased with the self-study design and the changes undertaken.

The extent and quality of participation in the Mercy self-study process were also high. The effectiveness studies proved to be useful and the legacy from the study of ongoing institutional research and decision making was substantial. Problems were identified, some changes or other responses were made, and the prognosis is presently for a rich harvest of additional benefits. The self-study document that was produced included a twenty-page description of the college, a description of the self-study process, a presentation of the results of the goals/effectiveness studies and the departmental discussions, a set of recommendations from the workshop, and a report of actions already taken on the more readily solvable problems. Also included were an extensive set of appendixes, including the recently reviewed master plan and the data from the various studies conducted.

The foregoing three case examples do not include all of the major approaches that can be used for self-studies. They do, however, include enough of the design elements to stimulate the reader to consider other than a rote prescription for a self-study process. A particularly interesting approach used by Brookdale Community College in New Jersey is outlined in Appendix D, and departmental or program-level approaches are presented in chapter 7. The potential to create useful processes exists. Use it.

Using Work Groups Effectively

The heavy use of the committee or work group in conducting self-studies has the potential for substantial organizational improvement from the high level of staff participation, diminished goal displacement and the possibly deepened staff member commitment to change. Reliance on the work-group approach also brings great problems. The weak link in an otherwise well-designed, internally motivated, potentially useful self-study is often the lack of skills among group members needed to solve problems and even to function well. When a group is the best format to solve a problem, skills are needed to clarify problems, to explore alternatives, to find the best resources in the group, and to develop and select creative solutions.

Many groups or committees at postsecondary institutions function very badly. The leadership of committees is often designated for the wrong reasons and most leaders have no training in the skills they need to work well with groups. Committee functioning is often typified by poor use of time, no "pretask" planning, poor or no choice of communication pattern, inadequate staff support, poor decision processes, and poor problem identification, clarification, and solution. The best resources in the group often remain unused; solutions arrived at may not be the best answers. Members are often used inappropriately, vested interests can easily prevail, and a climate necessary for action on the solutions is rarely created.

To function well, a given self-study process needs properly selected and trained group leaders and several people with the ability to design and conduct group efforts. The lack of people with such skills is a major weakness in many self-study processes.

A role exists for the prestudy planning group in making sure groups work well. Members should informally inventory the people on campus who can lead groups or help train group leaders. Psychology departments, social work programs, and management programs are often good sources for such people. Local industry can also be helpful. Large firms usually have a staff training director who establishes and often runs training programs for group leaders and team training workshops, as well as programs in listening skills, developmental communication, and problem solving. Several national organizations also offer such training, such as the National Training Laboratories in Bethel, Maine; the Higher Education Management Institute associated with the American Council on Education; and the United States Department of Agriculture Graduate School, Special Programs Branch in Washington, D.C. Each has an array of group and other management training opportunities. Finally, major universities often have personnel development programs with constituent short training courses that could be of value to group leaders and problem solvers in self-study processes. Do not forget to check your *own* or a nearby institution for a possible group skills training program.

Even though special training really ought to occur—it can be the first payoff attributable to the self-study effort—there are things any institution can do without special training sessions to improve the functioning of work groups in a self-study process.

1. *Promote trust and risk taking through increased knowledge and understanding among members.* The start of any work group should be an introductory exercise that is sufficiently deep and involving to begin the process of breaking down the interpersonal barriers. A biologist may distrust a social scientist until he finds out that they are both interested in sailing—and that, after all, "that guy is pretty sharp." A dinner, a social gathering, golf, tennis, and so on can work wonders by thawing the professional and often stiff demeanor academicians usually bring to a work group.

2. *Group leaders should always plan well each session of the group* (see chapter 1). Group leaders should be selected, in part, for their ability to promote effective functioning in the group. Beyond planning well for each session, they must *lead* the session: They should promote participation through questioning of group members and encourage listening among group members, as well as summarize continuously in order to focus discussion and to guide the development of creative solutions. They should use several techniques, not just ram-

bling or even guided discussion. Brainstorming, subgroups, debates, case analyses, and external stimuli (visitors and comparison information) are a few of the available techniques. Visual displays, diagrams, and summaries are others. Creative uses of staff assistance and ample and appropriate use of data are often helpful. Through such techniques the group leader stimulates the group members to apply their talents and expertise to the problems before the group.

3. *Schedule meetings carefully.* Do not meet for the sake of meeting. *A good work group brings together the right people at the right time with the right information to handle real issues.* If one of the ingredients is missing, reschedule the meeting until they are all present.

4. *Be attuned to the psychological dimensions of a work group.* Use intensive, brief activities so the participant can see a clear beginning and end to the activity. An assignment by the dean to serve on an eighteen-month task force can deaden interest. An assignment to solve a problem or to study a function over a two-month period—even if the group must meet six times for at least half a day—is far preferable.

Use the proper sequence of activities. Some tasks must follow other tasks. Yet self-study process after self-study process ignores this fact. All committees are started at once, despite the fact that several must use the results of one of the groups. The newly appointed work-group members often take three frustrating meetings to discover it. The planners of the process should not permit such wasteful scheduling to happen. Most of these occurrences can be foreseen by a steering group.

Leaders and planners should *share the context and the results* of any information-gathering activities with everyone who takes part in the process. If work-group members are worthy to participate in the self-study, they are worthy of a proper orientation and thorough explanation of how their work was received and used. Communicate constantly and people will respond.

Match the right person to the right job in a work group. It is discouraging to recount how many times a young instructor of music is asked to handle budget figures or a professor of engineering with much to bring to the steering process is buried in a committee to consider library holdings. Proper use of human resources involves checking, communicating, asking, discussing, and trying. It rarely results from "quick and dirty," nonparticipatory, or just politically acceptable schemes for the assignment of people.

Remember and reward. It is not always possible to thank everyone who participates in a process or who does a great job at a particular meeting by monetary reward or by promotion. But the biggest reward is often a sincere thank-you for a job well done, a commendation in that person's personnel file, and public recognition. If self-study is to be ongoing—and if people are to become more committed to their program and/or institution—these rewards are imperative. Of course, publicly acknowledging valuable participation is also the decent thing to do.

5. *Remember the political dimensions.* A brief refresher from Political Science I will help the planning of a self-study process. The mandate from the leader must be clear, strong, and repeated several times and in several ways. Funds must be committed to the effort or some faculty members will not believe it is real. Use a mixture of "natural" work groups (the usual work group for the members—their department, for instance) and mixed membership groups. Some tasks can best be handled in usual settings. Some require the lift of opposing experiences, backgrounds, or points of view. And, of course, be sure to involve representatives of the formal and the informal power structure. You will need both.

6. *Technical, procedural aspects* can be very important. Self-study processes are complex, time-consuming, and important. They *must* receive adequate staff support. Some released time for a faculty coordinator is probably a minimum requirement. Technical and typing support, data services, time on the computer, priority treatment for work to be done—these are all also necessary. There is no "free lunch" in the self-study business.

Finally, the process must be well steered. Waste must be averted. More on these matters appears in chapter 5.

Planning for Change

The prestudy planning group must begin to think about the ways that the agenda for self-study can be realized. Planning a useful self-study is a very good beginning, but recommendations for change that result from such studies too often are left on the doorstep of implementation. They are not heeded. The usual final resting place for the book of suggestions is the bottom shelf of the bookcase, covered with dust.

What can be done to change this situation? A look at some of the theories and models for change can give us guidance. Kurt Lewin (1947) spoke of the necessity in a change process to "unfreeze" the present condition, then to change the present condition, then to "refreeze" the situation, so things can function. Self-study should be a useful way to "unfreeze" things. People must be prepared for change. Jack

Lindquist (1978) helps us some more. His "strategies for change" include helping people discover for themselves that things need changing; helping them gain, in a nonthreatening way, some new knowledge about how others have solved similar problems; and providing the "process help" so people can solve their own problems. Beckhard and Harris (1977) indicate that organizational transitions (changes) are often very complex and that the change process, particularly the transition state to the new form, must be managed carefully.

These theories and models, plus some common sense, ought to guide us to plan for implementing changes that result from a study process. In planning for such change, the following points require attention.

1. The planning group must include in their published plan the expectation that changes will result from the process. They should expect the president or other leader to endorse this concept.

2. The critical importance of accomplishing a wide range of participation in the process cannot be overstated. If people can be involved in the building of a new approach, they can be counted on to carry it out. An isolated process that proposes changes that affect people's lives will be swept away—rebuffed by understandably alienated, even threatened, respondents. Involving people is painful. It is slow. It takes considerable skill. But there is no real substitute for it in the long run. People must "buy in" psychologically, or they will oppose the recommended new order.

3. The planning group must insist on an "open" study process. It should recommend that the subsequent steering group openly and frequently communicate orally and in writing. Once that open style is established, it is possible to state publicly the changes or improvements being recommended, an expected timetable for consideration, and some general task assignments and expectations—for all to see. Few people can escape the pressure such openness can generate, unless the management of the place is so chaotic as to permit no action or to snuff out even the strongest of initiatives.

4. The self-study process should not cease before a real and potentially effective group has been assigned to oversee the consideration and even some implementation of change suggestions. A periodic review to monitor progress should be conducted by the new group and enforced by the president, dean, or director. It is sometimes most effective if the new group can be a regular committee in the institution's or program's governance structure. Under certain circumstances, a totally new group is required.

5. Finally, the self-study process should not end until the first steps of a succeeding master plan or other planning process are at least visible on the institutional horizon. The self-study should be a prelude to planning, as well as a spur to change and improvement.

Seeking Approval and Acceptance for the Design

The prestudy planning group should seek approval for the design it develops. The chief executive officer and, of course, any accrediting or other outside agency involved should receive the study plan and should be asked to respond in writing. Such a response can function as a kind of contract and it can and should bring with it suggestions for enhancing the plan (Kirkwood, 1978).

Securing acceptance of the plan is even more important to the success of the process. The study group, with the chief executive officer present to convey his or her support, should offer the plan to all professional staff, at smaller institutions, and to the administrative council and/or senate, at larger ones. Study planners should remember that no proposal for a participative process is ever greeted eagerly. Thus, they should contrast, in their presentation, the value of a specially designed, locally oriented process with that of the more traditional often useless variety. They could also invite an outsider to speak about the need for a useful process and the listeners' responsibility to respond to the study in some way. The pride professionals hold for their work and for their institution is usually evident when the call for help comes forth. If the call proposes a useful process, it can receive a positive response. In any event, not to seek acceptance and participation will only lead to the planners' embarrassment and to a less than fruitful process.

Check lists for use by prestudy planning group members as they design a self-study process close this chapter.

References

Beckhard and Harris. *Organizational Transitions* (chap. 1).

Fordyce, Jack K., and Weil, Raymond. *Managing with People: A Manager's Handbook of Organization Development Methods*. Reading, MA: Addison-Wesley, 1971.

Kells, H. R. "An Alternative Model for Self-Study in Higher Education." *The North Central Association Quarterly*, Fall 1977, pp. 341–46.

Kells and Kirkwood. "Institutional Self-Evaluation Processes" (chap. 2).

Kirkwood, Robert. "Institutional Responsibilities in Accreditation." *Educational Record*, Fall 1978, pp. 297–304.

Lewis, Kurt. "Frontiers in Group Dynamics: Concept, Method, and Reality in Social Science; Social Equilibria and Social Change." *Human Relations*, June 1947, pp. 5–41.

Lindquist, Jack. *Strategies for Change* (chap. 1).

CHECKLIST

For Members of the Prestudy Planning Group

Desired Attributes of a Self-Study Process

Do we have—or how can we arrange to achieve—these attributes?

1. Internal motivation _____

2. Top leadership committed to the process

3. Design appropriate to circumstances _____

4. Goals clear, outcomes of goals studied and used _____

5. Participation (representative; extensive)

6. Good process leadership _____

   Training needed? _____

7. Problems assessed and solved _____

8. Change, improvement expected; during and as a result of self-study _____

9. A useful, readable report should result

10. A better system to study ourself should result _____

CHECKLIST

For Members of the Prestudy Planning Group

The Agenda

What are out major intentions for this study process? (What should be our primary agenda? What should we expect to get out of it?)

1. _____
_____
_____
_____
_____
_____
_____
_____
_____
_____
_____
_____

2. _____
_____
_____
_____
_____
_____
_____
_____
_____
_____
_____
_____
_____
_____
_____
_____

3. _____
_____
_____
_____
_____
_____
_____
_____
_____
_____
_____
_____
_____
_____
_____

4. _____
_____
_____
_____
_____
_____
_____
_____
_____
_____
_____
_____
_____
_____

CHECKLIST

For Members of the Prestudy Planning Group

The Design Questions

1. What is the status of *institutional research* at the institution, and what is the status of the data base concerning students, staff, programs, resources, and goal achievement (outcomes)? Should the self-study process leave improved capacities for ongoing study in these areas? Which areas? _____
   _____
   _____
   _____
   _____

2. What is the status of *master planning* at the institution? How recently has a thorough planning process been conducted? When is the next cycle to be conducted? What studies would enhance the next planning process?
   _____
   _____
   _____
   _____
   _____

3. What is the status of the statement of *goals* for the institution, its subunits, and/or the program in question? Are goals clearly stated, complete, and current? Is there a reasonably useful consensus on them? Are they commonly understood and used as the basis of program and institutional management? What work remains to be done in this area? _____
   _____
   _____
   _____
   _____

4. Have there been *recent, useful study* processes at the institution? What written evidence is available that resulted from such processes? How can the current study process build on and complement what was done in these studies? _____
   _____
   _____
   _____
   _____

5. What has been the level of *turnover* in institution or program leaders and/or staff members? What are the orientation needs of any new members of the community? How can the study process meet these needs?
   _____
   _____
   _____
   _____
   _____

6. What is the level of *morale* at the institution or in the program? What *historical and/or political factors* must be considered? What implications will these factors have for the level of participation in the study, and in the timing or sequence of its separate elements?
   _____
   _____
   _____
   _____

7. Is there a reasonably useful consensus among the formal and informal leaders at the institution concerning the major problems which the institution or program faces? What are they? Should the study focus on these? How? Should we gather more opinions and evidence about what the problems are? _____
   _____
   _____
   _____

8. How prepared is the staff, *psychologically,* in terms of their *readiness* to undertake a major participatory venture in self-analysis? What are the implications for the design?
   _____
   _____
   _____
   _____

9. What *other accreditation relationships* and state-related or other activities or responsibilities does the institution or program have or must it complete in the near future? Is it possible to combine the processes and perhaps synergistically to produce better results from all such processes? _____
   _____
   _____
   _____

10. What accommodations must be made to the *size and complexities* of the institution or program? _____
    _____
    _____
    _____

11. What self-study model seems to be most appropriate in light of all of the above? Can it be depicted diagrammatically? _____
    _____
    _____
    _____

5

Organizing for Self-Study

In accordance with the proposed general sequence for the self-study process, this chapter is about the organization of the study. The organizational steps follow the plans produced by the prestudy planning group. They flow naturally from the design and from the obvious need to move as effectively as possible into the study process itself. Organization concerns roles, relationships, and resources. Since in this book we have added the traditional "staffing" function to our organization step, we must also consider the selection and proper orientation of the people who will conduct the study. We begin the examination of these issues by reviewing the experiences of others in organizing self-studies.

What Others Have Done and Perceived

As indicated earlier, the accrediting agencies are the organizations which have been associated most with self-study processes. Therefore we can learn the most about what practices have been by examining their experiences. These entities publish self-study handbooks recommending that a steering committee be used, that committees be established to address the constituent areas of the institution or study issues, and that a professional be released from some regular duties to coordinate the study. When an institution is conducting a self-study for accreditation purposes, the organizational assistance provided by the handbooks is augmented by consultation from an accrediting agency staff member.

Until recently, the actual patterns of organizations used by colleges in self-studies in the 1970s had not been documented. Thus, I undertook with Robert Kirkwood to examine self-study processes at over 200 institutions in the Northeast of all sizes, types, and ages in 1978–79 (Kells and Kirkwood, 1979). The following summary tables permit us to see what the practice has been in institutional self-study. *The reader should not conclude that what has been is what should be, or that what was found about college- or universitywide studies applies to program or departmental efforts. The latter have been little studied and are addressed in chapter 7.*

None of the process characteristics indicated in the following tables was found to correlate positively and significantly with perceived success. As noted in chapter 4, only strong leadership, internal motivation, and the appropriateness of the design were shown to be so correlated.

The median characteristics from table 5.1 are: length of study, fifteen months; funds directly expended, $2,501–$5,000; number of work groups, 4–6; and average size of work group, 7–9. The amount of funds directly expended is surprisingly small considering the size and potential benefit of the processes conceived. In table 5.2, the participation levels in the self-study processes examined are presented. Several

TABLE 5.1. Characteristics of Institutional Self-Study Processes, 1971–77
(N = 208)

Characteristics	Percentage of Institutions
Length of the study	
6 months	7
9 months	11
12 months	20
15 months	21
18 months	21
21 months	6
24 months	10
>24 months	4
Funds directly expended, including estimated released time, printing, mailing, data processing, supplies, secretarial, etc.	
Have no idea	17
$ 0–$ 2,500	24
2,501– 5,000	23
5,001– 7,500	9
7,501– 10,000	5
10,001– 12,500	8
12,501– 15,500	5
15,501– 17,500	2
17,501– 20,000	0
>$20,000	7
Number of committees, task forces, or other work groups, in addition to the steering committee	
No committees	5
1–3 committees	14
4–6 committees	34
7–9 committees	23
10–12 committees	14
13–15 committees	2
>15 committees	6
Average size of the committees	
1–3 people	9
4–6 people	36
7–9 people	25
10–12 people	14
13–15 people	7
>15 people	3

TABLE 5.2. Participation Levels in Institutional Self-Study Processes
(N = 208)

Constituent Group	Percentage of Institutions
Number of persons who served on committees or work groups of any kind or who carried out specific assignments in the process	
0–25	17
26–50	25
51–75	22
76–100	15
101–125	10
126–150	2
151–175	1
176–200	0
>200	6
Percentage of constituent group that the number above represented, by group; *example*, What percentage of the total faculty (full- and part-time) did the faculty members in the above group represent?	
Faculty	
1–5 percent	5
6–10 percent	6
11–15 percent	10
16–20 percent	6
21–30 percent	11
31–40 percent	5
41–50 percent	14
>50 percent	40
Administration	
1–5 percent	8
6–10 percent	12
11–15 percent	5
16–20 percent	12
21–30 percent	14
31–40 percent	6
41–50 percent	12
>50 percent	29
Students	
0 percent	9
0.1–0.5 percent	29
0.51–1 percent	10
1.1–1.5 percent	7
1.51–2 percent	7
2.1–3 percent	6
3.1–4 percent	3
4.1–5 percent	5
>5 percent	21
Board members	
0 percent	48
1–10 percent	31
11–20 percent	8
21–30 percent	3
31–40 percent	1
41–50 percent	1
>50 percent	5

interesting aspects deserve comment. First, it is important to recognize that despite the presence of almost 30 percent of the sample institutions with enrollment over 5,000 students and corresponding professional staffs of 500 or more, 90 percent of the institutions were able to secure the participation of only 125 or fewer people in the study process. This statistic is important and not unexpected when one considers the possible span of control in any given process. Apparently, a given steering mechanism can manage only 100–125 people at the most in a self-study process. Large institutions would be wise to consider multiple or phased processes if more participation is desired.

The other interesting item in table 5.2 is the relatively high percentage of institutions indicating over 40 percent participation of the faculty. This figure is encouraging, but probably somewhat deceiving. The Middle States region in which the 200 institutions studied are located has a high percentage of small institutions. Also, the relatively low participation of trustees in self-studies is disappointing, though not surprising.

Finally, in table 5.3 is presented a list of the statistically significant relationships between institutional types, sizes, and structures (institutional characteristics) and how the process was carried out. Three particularly interesting aspects should be noted. First, the most persistent possible intervening factor in process formulation and management appears to be *institutional size.* Size appears to be significantly associated with:

- Form of study chosen
- Number of committees employed
- Percentage of faculty on the steering committee
- Cost of the self-study process
- Number of people involved
- Percentage of all faculty members involved
- Use of outcome studies

Some of the apparent relationships between the process characteristics and degree level and disciplinary profile of the institution are probably related to or may even be caused by size. Baccalaureate-granting liberal arts institutions, in great number in the sample and almost all small or very small in size, showed the same pattern of relationships as was seen with size.

TABLE 5.3. Self-Study Process Characteristics Significantly Associated with Institutional Characteristics (N = 208)

Process Characteristic	Institutional Characteristic	Significance	Explanation
Form or model of self-study	Several	<0.040	Size, degree level, sponsorship, number of schools.
Number of committees	Size	0.023	Positive correlation.
Percentage of steering committee as faculty members	Size	0.032	Very small and very large institutions used fewer faculty members.
Cost	Size	0.036	Positive correlation.
	Level (degree)	0.035	Master's and doctoral level institutions cost disproportionately more.
	Collegiate structure	0.023	>5 colleges, disproportionately higher cost.
Number of people involved	Size	0.000	Positive correlation.
	Level (degree)	0.021	Associate and baccalaureate institutions disproportionately more people; master's and doctoral, disproportionately fewer.
	Collegiate structure	0.028	>5 colleges, disproportionately more.
	Disciplinary profile	0.003	Disciplinary profile follows size pattern.
	Time since last study	0.001	5 years, disproportionately fewer; 10 years, disproportionately more.
Motivation:			
External	Disciplinary profile	0.050	Professional schools disproportionately high.
Internal	Disciplinary profile	0.006	Liberal arts schools disproportionately high; professional schools disproportionately low.
Percentage of all faculty members involved	Level (degree)	0.001	Master's and doctoral institutions disproportionately less; associate and baccalaureate, disproportionately more.
	Size	0.043	Large institutions disproportionately less.
Improvement motivation (when listed as a strength)	Level (degree)	0.001	Baccalaureate institutions disproportionately more; master's and doctoral disproportionately less.
	Disciplinary profile	0.017	Liberal arts institutions disproportionately more; professional schools disproportionately less.
Use of goal achievement (outcomes) studies	Size	0.001	Large institutions disproportionately fewer.
	Level (degree)	0.000	Master's and doctoral level disproportionately fewer.
	Collegiate structure	0.001	>5 colleges disproportionately fewer.

Source: Adapted from H. R. Kells and Robert Kirkwood, "Institutional Self-Evaluation Processes," *Educational Record,* Winter 1979, p. 40.
Notes: The Kruskal-Wallis test was used to determine significance (<0.050). All other characteristics showed no significant relationship with process characteristics.

The second noteworthy item in table 5.3 shows the relatively high incidence of externally motivated self-studies in professional schools, which could be explained by the pervasive influence of specialized, usually prescriptive program-accrediting agencies in these fields. Professional school staff members may tend to feel that one must look first at indicators of "good practice" in the field rather than at what works well in the institution as a basis for study and improvement.

Finally, it is not surprising—though again it is disappointing—to find that master's and doctoral level institutions—often larger and more attuned to high ability, high performance, and more professional students and staff members—are reported as being disproportionately less motivated for improvement in the self-studies and as using disproportionately fewer outcomes studies to test goal achievement than are other schools.

Satisfaction with Self-Study Processes. Several measures were employed in the retrospective study which related perceived satisfaction with the self-study processes. Results with four of the items are reported in table 5.4. It appears that people who have been intimately involved in designing and coordinating self-studies are very enthusiastic about the benefits that result. The level of satisfaction found in this study is higher than that determined by Romine in his study of some entire accreditation processes (Romine, 1975), but that is understandable since the self-study aspect is likely to be (or likely to be seen as) the most beneficial aspect of the accreditation process. The perceptions about how aware and positively inclined most members of the general groups in the academic community were about the self-study processes ranged from a high of about 90 percent for administrators to a low of 20 percent for students.

The perceived major strengths and weaknesses of the self-study processes are recorded in table 5.5.

When all of the institutional characteristics, all of the process characteristics, and the perceived major strengths and weaknesses were examined in association with two of the major satisfaction measures—whether improvement was perceived to have occurred and whether most people involved with the process were perceived as feeling it was useful—*only three*

TABLE 5.4.   Satisfaction Measures for Institutional Self-Study Processes
(N = 208)

OPINION	PERCENTAGE OF INSTITUTIONS	OPINION	PERCENTAGE OF INSTITUTIONS
The self-study process resulted in real improvement at the institution (in program or policies or procedures):		Most of the people actively involved in the self-study process thought it was	
Definitely yes	52	Very useful	39
Probably yes	40	Useful	58
Probably no	7	Not very useful	3
Definitely no	1	Not useful at all	1

	PERCENTAGE OF INSTITUTIONS			
	MOST BOARD MEMBERS	MOST ADMINISTRATORS	MOST FACULTY MEMBERS	MOST STUDENTS
Regarding the self-study process, most people on campus:				
Were really unaware of it	3	1	2	31
Were aware but had no opinion because of lack of information	12	1	7	33
Were aware of it and thought it was useful	69	89	66	20
Were aware of it, but thought it neither useful nor harmful	8	5	20	14
Were aware of it, but thought it was harmful (wasteful, too costly, diverting)	1	3	3	1

	PERCENTAGE OF INSTITUTIONS
In general, in light of the institution's reasons for choosing it, the self-study form turned out to be a good choice:	
Generally, yes	87
Qualified, yes	11
Generally, no	2
Definitely no	1

TABLE 5.5. Perceived Major Strengths and Weaknesses of Institutional Self-Study Processes

(N = 208)

EVALUATION	PERCENTAGE OF INSTITUTIONS
Major strengths of the self-study process:	
Great commitment existed to conduct study for institutional improvement	45
Strong, appropriate support and leadership were provided at the top of the institution	69
Active participation by desired people was achieved	72
Goals were reexamined and/or clarified	76
Action to solve problems was initiated	59
Improvement occurred in one or more major areas	60
Morale and awareness were enhanced on campus	46
Other	5
Major weaknesses and/or disappointments of the self-study process:	
Broad commitment to conduct the study for institutional purposes was missing	14
Support and leadership from the top were absent or weak	8
Adequate amount of participation was never really achieved	13
Representative participation was not achieved	11
Consensus on problems was never achieved	16
Problem solving was not initiated	14
Little improvement ever resulted	14
No real effort was made to study educational outcomes	18
Increased morale and institutional awareness were not achieved	18
No relationship existed of self-study to planning	17
Other	8

Note: Multiple responses were possible.

factors seemed to be significantly associated. Table 5.6 presents these results. No institutional variables were found to be significant. Only perceived primary motivation (with internal improvement-oriented motivation being positively associated with satisfaction and vice versa), perceived commitment of top leaders at the institution (similarly associated), and satisfaction with the choice of self-study form in light of institutional circumstances were significantly associated with perceived satisfaction. No other factors seemed to be substantively or statistically significant. When listed as a strength of the process, high participation levels on campus were significantly associated, but reported *actual* participation levels were not.

That no basic institutional characteristics such as size, age, degree level, or general disciplinary profile were significantly associated with satisfaction is a hopeful finding for those interested in improving such potentially useful processes, for it would seem that any type of institution could organize and conduct a satisfactory self-study. That none of the mechanical or organizational aspects of the process steps examined was importantly associated with satisfaction is a similarly reassuring finding, for it has long been assumed by most knowledgeable practitioners that any organization or process can be made to work—that is, to achieve goals—if one *wants* to make it work.

The Steering Committee

The structural organizations used in self-studies are very important process dimensions. Central to the total process is usually a steering committee that organizes the study in light of the agreed-upon design, usually selects the work groups and their members, and coordinates the ongoing activities. It is also usually the key body in interpreting the results of the studies and deliberations, as well as in formulating recommendations for institutional change and improvement. Before describing the activities of the steering committee in more detail, let us examine the data from the 1979 retrospective study on steering committee composition.

As indicated in table 5.7, the median respondent institution used a steering group with ten to twelve members, and 55 percent of the institutions had steering groups with seven to twelve members. The median institution had a steering group membership of about 30 percent administrators, 50 percent faculty members, and 10 percent students. It had no trustees, no local community members, and no alumni. The entire membership profile included administrators up to a level of about 60 percent of the steering group composition; faculty membership spread throughout the range, all the way to 80–90 percent of the composition; 30 percent student participation; and only 10 percent participation each for trustees, community members, and alumni. Faculty membership seemed to vary most according to institutional circumstances (see table 5.3). The respondent institutions in the retrospective study used administrators as the self-study coordinators or chairpersons of the steering committee about 55 percent of the time, and nearly 45 percent of the institutions used faculty members. Of these, approximately 60 percent were released from regular teaching duties to some extent. Forty-three percent of these were relieved of one-quarter load or less of teaching duties, and 85 percent of the faculty members were relieved of one-half load or less. In my judgment, the coordinator of a self-study process, who chairs the steering committee,

TABLE 5.6.   Factors Associated with Satisfaction in Institutional Self-Study Processes
(N = 208)

FACTOR	SATISFACTION MEASURES		EXPLANATION
	PERCEPTION THAT IMPROVEMENT RESULTED	PERCEPTION THAT MOST PEOPLE INVOLVED THOUGHT PROCESS WAS USEFUL	
External motivation	0.004	NAS*	Disproportionately less improvement when motivation was perceived as external.
Internal motivation	0.002	0.000	Disproportionately more improvement and perceived usefulness when motivation was perceived as internal.
Improvement motivation (when listed as a strength)	0.006	0.015	Disproportionately higher satisfaction on both measures when improvement motivation was listed as a strength of the process.
Lack of improvement motivation (when listed as a weakness)	0.000	0.001	The reverse of the previous item.
Supportive leadership (when listed as a strength)	0.023	NSA*	Disproportionately more improvement when leadership support was listed as a strength of the process.
Lack of leadership support (when listed as a weakness)	0.000	NSA*	Disproportionately low levels of satisfaction when low participation was listed as a weakness of the process.
Good choice of process form	0.030	NSA*	Disproportionately more improvement reported when the form chosen was perceived as a good choice.
Particular form of process chosen	NSA*	0.037	Forms 1 and 4 had disproportionately higher responses under perceived usefulness.
Participation level high (when listed as a strength)	0.001	0.008	Disproportionately high levels of satisfaction when high participation listed as a strength of the process.
Participation level low (when listed as a weakness)	0.002	NSA*	Disproportionately low levels of satisfaction when low participation was listed as a weakness of the process.
Goals examined (when listed as a strength)	0.050	NSA*	Disproportionately high levels of perceived institutional improvement when work with goals was listed as a strength.

Source: Kells and Kirkwood, "Institutional Self-Evaluation Process," p. 43.
Notes: No significant association with satisfaction was found with any other institutional or process factors. The Kruskal-Wallis test was used to determine significance (<0.050).
*NSA means "Not significantly associated."

directs the activities of any clerical or administrative help, and is the constant proponent for the process, should receive at least one-half load reduction in teaching duties. The coordinator's job is a major administrative assignment of considerable importance to the institution.

Composing the Steering Group

The composition of the steering group usually follows naturally from that of the prestudy planning group. During that experience some participants probably developed specific interests, and natural leaders may have emerged. In any event, the chairperson of the planning group, in consultation with the executive staff of the institution, may wish to augment the steering group in light of the self-study design, the tasks to be attempted, and the political and other human realities of the institution. The following things must be considered in composing the steering group:

1. Who are the natural leaders with good organizational and conceptual skills?
2. What subtasks must be accomplished in the study? If the steering group is to have an interlocking membership with each major subgroup, how many members are needed? Remember, some of the tasks can be performed in tandem order, and every task need not be done by a committee.
3. What important informal leaders might be very important and useful as members of the steering group, whether or not they ever serve on a subcommittee or accept an individual assignment?
4. What constituencies must really be represented on the steering group? Remember, an overly representational body will usually be too large and may not be able to forget the interests of the constituency when institutionwide statespersonship is required.
5. Must or should some members be elected by the

TABLE 5.7. Composition of Steering Committees in Institutional Self-Study Processes
(N = 208)

Composition Characteristic	Percentage of Institutions	Composition Characteristic	Percentage of Institutions
Size of committee or coordinating groups used in the process:		(continued)	
3 or fewer people	2	Approximate percentage of members who were	
4–6 people	14	Students	
7–9 people	30	0 percent	30
10–12 people	25	1–10 percent	26
13–15 people	14	11–20 percent	26
>15 people	14	21–30 percent	10
N/A	1	31–40 percent	3
		41–50 percent	1
Approximate percentage of members who were:		Board members	
Administrators		0 percent	69
0 percent	1	1–10 percent	21
1–10 percent	16	11–20 percent	6
11–20 percent	18	21–30 percent	1
21–30 percent	25	31–40 percent	0
31–40 percent	17	41–50 percent	1
41–50 percent	9	Community members (local area)	
51–60 percent	7	0 percent	91
61–70 percent	2	1–10 percent	7
71–80 percent	2	11–20 percent	1
81–90 percent	2	21–30 percent	0
91–100 percent	1	31–40 percent	0
Faculty members		41–50 percent	0
0 percent	1	Alumni	
1–10 percent	5	0 percent	80
11–20 percent	9	1–10 percent	13
21–30 percent	12	11–20 percent	5
31–40 percent	16	21–30 percent	0
41–50 percent	20	31–40 percent	0
51–60 percent	15	41–50 percent	0
61–70 percent	7		
71–80 percent	10		
81–90 percent	5		
91–100 percent	1		

senate or a comparable group? If that is the case, the executive staff usually must also appoint some members in order that adequate levels of expertise, necessary overview, and access to data and certain staff services are provided.

6. What campus citizens with current, useful planning, organizational development, research, problem-solving, writing, editorial, and other skills and experience needed for self-study are available? *Caveat:* Beware of the volunteer who "did it last time" unless you know that the last experience was useful and worth the effort.

7. A group with more than ten to twelve members becomes unworkable at times. Even when one considers that some of the members may miss some sessions, staff aides and others in attendance ex officio can swell the size to a barely manageable one. This writer's preference for an institutional self-study is about eight members with aides and visitors coming and going as

needed. For a program self-study, a steering group of two to four people is usually adequate.

Finally, after all of the juggling and planning is finished, if the steering group members are strong, mature campus citizens who trust one another and who are committed to accomplish the task, the study goals are more likely to be achieved.

The Work of the Steering Group

In figure 4.1, a representation of an entire self-study process is presented. The work of the steering group is depicted for both the organizational phase and for the actual conduct of the study. The role of the steering committee is a crucial one. It is the central, unifying element in the process.

In the organizational phase, the steering group must translate the design developed during the prestudy planning into the tasks, roles, structures, and sequences of activity that will form the process. One of the first items to be considered is the possible assignment of parts of the total task to groups and to individuals. It is at this point that the "do it by committee" mode so prevalent at colleges and universities can be carried too far. Consistent with the desire to provide ample opportunity for participation in the process—and work groups are excellent vehicles for achieving this goal—is the notion that some tasks are better done by an individual. The collecting of data, the drafting of position papers, and, in the absence of very strong group leadership skills, the resolving creatively of certain problems are often best done by individuals. Groups are best used when the issues or questions are complex, when the need is to stimulate "ownership" through participation in the creation of solutions or new ideas, and when there is sufficient time. A mixture of brief individual assignments with a well-defined charge to the right person and the carefully sequenced use of work groups directed by strong, well-trained group leaders constitute the best approach to a self-study or a planning process. For a further exposition of the choice between group or individual assignments, see Sherwood and Hoylman (1978).

Keeping these points in mind, the steering group should move ahead to define the tasks to be completed, the work groups to be used, and the roles each member of the steering group will play as liaison to one of the work groups. The overall committee and other structures of the self-study process should be kept as simple and as small as possible. Most large structures are very hard to coordinate and to use effectively.

The steering group should establish a schedule for the process, including a carefully developed sequence of activities that will allow most efficient use of human resources and that flows naturally from the nature of the tasks. That is, some tasks *must* be completed before others begin; some may just fare better if they wait until services, certain data, or psychological energy are available for them to proceed (see chapter 4). In any event, the schedule should be formulated and deadlines and target dates established.

The steering group must now begin selecting work-group chairpersons, creating the work groups, and compiling a clearly written charge for each work group for distribution, perhaps at an orientation session at which the members of the groups will be able to discuss their roles, see their roles in light of the whole design, ask questions, and arrange for needed help. The steering committee should then provide or arrange for any needed training for group leaders (on leadership, questioning, problem-solving, and communication skills) and any obvious technical assistance for the first stages of the work. (A sample charge to a work group appears at the end of this chapter.)

Before the first work group is commissioned, and the first steps in the process commence, the steering group must assure itself that the institution will provide the needed resources to accomplish the task—staff, travel, printing, data processing and typing, and access to materials and records as well as the assistance needed to interpret these. Ideally, a budget should be established which the steering group chairperson can manage, and access to a computer-based text-editing system should be arranged. This kind of capability is ideally suited to study processes which involve large amounts of text materials, minutes, tables, instruments, reports, and sequential drafts.

Finally, steering group members should plan how they will help the work groups communicate with one another to avoid duplication of effort. Such mechanisms will provide the ways in which the steering group will also keep the entire academic community aware of the activities, progress, and needs of the process; through them, it will solicit input, reaction, and discussion regarding the issues. Various means some steering groups have used to achieve this communication have been interlocking membership between work groups and the steering committee; reports at faculty meetings; newsletters; brief work-group minutes (progress reports, requests for help) to all community members; a periodic report in the campus newspaper, complete with pictures, group membership, and short progress statements; and open work-group sessions.

One steering task deserves special mention here. The steering group should coordinate and perhaps approve all data-collection efforts and particularly all "home-grown" or other data-gathering instruments (see chapter 6). The protection of innocent registrars, computer center aides, and possible respondents to questionnaires demands such coordination. One request for information can then meet the needs of several possible work groups, and one instrument can contain the elements needed by several users, as well as being reviewed by professionals before use.

The Importance of Staff Work

One of the things which has become clearly evident in a decade of experience with self-study and other related processes is that adequate staff work is absolutely essential. Both the steering group and the committees it initiates and monitors must have help. They must have the descriptive materials and data

Committee Name: <u>Admissions and Student Services</u>

Members: Mr. Igor Beaver, Chr.   (tel. no.; address)
           Dr. Augusta Wind   ("   )
           Dr. Faith Bilder   ("   )
           Dr. Noah Count   ("   )
           Dr. Hesa Goodwon   (" / Liaison with Steering Committee)
           Ms. Imno Help   ("   )
           Mr. Rick O'Shea   ("   )
           Dr. Alfredo D. Dark   ("   )

Charge:
1. Review the college and any departmental or program admissions policies in light of the mission and goals of the college and the past performance of admitted students.
2. In light of the data provided about students (incoming, first-time and transfer, nontraditional, handicapped, etc.), review the goals of the Student Services Division and assess the effectiveness of the services provided to students at the college in light of these goals. Communicate needs for additional data or studies to the steering committee and Institutional Research office.

Materials to be provided:
1. Complete data compilations on the student body for the last three years.
2. Description of the admissions process, office organization, and staffing.
3. Description of each student service including objectives, staffing, budgets, and activity levels. Annual reports of each office.
4. Any previous surveys of effectiveness or student follow-up data.

Additional Resources:
1. Master plan materials.
2. Stated admissions policies and statement of goals for the Student Services Division.
3. Student services guidelines from national organizations and accrediting agencies.

Dates to be observed:
   Orientation: _____   Status report due: _____

   Submit plan of activities and needs: _____   Draft report due: _____

Figure 5.1. Sample "Charge" to a Work Group

they need to begin their work. They need assistance with interpretation, and they need a whole array of services which too often have been expected of committee chairpersons inexperienced in negotiating the administrative morass. Such expectations are usually shortsighted, expensive in many ways, and generally destructive of morale and work-group performance. Indeed, I am convinced that our organizations, in general, use their work groups improperly. The groups are usually offered "assistance, when needed" instead of receiving what they often do not realize they need. They are often offered data without interpretation or they are asked to define their data needs independently, and often asked to collect the data themselves—a most wasteful procedure.

What I recommend and what creative institutions have discovered is that work groups should provide the brain power, the mechanism for enlightened self-discovery, and the special interpretations, conclusions, recommendations, and commitments to change. Providing the groups the opportunity to do those things is the job of the staff. When this occurs,

the staff is happier because the groups get useful information in ways the staff knows best and the work-group chairs and members are delighted because they are not expected to act like administrators. Rather they can do the job they are needed to do—better and more extensively. An example of a committee "charge" which carefully distinguishes between administrative staff roles and the duties of the committee is presented in figure 5.1. Note that the committee described in the "charge" is *provided* with the description of the area or service it is asked to examine. In my experience most self-study work groups spend inordinate amounts of time and effort collecting and writing descriptions. Such work is better done by the administrative staff. The committee may decide to augment or refine the description once it is provided to them, but a group should not be asked to do what an individual usually can do better. Note also that the specific work-group models presented in chapter 4 clearly indicate this approach.

When the self-study steering committee moves the study process into the operational stage—that is, when the first activities (often a review of goals) begin—it must start coordinating the work of the individuals and the work groups. At this point, the steering group must undertake many important activities: providing assistance to work groups; solving any problems that arise; selecting people for tasks; scheduling activities; reviewing progress reports; eliminating duplicative activities; coordinating data needs; motivating people to complete tasks; reporting progress and representing the workers in the process to the larger academic community; and generally providing what is needed to achieve the goals for the self-study process.

References

Kells and Kirkwood, "Institutional Self-Evaluation Processes" (chap. 2).

Romine, Stephen, "Objectives, Objections, and Options: Some Perceptions of Regional Accrediation." *North Central Association Quarterly*, Spring 1975, pp. 365–75.

Sherwood, John J., and Hoylman, Florence M. "Utilizing Human Resources: Individual Versus Group Approaches to Problem Solving and Decision Making." *The 1978 Annual Handbook for Group Facilitators*, pp. 157–62. La Jolla, CA: University Associates, 1978.

6

Mechanics of the Self-Study Process

The study process itself, and the individual and work-group activities it encompasses, will be the topic of this chapter. We will begin with the type of tasks usually assigned—how they may vary depending on the nature of the design, and where "starting points" for discussion may be obtained. We will then discuss working with goals; goal achievement (outcomes) studies; studies of input, environment, programs, and processes; and using instruments in the process. The concepts and general procedures presented in this chapter are applicable to institution-wide and to program or departmental situations. The examples used are institutional in nature. Departmental and program examples and any special contextual or other dimensions of studies conducted in such settings are presented in chapter 7.

THE NATURE OF THE WORK

As was indicated in chapter 5 and illustrated in figure 4.1, the steering committees of most self-study processes use both individuals and work groups to accomplish the study task. To achieve the intentions for self-study—to improve the program or institution, to assess and solve problems, to review goals and to study goal achievement, and the like—the following kinds of activities must be conducted.

- The process of study must be managed.
- Records must be reviewed.
- Data must be assembled from within the institution.
- Facts and opinions must be gathered from individuals.
- Questions must be posed.
- Answers to questions and solutions to problems must be sought.
- New ideas must be generated.
- Materials must be drafted.
- Discussions must be held about drafted materials.
- Written opinions and reactions must be sought.
- Editing must be done.
- Final documents must be produced.
- The results must be discussed and implemented, often in light of strategies developed during the process.

The work in a self-study process can also be thought about in other ways. Some of the activities are *managing* activities, others are *gathering* activities. Some tasks have the purpose of *eliciting reactions*, and *revealing new perspectives or solutions*. Some tasks are to *produce and use written and other results*.

Clearly, some of these items are best attempted by individuals, either working alone or as part of a group. Other tasks are best done by the group. For example, a work group studying the nature of student experiences at a college in recent years might decide, as a group, the general outline of their task. Members might then decide to ask one person to prepare a written agenda and another, to meet with student representatives. The group might request of the registrar or the institutional research officer a cohort attrition analysis for two recent classes. The group might ask a member to explore available instruments to gather student reactions to the college, its programs, services, and so on. The steering group, however, might not assign some tasks to any work group. Collecting certain data that would serve several work groups, editing drafts, and the like, might better be contracted by the central steering committee with certain individuals and the results shared with other work groups and with operating offices or committees of the institution.

THE IMPORTANCE OF STAFF WORK

The reader is once again reminded that the work of individuals and groups in any study effort will be greatly eased and perhaps much more appropriately focused if the worker(s) do not have to attend to all of the administrative activities which support the effort. As indicated in the design diagrams in chapter 4 and in the section on organizing the effort in chapter 5, the leaders of the institution or program must assign adequate staff assistance to the study effort. This assistance is just as important in the active part of the process as it is in the design stages. Because data needs rise during this part of the self-study and because materials must be recorded in various ways (and often revised several times), staff assistance is critically important.

One recent procedural innovation which can transform self-study work as perceived at the worker or work-group level is the use of computer-based text editing or word processing systems. If such staff assistance is provided to enable self-study committees essentially to ignore the clerical aspects of the task and focus on issues, analysis, and strategies for improvement, then more results, less fatigue, and a more positively perceived participation level can result. Another very important aspect of staff work is data for the study.

GENERAL DATA NEEDS

The data used are of two general kinds—facts and opinions. The facts are usually gathered from records or from individuals in written form. The opinions are gathered either in person or via instruments. If instruments are to be used, particularly if they are developed locally, great care must be taken to confirm that the language is clear and that it has at least face validity (it is understood generally to mean what was intended by the writer). Pretesting of the instrument is necessary and the results must be used cautiously. (See the later section in this chapter on instruments). The data used in the study may also be seen as being related to two kinds of matters—descriptions of things (sizes, trends, work loads, credits, degrees) and ideas, issues, problems, and goals. They may also, of course, be about inputs to the institution or program, about processes (programs, procedures, services) and about outputs (goal achievement studies).

FOCUSES FOR WORK GROUPS

As pointed out in chapters 4 and 5, the extent to which data must be generated *de novo* to support the study efforts depends on the status of the institution's data base and the sophistication and utility of the institutional research function. In situations where useful data are readily available, the person providing the staff assistance to the work group assists in the phrasing of useful questions and the resulting data are arrayed for the group to discuss. In those more usual situations where useful data are scarce, the staff role is even more critical, as is the eventual longer-term result for the institution. The institution learns via this cycle of the study process what it ought to collect regularly and use for its ongoing decision-making and problem-solving processes.

As pointed out in chapters 4 and 5 the exact configuration of work group and other assignments will vary depending on the study design. A comprehensive self-study process usually employs nine to twelve work groups, appointed in some sequence that will work for the institution in question, and charged with considering the status, strengths, weaknesses, problems, and any new solutions for the following areas:

Goals (or mission, goals, and objectives)
The student body
The faculty (or faculty and instruction)
The program (possibly undergraduate and grad-
    uate separately)
Student services
Academic services (possibly a separate group for
    the library or learning center)
Administrative services (including physical plant)
Organization and governance
Finances
Research (if research is a goal of the institution)

Public services (or continuing education or community services)
Goal achievement (outcomes)

A less comprehensive study may touch on some of these areas. Such a study may also employ work groups for various periods of time to explore special topics in depth, according to the design developed for the study. Of special concern, and therefore receiving special attention, may be governance, financial planning, the relationship between liberal and career studies, financial aid problems, or basic studies programs. The self-study outlines in appendix D reflect the results of various study emphases and configurations.

In some cases, the use of specially established continuing work groups may not be appropriate in a study process. Rather, such processes may focus more on problem identification in natural work groups, individual task assignments, special short-term workshops, and the like. The Mercy College case explored in chapter 4 is an example of this circumstance.

STARTING POINTS FOR DISCUSSION AND STUDY: SOURCES

In light of the picture of the total process presented in chapter 4 (figure 4.1) and the foregoing discussion, one might ask about the *substance* of the work for the work groups. Beyond the notions that every program or service at an institution should be related to and advance institution or program goals; that problems should be assessed and normal functioning examined; and that the outcomes of (or at least people's opinions about) the programs or service objectives should be assessed—*where* does one look for specific issues to shape the work group's work? In a variety of sources, including the following:

1. The design of the self-study, its specific charge, and the report of any predesign diagnostic meetings at which problems or key issues were identified (see chapter 4);
2. The goals or objectives for the program, service or other activity a work group is to study;
3. Any annual reports, consultant reports, or review team or other documents for the school or program that reveal concerns, problems, issues, general activities, dimensions, and human and other profiles;
4. The institutional or program catalog and any master plan document;
5. The last self-study document and any visitor's report;
6. The list of standards and the self-study guide

from any regional accrediting agency with which the study may be related that outlines specific issues of concern to the agency (see figure 6.1);

7. The materials from any related professional society such as the self-study guide produced by the National Association for Foreign Student Affairs, the many guides produced by the National Association of College and University Business Officers; and the self-study guide of the Association of Governing Boards for boards of trustees. In the student services/student affairs/student development areas, several recent manuals of instruments and suggested procedures for needs assessment have been developed (Baird, Hartnett et al., 1980; Harpel, 1976; Washington State Student Services Commission, 1977; State University of New York, 1977). For the general administrative areas, one might examine the guidelines of the self-regulation office of ACE or the guide prepared by Griffin and Burks (1976). (See appendix B.) Those studying academic libraries should review the work of Casserly (1983). Johnson (1982) and Kania (1983);

8. The detailed standards of any specialized accrediting agencies concerned with the area in question (see chapter 7);

9. The useful book by Richard I. Miller (1979) which details suggestions for subtopical analysis concerning students, faculty, academic programs, support staff and facilities, administrative effectiveness, fiscal management, and governing boards; a piece in the New Directions for Higher Education series concerning the assessment of financial health (Frances and Coldren, 1979); and one produced by the staff of the University of the State of New York (1979), which offers some brief guidelines, case experiences, and several short essays.

Other mechanisms for centering the work group's attention on developing "work plans" are:

● The commercially available instruments for gathering data and opinions. These should be reviewed for ideas and applicability by one or more of the work groups. These tests have been developed with average two- and four-year colleges or constituent schools at a university in mind. The items in the instruments might serve as starting points for discussion, even if the instruments are not used. See appendix B.

● "Brainstorming" or some other group technique by which members can draw up lists of key issues, needs, problems, and opportunities

STANDARD SIX: STUDENT SERVICES

Standard 6.A.

Student services are available to support the objectives of the educational programs.

Education takes place outside as well as inside the classroom. Much of this out-of-class educational experience can be encouraged by well-organized and imaginative student services. Most postsecondary institutions, therefore, consider student services an important educational function. The purpose is to assist students to use their own capabilities and to develop self-reliant, responsible behavior. In addition, such services as financial aid, housing, and health care are appropriate.

Some, though by no means all, components of this standard are:

6.A.1.	Orientation is provided for new students.
6.A.2.	Academic and personal counseling is provided for students.
6.A.3.	Career or placement services are available to students and graduates, and are administered in accordance with clearly stated policies.
6.A.4.	Clear and publicized policies on student rights, student conduct on campus, student discipline, and due process are available to all students.
6.A.5.	Clear and publicized policies on the role of student publications and student government are available.
6.A.6.	If the institution is engaged in inter-collegiate athletics, clear and public policies are available, and the program is conducted in perspective to the purposes of the institution.
6.A.7.	The student financial aid program is well-organized, well-publicized, and periodically evaluated.
6.A.8.	The institution has a well-publicized and uniformly administered policy regarding fee refunds, consistent with customary standards.
6.A.9.	Residential colleges provide adequate student housing, facilities, and appropriate staffing.
6.A.10.	A well-stocked and efficiently managed bookstore supports the educational program, contributes to the intellectual climate, and, in a residential institution, serves other student needs.

Figure 6.1. Example of a regional accrediting agency standard as a starting point for work group activity. *Source:* "Standards for Accreditation," in *Handbook of Accreditation* (Oakland, Calif.: Western Association of Schools and Colleges, Accrediting Commission for Senior Colleges and Universities, January 1979), pp. 30-31.

(Fordyce and Weil, 1971). An experienced process consultant can assist a work group in this regard.

- For the work group seeking a specific agenda for study in a service or program area, engaging a consultant to look at available materials, interview professionals and students, and recommend some issues for study.

The important thing to remember at this point is that the study is your study. It does not belong to an outside agency or some other entity. If question guides, standards, or other "starting point" source materials are used, you, as work-group members, must be selective in choosing from among them. You must adapt, augment, and enhance these materials to make them consistent with your needs. Do not become enamored of a technique or list of questions because someone else thinks they might be useful.

WORKING WITH GOALS

Contrary to a belief expressed to me by many academics, goals can be very useful. It is fashionable, and has been for several decades, to belittle the statements in college catalogs concerning the mission of the institution. The generalities are pointed to as useless in planning and in evaluation and as consumer information. Generally, these criticims are correct, but misguided. The presence in catalogs of general mission statements that merely inform the reader about the *kind* of institution and the general commitments that are intended is not a problem; the absence of complementary, specific, usable goal statements *is* a problem. It is here that the self-study process must start, because clear statements about what is intended to be accomplished by the programs and services of an institution are the bedrock upon which study processes are built and plans are laid.

Although developing these statements during a self-study often is a difficult exercise that frustrates the participants, it is possible to move through it usefully. This utility can be achieved if the leader of the goals group is strong, if the leader and members become acquainted with the relatively recent useful literature about using goals, if they adopt a workable construct for their situation, and if they realize that, just as self-study and planning are cyclical, so is work with goals. The first or second cycle will not usually produce an ideal, clear, and completely useful set of goals for such complex entities.

Definitions

One should start with a few definitions related to goals before attempting to develop or review a set of one's own goals. *Mission* or *purpose* statements are general in nature and are intended to indicate the type of institution and the more overall intentions of the organization. They describe the tone of the institution and delimit generally its nature and perhaps its market. They are useful to potential members of the community and they generally guide the leaders and the work force. Some examples:

College A seeks to be a small Christian, value-oriented institution with a primary focus on the transmission of knowledge and the preparation of graduates to serve humanity.

A military institution, College B prepares leaders in an atmosphere that trains the mind and the body. It is committed to the preservation of democratic society. It is selective in its admission of students and has a national focus.

College C is a community college that has three basic purposes—to offer transfer programs in the first two years of collegiate study; to offer career and vocational programs meeting local employment needs; and to offer a wide range of community programs and services.

University D seeks to achieve three purposes—the creation of knowledge, the transmission of knowledge, and service to the State. It seeks to create an atmosphere of excellence and is firmly committed to academic freedom—the freedom to teach and the freedom to learn. It believes that sustaining a large, active, and diverse community of scholars is the best way to achieve its mission.

These mission statements indicate to readers something about the general type, tone, and extent of the organizations. They do not, however, provide the specifics needed to guide program development and to assess progress. *Goal* statements, which complement and flow from the mission statement and which indicate how the mission is to be achieved, are needed. These statements may be of three kinds:

input goals, which describe the type of human and other resources, including students, that are desired in or for the organization; *process goals*, which describe the environment to be created or specific types of programs or services to be offered to promote the mission; and *outcome goals*, which state the expectations with regard to outcomes of the process—what is to be achieved as a result of the process.

Some examples of these goal types follow for College A:

(Input goal) College A will seek students who can benefit from its programs and who are serious about exploring their knowledge of God and their ability to serve mankind.

(Input goal) College A will recruit a staff able to carry on the dual role of providing a first-class liberal education for students and of committing themselves to working closely with students in a Christian community

(Process goal) College A will maintain an open community with active participation in campus governance by all interested parties.

(Process goal) College A will offer a full liberal arts program with special emphasis on living/learning work experiences, particularly in the social science and social service areas.

(Outcome goal) College A will graduate students committed to serving mankind who will become active members of their community.

(Outcome goal) The graduate of College A will be able to demonstrate—

1. Oral and written fluency in his or her native language and in one other language;
2. In-depth knowledge of one area of study;
3. An understanding of the approaches to the social sciences, an appreciation of the humanities and fine arts, and a basic knowledge of the natural sciences; and
4. The ability to identify and clarify values.

These goals do not completely express all possible goals for an institution like College A. However, it is not possible to prepare and use goal statements for every process and outcome at a college. What should be attempted is the creation of a set of goals of sufficient coverage and specificity to guide the further development of the institution and to form the basis of useful, continuous, improvement-oriented study.

Some institutions or programs create statements of even greater specificity, which are usually quantifiable. These are called *objectives*. The objectives amplify each goal statement and provide short-range statements of process or intended outcome. These results can be examined, through the prism of written, locally determined criteria, for purposes of guiding the management effort over time. The case study later in this chapter demonstrates the function of objectives, but does not employ acceptable criterion levels.

In light of the definitions of mission and goals, what is the task of the goals review work group in the self-study process? First, the steering group must recognize the importance of this task by providing adequate staff assistance, by securing experienced, hardworking group members, and by monitoring the progress so the process does not become bogged down. Well-run, properly staffed work-group meetings with adequate preparation are required or a goals effort can easily lapse into a seemingly endless set of meetings in which statements are rewritten by committee.

The Tasks

In general, the goals work group should undertake the following tasks:

1. Review the mission and any charter statement for the college.
2. Review the existing statement of goals:
   a) Classify the goals by input, process, and outcome designations;
   b) If appropriate, examine knowledge of the market for programs;
   c) Examine the statement for adequacy of coverage, given the existing patterns of program and services;
   d) Examine each goal statement for clarity;
   e) Assess the degree of understanding of changes needed in and agreement on the goals by the members of the professional staff and the board of trustees. Instruments are available to assist in such efforts (see the later description in this chapter of goal inventories and similar data-gathering devices).
3. Update the statement of the goals. Each succes-

sive, effective review should require less change as the community becomes better acquainted with and better able to use the goals. What is desired is an adequately comprehensive, yet specific statement of input, process, and outcome goals. Any priority among the statements should be determined and noted.

4. Present the updated statement for approval by the governing bodies, particularly by the board of trustees. Once consensus is achieved, the statement can then be used by the outcomes (goal achievement) group and other groups. The outcomes group, which in some instances may be the goals group with an extended charge, may have already started its work, since most goals groups determine that some existing goals can be retained. Also the outcomes work group will want to assess achievement of the goals in effect over the last few years. The goals statement will also guide much of the work of the other study groups.

The leaders of the goals review will want to become acquainted with the work of similar institutions that have recently clarified their goals and with the literature that explains and supports the use of goal instruments (Peterson, 1978; Romney and Bogen, 1978; Romney, 1978; Educational Testing Service). If the study is being conducted at the program or departmental level, the group will also want to check the *consistency* of the program goals with those of the whole college. Members will want to examine the program goals in light of any collegewide priorities. These might include ensuring that students develop basic cognitive skills, writing proficiency, and such higher-order cognitive skills as critical thinking, evaluation, and synthesis. This comparison of program and college goals should occur in addition to the *coverage*, *clarity*, *priority*, and *consensus* tasks described above.

Advice on goal clarification is intended not just for small, struggling institutions. Most large prestigious institutions are also strongly advised to work with goals, as many are already doing. For example, the curriculum reform proposal prepared by the Harvard faculty betwen 1974 and 1978 essentially defined the outcome goals for liberal education there by stating that "an educated person" must—

Be able to think and write clearly and effectively.
Have an informed acquaintance with the five basic academic areas.
Be able to use his or her experiences in the context of other cultures and other times.
Have some understanding of, and experience in thinking about, moral and ethical problems.

Have achieved depth in some field of knowledge. (Fiske, 1978)

More extensive lists of attributes, competencies and skills, all potential elements in academic outcome goal statements, were presented by Breen (1981) and by a report on a recent College Board project (*Chronicle*, 1981).

Using a Goals Inventory

To promote awareness of goals, identify goal priorities, and assess consensus on what the academic community feels the goals of the institutions are and should be, some institutions or programs may wish to use a commercially available goals inventory to start clarifying and updating them. The most widely used instrument is the Institutional Goals Inventory (IGI) developed by the Educational Testing Service. This instrument has the following characteristics:

1. It uses an "is" and "should be" Likert-scale item structure to gather respondent opinions concerning ninety general goal items in ten outcome goal categories and ten process goal categories (see figure 6.2). Essentially, the respondent indicates the extent to which he or she feels the particular goal item *is* important at the institution (based on what is happening there now) and *should be* important at the institution.

2. The IGI can accommodate up to five categories of respondents (for instance, administrators, full-time faculty, part-time faculty, faculty by discipline, board members, etc.).

3. Local, specific institutional goal items can be entered into the instrument and handled just as the general goal items are. *This is a very important aspect.*

4. Special goal inventory instruments are available for small, liberal arts colleges and for community colleges, in addition to the general version for use at most other kinds of institutions.

5. Background data are gathered about the respondents to permit analysis of the respondent group and cross-tabulation of the data.

6. Data can be analyzed (ETS does it for a fee) in several ways: by item; by goal area; goal area priority; by respondent group; goal areas by rank order in the "is" category and in the "should be" category; and goal areas by rank order discrepancy between "is" and "should be." It is possible to use these data to examine the consensus and priority aspects of a goal review and to generate much material for discussion in the work group.

The IGI can be useful if it is possible to obtain a reasonably high response from the desired respondent groups on campus. One must remember, though, that the instrument is a tool; in this use, since exacting research methods are not being followed, the data are not necessarily accurate enough to prove anything. The object is not to prove statistically that a goal or goal area is important or neglected, but to formulate general impressions about opinions in the academic community. Furthermore, even if the data are fairly reliable—as they may be—they may not represent what *ought* to be at a particular institution. Rather, they are a valuable starting point for discussion (see the example below).

An example of the use of the goals inventory is contained as part of the process described in the following case study.

CASE STUDY: The Review of the Mission, Goals, and Objectives of Middlesex County College (MCC), Edison, New Jersey

Early in the two-year self-study at MCC (1978–80), a work group, headed by a divisional dean and made up of eight faculty members and administrators, was formulated to review the college's statement of mission, goals, and objectives. The group received a charge and first gathered the written evidence of the stated purposes and objectives of the college. The starting point for the current deliberations was a 1974 statement in the bylaws of the board of trustees:

Purposes. Recognizing the broad range of needs for greater educational opportunity beyond high school in the community, the Middlesex County College will offer programs of study to meet the following major purposes:

1. Associate degree programs in the organized occupational fields of business, health services, and commerce- and industry-related technologies for full-time day students.
2. Associate degree programs in the fields of the liberal arts and science for full-time day students.
3. Associate degree credit courses in both college parallel and occupational areas for part-time evening students.
4. Extension and community-centered programs of both degree-credit and noncredit value, of varied length and character in response to the particular educational, occupational, and cultural needs evidenced by the people of Middlesex County.

Objectives. The College serves as a guide in providing the environment and experience conducive to integration of knowledge, proficiency, and attitudes in students. These three objectives are also planned to aid students in the promotion of their individual growth, technical competence, and social responsibility.

OUTCOME GOALS

General Education—has to do with acquisition of general knowledge, preparation of students for further academic work, and the acquisition of skills and knowledge to live effectively in society. (1,4,6,9,)*

Intellectual Orientation—relates to an *attitude* about learning and intellectual work. It means familiarity with research and problem solving methods, the ability to synthesize knowledge from many sources, the capacity for self-directed learning, and an openness to new ideas and ways of thinking. (2,5,7,10)

Lifelong Learning—means providing noncredit courses to community residents who can pursue a variety of interests, instilling in students a commitment to lifelong learning, providing learning opportunities to adults of all ages, and awarding educational credit for knowledge and skills acquired in non-school settings. (3,8,11,13)

Cultural/Aesthetic Awareness—entails a heightened appreciation of a variety of art forms, encouraging study in the humanities and art beyond requirements, exposure to non-Western art and literature, and encouragement of student participation in artistic activities. (14,17,20,23)

Personal Development—means identification by students of personal goals and the development of ways of achieving them, enhancement of feelings of self-worth, self-confidence, and self-direction, and encouragement of open and honest relationships. (15,18,21,24)

Humanism/Altruism—reflects a respect for diverse cultures, a commitment to working for peace in the world, an understanding of the important moral issues of the time, and concern about the general welfare of the community. (16,19,22,25)

Vocational/Technical Preparation—means offering specific occupational curricula (such as accounting or air conditioning and refrigeration), programs geared to emerging career fields, opportunities for upgrading or updating present job skills, and retraining for new careers or new job skills.(26,30,36,38)

Developmental/Remedial Preparation—includes recognizing, assessing, and counseling students with basic skills needs, providing developmental programs that recognize different learning styles and rates, assuring that students in developmental programs achieve appropriate levels of competence, and evaluating basic skills programs. (27,31,32,41)

Community Services—is concerned with the college's relationship with the community: encouraging community use of college resources (meeting rooms, computer facilities, faculty skills), conducting community forums on topical issues, promoting cooperation among diverse community organizations to improve availability of services, and working with local government agencies, industry, unions, and other groups on community problems. (28,34,35,37)

Social Criticism—means providing critical evaluation of current values and practices, serving as a source of ideas to change social institutions, helping students learn how to bring about change in our institutions, and being engaged, as an institution, in working for needed changes in our society. (29,33,39,40)

*The numbers in parentheses are the four goal statements that make up each goal area.

PROCESS GOALS

Counseling and Advising—means providing career counseling services, personal counseling services, and academic advising services for students and providing a student job-placement service. (44,47,50,51)

Student Services—means developing support services for students with special needs, providing a comprehensive student activities program, providing a comprehensive student financial aid program, and making available health services that offer health maintenance, preventive medicine, and referral services. (42,45,48,52)

Faculty/Staff Development—entails a commitment of college resources to faculty and staff development activities designed to improve instructional programs, by providing opportunities for professional development of faculty and staff, by maintaining a consistent and equitable method of faculty evaluation, and by providing flexible leave and sabbatical opportunities for faculty and staff. (43,46,49,53)

Intellectual Environment—means a rich program of cultural events, a college climate that encourages student free-time involvement in intellectual and cultural activities, and one in which students and faculty can easily interact informally, and a college that has a reputation in the community as an intellectually exciting place. (54,57,60,63)

Innovation—is defined as a climate in which continuous educational innovation is an accepted way of life. It means established procedures for readily initiating curricular or instructional innovations, and, more specifically, it means experimentation with new approaches to individualized instruction and to evaluating and grading student performance. (55,58,61,64)

College Community—is defined as fostering a climate in which there is faculty and staff commitment to the goals of the college, open and candid communication, open and amicable airing of differences, and mutual trust and respect among faculty, students, and administrators. (56,59,62,65)

Freedom—has to do with protecting the right of faculty to present controversial ideas in the classroom, not preventing students from hearing controversial points of view, placing no restrictions on off-campus political activities by faculty or students, and ensuring faculty and students the freedom to choose their own life-styles. (66,69,73,76)

Accessibility—means maintaining costs to students at a level that will not deny attendance because of financial need, offering programs that are convenient for adults in the community, recruiting students who have been denied, have not valued, or have not been successful in formal education, and, with a policy of open admissions, developing worthwhile educational experiences for all those admitted. (67,70,74,77)

Effective Management—means involving those with appropriate expertise in making decisions, achieving general consensus regarding fundamental college goals, being organized for systematic short- and long-range planning, and engaging in systematic *evaluation* of all college programs. (68,72,75,78)

Accountability—is defined to include use of cost criteria in deciding among alternative programs, concern for the efficiency of college operations, accountability to funding sources for program effectiveness, and regular provision of evidence that the college is meeting its stated goals. (79,81,83,87)

Miscellaneous goal statements not included in goal areas (12,71,80,82,84,85,86,88,89,90)

Figure 6.2. The CCGI goal areas of the Educational Testing Service. Used by permission.

The work-group members felt that a much more specific useful statement was required. They decided to begin discussing the statement and to collect systematically information from a wide-ranging sample of the academic community. It authorized the institutional research office to use the Community College Goals Inventory (CCGI) with all members of the full-time faculty, the academic administration, the trustees, the non-academic administrative staff, and the members of the career program advisory boards. The response from the full-time faculty was about 60 percent, and higher response rates were achieved from the other groups. A total of 363 responses were received in all groups.

The CCGI data were tabulated and the following summary results were discernible.

1. The degree of consensus was high across the five respondent groups in the twenty goal categories regarding relative priority. For example, on the goal area "General Education" (items 1, 4, 6, 9 in the instrument), the following levels of agreement were obtained.

"Is" MEAN	RESPONDENT GROUP	"SHOULD BE" MEAN
3.54	Total	4.13
3.55	Faculty, full-time	4.17
3.69	Academic administrative staff	4.26
3.44	Trustees	4.09
3.46	Nonacademic administrative staff	4.09
3.56	Advisory boards	4.04

This pattern was typical of the level of agreement.

2. The results of the priority rankings by goal area reinforced the items that had been added tentatively to the goal statement in the work group's first discussions of coverage, priorities, clarity, and consensus regarding goals and objectives.
3. Several useful considerations emerged from the general goal area rankings (see figure 6.3) that would be very important starting points for the other self-study work. For instance:
   a) The data clearly indicate relatively strong perceived priority for only two of the three basic purposes of most community colleges. The community services goal area was fifteenth, eighteenth, and fifteenth respectively on the "is," "should be," and discrepancy rankings. Here is an example where the self-study groups may be starting with data that, though widely supported on campus, may not represent what sponsoring agencies think ought to be.

   b) The need to develop attitudes, programs, and activities to promote a sense of "community" on campus is very strongly indicated in the data (the "is" ranking is fourteenth; "should be," fourth; discrepancy ranking, first).
   c) The college community seems to be well satisfied with previous efforts to provide accessibility. What they seem to want now is a focus on personal development, remedial/developmental services, counseling and advising, and faculty/staff development required to do a good job with the wide range of students who have access to MCC. They also would like to see more attention to intellectual orientation on the campus.

The CCGI data are just a beginning for the MCC self-study, and the above analysis is cursory. MCC will do much more as it proceeds through successive study efforts.

The final steps in the MCC review of mission, goals, and objectives was the production of a clearer, more comprehensive, more useful statement. After three or four drafts, discussion on campus, work with a consultant, and several meetings, the work group produced the statement that follows.

STATEMENT OF THE MISSION, GOALS, AND OBJECTIVES OF MIDDLESEX COUNTY COLLEGE

Middlesex County College is a comprehensive publicly supported, multipurpose, two-year institution of higher education committed to serving all of those who can benefit from postsecondary learning opportunities. The College offers a wide range of curricula and programs that provide access to the educational process for diverse populations within its service area in a lifelong learning context. The College views the creation of an environment responsive to the career and personal needs of individuals as essential to the fulfillment of this mission.

In order to accomplish this mission the College sets for itself the following goals and objectives.

Goals

- offer occupationally oriented degree and certificate programs that prepare students both for immediate employment and for continuing career education.
- provide lower-division programs which prepare students for transfer to four-year colleges and universities.
- provide opportunities for general education that foster students' awareness of the broad

GOAL AREA SUMMARIES RANK ORDERED

For "Is" Means	Mean		For "Should Be" Means	Mean
1. Vocational/technical preparation	3.58		1. Vocational/technical preparation	4.21
2. General education	3.54		2. Intellectual orientation	4.15
3. Accessibility	3.40		3. General education	4.13
4. Counseling and advising	3.33		4. College community	4.09
5. Lifelong learning	3.22		5. Counseling and advising	4.08
6. Accountability	3.19		6. Development/remedial preparation	4.05
7. Effective management	3.12		7. Personal development	3.98
8. Freedom	3.05		8. Faculty/staff development	3.95
9. Intellectual orientation	3.02		9. Lifelong learning	3.92
10. Student services	3.01		10. Effective management	3.91
11. Developmental/remedial preparation	2.99		11. Intellectual environment	3.84
12. Faculty/staff development	2.89		12. Student services	3.75
13. Intellectual environment	2.84		13. Accountability	3.73
14. College community	2.80		14. Accessibility	3.72
15. Community services	2.79		15. Humanism/altruism	3.63
16. Personal development	2.78		16. Innovation	3.61
17. Innovation	2.60		17. Freedom	3.46
18. Humanism/altruism	2.50		18. Community services	3.45
19. Social criticism	2.40		19. Cultural/aesthetic awareness	3.19
20. Cultural/aesthetic awareness	2.38		20. Social criticism	3.16

Rank Order, By Discrepancy Between "Is" and "Should Be"

	Discrepancy
1. College community	+1.29
2. Personal development	+1.20
3. Intellectual orientation	+1.13
4. Humanism/altruism	+1.13
5. Developmental/remedial preparation	+1.06
6. Faculty/staff development	+1.06
7. Innovation	+1.01
8. Intellectual environment	+1.00
9. Cultural/aesthetic awareness	+0.81
10. Effective management	+0.79
11. Social criticism	+0.76
12. Counseling and advising	+0.75
13. Student services	+0.74
14. Lifelong learning	+0.70
15. Community services	+0.66
16. Vocational/technical preparation	+0.63
17. General education	+0.59
18. Accountability	+0.54
19. Freedom	+0.41
20. Accessibility	+0.32

Figure 6.3. Summary tabulation of the CCGI data for the Middlesex County College, 1979.

outlines of human knowledge and in the development of intellectual, personal, and social values.

- foster self-awareness, personal growth, and career development through student services.
- provide accessibility to education for a broad spectrum of student subpopulations.
- play a major role in enhancing the social, cultural, recreational, and economic life of the community.
- encourage the pursuit of lifelong learning.

Objectives

- design educational delivery systems that accommodate individual differences in learning styles and ability.
- conduct educational programs that are responsive to the changing needs, problems, and requirements of the community.
- periodically reassess general education requirements and offerings so that they reflect emerging needs, interests, and priorities.

- develop students' ability to define and solve problems and to synthesize knowledge from a variety of sources through content and activities of instructional programs and services.
- encourage student leadership and involvement through collegiate governance and extra curricular activities.
- develop students' ability to think clearly and use language effectively through content and activities of instructional and extracurricular programs.
- provide comprehensive, accessible counseling and advisement services through faculty advisors and career and personal counselors.
- offer basic skills and developmental programs and services to meet the special needs of traditional and non-traditional students.
- integrate credit and non-credit programs to develop accessible "career ladder" occupational programs responsive to our community's employment needs.
- maintain ongoing assessment of community needs.
- maintain a staff development program for administrative personnel, faculty, and staff.
- maintain a climate of mutual trust among students, faculty, administrators and the Board of Trustees in which communication is open and candid.
- evaluate institutional programs and services in terms of objectives and outcomes.

(June 6, 1979)

As the MCC statement indicates, it is possible to make substantial progress in clarifying the mission, goals, and objectives of an institution. It is possible to involve people directly and indirectly, via survey and reaction to drafts, in the effort. It is possible to complete this task in a matter of weeks. Clearly, if a goals inventory is used, sixty to ninety days will be required for that activity, but the rest of the workgroup activities can be accomplished in a few weeks before and after such a survey is run and the data analyzed.

The ideal set of mission and goal statements is not likely to be achieved in any given review process. The object is to make steady progress on developing a more useful statement that is more widely used than the preceding statement was on the campus.

Goal Achievement (Outcomes) Studies

In the last half of the 1970s, the subject of "outcomes" measurement received a great deal of attention. Little of this attention resulted in concepts and procedures that can help an institution or program seeking to study itself usefully. As early as the first half of the decade, as the push for accountability was made and as the standards and procedures of regional accrediting agencies were questioned (Koerner, 1971), some calls came forth for increased use of outcome studies (Kells, 1972, 1976; Micek and Walhaus, 1973). More recently, complete structures and classifications for considering the outcomes of postsecondary programs and institutions have been developed (Lenning, 1977) and several accrediting agencies are shifting their emphasis in a major effort to develop and utilize techniques to measure outcomes (Andrews, 1978).

Most of what has been reported in the literature to date is of limited value to the institution or program conducting a self-study process, primarily because it has been proffered for the wrong reasons. The warnings of Romney and Bogen (1978) that outcomes assessment may bring political problems, that it suffers from methodological faults, and that it is costly for the returns received may be sound, indeed, particularly since the reasons inferred in many of the popular arguments for outcomes studies *are poor ones.* These reasons include the notions that outcomes studies will provide proof of institutional or program effectiveness, that much public relations value will accrue, or even that comparative advantage for an institution or program can be achieved by conducting such studies. However, the reasons of proof and comparison are not functional. Providing data to demonstrate these is not possible because in the absence of controlled conditions, an institution or program conducting follow-up studies or economic impact studies cannot distinguish the impact of the program(s) in question from the effect of the input variables and the external or other intervening variables. It is not possible to *prove* that your program caused the particular outcome that you may be fortunate enough to measure accurately. For more on this matter, see Hartnett (1974).

Necessary Ground Rules

Where does this conclusion leave us? With a lot of new and highly touted techniques that cannot prove anything? Yes and no. One can build a very strong case for conducting outcome studies if one recognizes the limitations, emphasizes the correct motivation, and defines the terms and procedures carefully. This writer believes that outcomes studies are important. I have argued strongly for their inclusion in self-study processes and regular institutional research programs for more than ten years, but I believe they can be useful only if the following are ground rules used as a guide.

1. *Outcome studies should be defined and conducted as goal achievement studies.* There are outcomes that probably result from the programs and services of institutions that are not defined in goal statements. These unintended outcomes are sometimes interesting and may present themselves in a helpful way as a matter of course in the outcomes studies; but this result is a relatively rare occurrence. Some other educational intentions are too complex or subtle to be described as goals and examined as outcomes. These are things we believe in and hope for but cannot define very well. On the other hand, there exists also a useful and doable set of outcome activities. Indeed, the major thrust of outcomes studies must be to see whether the institution's programs, along with the effects of external and other forces, yield the pattern of results intended— that is, those specified as goals for the enterprise. It is this basic set of examinations that can help steer the institution and improve its products.

2. *Goal achievement (outcomes) studies should be conducted primarily, if not exclusively, for purposes of institutional improvement.* Proof and comparison with other institutions should not be the motivations for goal achievement studies. Basically, one should search for patterns of activity and outcome that do not occur when called for by the goal statements or that do not occur in adequate amount in relation to locally defined criteria. This knowledge should then be the basis of attempts to improve the processes and programs or to change the inputs or even the goals until the desired outcomes appear consistently.

3. *Goal achievement (outcomes) studies should focus on several types of goal statements*—input goals, process goals, and outcome goals—*and should be developed locally using various approaches* ("hard" and "soft," that is, fact gathering and opinion collection) *for each goal.* The development should proceed in stages, during several self-study cycles, and should focus on those kinds of information that the local professionals find they can use to improve their programs.

4. In addition to the attempts to measure goal achievement, outcomes study ought to *include attempts to assess user or recipient satisfaction and suggestions for improvement* regarding each of the inherent program elements or services related to each goal or goal area. Such an effort would, for instance, seek comments about the admissions process that is called for in a particular input goal, or about the adequacy of counseling or a particular set of courses that are conducted to achieve a given process or outcome goal. Such useful feedback is almost universally missing or underrepresented from the recent outcomes systems and classifications, yet it must be an important part of any attempt to use the results of outcome studies.

5. *The process of considering the goal achievement results and concomitant feedback may be as useful and at times more useful than the evidence or opinions collected.* If one can achieve the state under which the professionals in a program regularly convene to discuss what seems to be happening and not happening as a result of their efforts, one probably has a healthy, responsive, effective institution.

These ground rules comprise a different approach from the attempts to prove, to ascribe cause and effect, or to compare one institution's purported impact with another's. The scheme recommended here has been used quite comfortably and effectively in program improvement efforts with which this writer has been involved and it is completely consistent with the concepts reported in chapter 1 about the assessment of organizational effectiveness (Campbell, 1977) and compatible with the recent recommendation of Bowen (1979), who called for useful, broadly conceived approaches to outcomes assessment.

The Task

To build a usable system of goal achievement studies based on the foregoing ground rules, the procedures would be generally as follows. Note that the ground rules assume that each institution or program is different and that the stated goals and any objectives associated with them are the starting point for the scheme. The work group charged with establishing or enhancing any existing system of goal achievement studies would begin by working with the goals and objectives statement produced by the goals work group or otherwise available from another recent review process. The work group, after some appropriate staff work and suggestions from the institutional research officer assigned to assist the group, should create for each goal and objective statement a list of all the possible ways in which the evidence—facts and opinions—could be gathered concerning the extent to which the goal is being achieved. If no useful, locally appropriate and acceptable criteria of achievement have been stated for the goal, the group should establish these after consultation with those involved at the operating level. The list of possible approaches for gathering goal achievement evidence could include examination of existing records and collection of new facts, interview data, standardized test results, and survey data from staff, students, alumni, employees, and community members. It may call for gathering of facts and opinions with locally produced instruments or with commercially available instruments. The first work of the group should produce

Specific Goal	(*Example:* Students will acquire general knowledge of principles of the social sciences)
	Procedure for Analysis: validated (locally) normative tests, area and item analysis of the data
	Procedure for Analysis: performance of graduates, further academic work in social sciences
	Procedure for Analysis: information from employers; suggestions
	Procedure for Analysis: oral examinations; review of student projects, research, etc.
	etc.
	etc.
Specific Goal	(*Example:* Communication skills; oral, written)
	etc.
	etc.
Specific Goal	(*Example:* Vocational or career skill[s])
	etc.
	etc.
Specific Goal	(*Example:* Independent study ability, self-direction)
	etc.
	etc.
Specific Goal	(*Example:* Religious values)
	etc.
	etc.

Figure 6.4. A format for an initial-outcomes (goal achievement) group.

something not unlike the format illustrated in figure 6.4.

The work group should then discuss the list of proposed study approaches with representatives of departments and offices concerned and with those expert in data collection, surveying, testing and the like, to compare the various approaches—the mechanisms required for each, the costs, the expected levels of cooperation or opposition, the time required, etc. Sample materials can then be examined and tentative draft instruments can be examined, authorized, and discussed with the steering committee to prevent any duplication of effort.

Building a Multiyear Plan

There are two objectives in listing and comparing approaches to goal achievement studies for a self-study. First, the work group should produce a multiyear plan for goal achievement studies that weighs for each the factors of cost, time, expected participation, and so on, as well as the potential usefulness of each step in light of the profile of needs and opportunities on the campus. Every goal achievement study probably cannot be conducted in one year; many need not be conducted each year. If ten goal achievement studies are required during a self-study, five might be undertaken in the first year and the other five in the second year. In year 3, six studies might be completed; the remaining four could be completed in year 4 (see figure 6.5)

Second, the work group must select those studies

to initiate in the first year of the self-study. It must supervise the development and organization of the procedures, review draft materials, gather suggestions for any instruments drafted, authorize the studies, review the results using any expert help required, and parcel out the results, recommendations, and stated implications to the work groups and departments concerned. If the work group is effective, the results of such efforts can be extremely valuable to the other work groups and to the ongoing study capacity of the institution or program.

The First Attempts

The particular goal achievement studies chosen in the initial effort vary from institution to institution; which are selected appears to be influenced by lack of activity in an area in previous years. In my experience, most work groups decide to conduct cohort attrition studies to examine student staying power at the institution, student retention being an objective inferred in many goal statements. They also focus increasingly on basic skill capacities, follow-up studies of recent graduates, and general education knowledge measures. The group at Mercy College (see chapter 4) chose to do the following studies:

1. Cohort attrition analysis of two recent classes.
2. A survey of senior students' reactions to services

GOAL ACHIEVEMENT STUDIES	Year 1	Year 2	Year 3	Year 4
1	●		●	
2		●		●
3	●			●
4	●	●	●	●
5		●		
6			●	
7	●	●	●	●
8			●	
9		●		
10	●		●	

Figure 6.5. Example of a multiyear schedule of goal achievement studies.

and programs and their suggestions for improvement.

3. A statistical "backward look" at a graduating class to find out which kinds of students were graduating.
4. An inventory of staff members' reactions to the way the college is run.
5. A goals inventory.
6. A follow-up study of recent graduates' activities, opinions of courses and services at the college, and suggestions for improvement.
7. A survey of community leaders' perceptions of college and community needs and suggestions for the college.

The need for these studies was ascertained by examining the college's stated input, process, and outcome goals. Subsequently each study served several needs and most produced useful information.

The use of major types of goal achievement studies at a large sample of institutions of all types for 1972-1977 (Kells and Kirkwood, 1979) was found to be as follows:

	INCIDENCE (%)
Follow-up studies of graduates	69
Attrition/retention studies	68
Surveys of current students about programs and services	66
Basic skill studies (competency)	36
Subject matter tests (knowledge)	28
Studies of higher cognitive skills (critical thinking, evaluation, etc.)	14
Studies of career/vocational competencies	14

Examples of instruments that have been used to accomplish some of these studies are presented later in this chapter.

Whatever studies are attempted initially, it should be remembered that one does not build the system overnight. Some attempts will require polishing. Some will not prove useful and will be abandoned. Using, over time, a battery of complementary goal achievement studies that are increasingly sophisticated and incorporating these into the regular operations of the institution is the desired product.

Examples of Basic Constructs

One serviceable exercise I have advised colleges and programs to conduct is depicted in figures 6.6 and 6.7. Basically, the outcomes work-group members, and any other appropriate participants, are asked to display on the blackboard, on "newsprint" sheets, or on blank forms the apparent relationship between the stated goals for the college or program and any specific steps the college takes to implement those goals. These two columns of information are then augmented with the plan for outcomes studies and space for eventual conclusions and any suggestions for improvement or further study.

Interesting and useful things begin to happen when the processes/activities column is addressed. Some college and program administrators are dismayed to find that the work-group members (and often others) cannot think of *anything* special the college does to try to assure that a particular goal is achieved. Before studying any outcomes, these administrators have learned that they must systematically attempt to identify, perhaps enhance, and communicate the program or process steps they take to achieve their goals. Such information can immediately be routed through the self-study

GOALS	PROCESSES/ACTIVITIES	OUTCOMES MEASUREMENT OR OTHER ANALYSIS	CONCLUSIONS/ SUGGESTIONS
M.C. will remain committed to the liberal arts and sciences, (yet will employ) diversity, flexibility, and novel methods and approaches	(To be _____ filled in _____ by outcomes _____ work group) _____ (tradt'l. elements in curric.) (flexibility in processes) (new teaching methods) (new curric.)	• Faculty Questionnaire (re use of various approaches and attitudes about them) • Student and grads. questionnaires • Admin. Questionnaire • College Records • IFI data	1. _____ 2. _____ 3. _____
(from Master Plan, p. 3) (M.C. students should accomplish:) • ability to communicate effectively and to interpret intelligently the communication of others	• Diagnostic testing of incoming freshmen • Developmental services _____ • _____ (courses available) • _____ (writing, speaking opportunities)	• Testing of random sample of seniors • GRE and NTE (and/or other) verbal scores • Analyze writing samples • Any experience with oral exams • Questionnaire of Srs. and faculty	1. Pretest all students* 2. Improve Learning Resources Center* 3. Multi-mode *ad libitum* skill development services*
some sense of literary and artistic form	• _____ (course work) • _____ (shows, events) • _____ (curric. rqmts)	• Questionnaire of Srs., grads and faculty • Undergrad. Record and NTE exams for these areas. • (Either all or random sample of seniors)	1. _____ 2. _____ 3. _____
an awareness of history, behavioral sciences and the natural sciences (etc.)	• curric., courses, rqmts. • special programs, lectures, etc. • role models—activities, research	• GRE, NTE and/or other testing of seniors • Questionnaire of Seniors • Results of any student projects	1. _____ 2. _____ 3. _____

*Suggestions from first Workshop during self-study process.

Figure 6.6. Work sheet used in Mercy College self-study process.

PROGRAM GOALS	RELATED PROGRAM ACTIVITIES	OUTCOME MEASURES	USE OF RESULTS
Goal: Graduates of "X" should be able to function well as professionals in the social service field.	• Basic core courses in social science. • special social work tracks. • advisory committee used to design and review. • internships. • visitors to campus. • staff chosen for practical knowledge. • senior colloquium.	• Area tests on social science principles—all graduates. Use local criteria; use item/subarea analysis. • social work skills exam; all graduates; analyze. • follow up graduates every 2 years; diary analysis; skill needs; problems; suggestions. • detailed interviews with employers; 10 per year; strengths, problems, suggestions. • attrition/retention analysis; a "backward look" at the graduating class. • senior student anonymous questionnaire.	• Review results of tests in detail with social science faculty; dean; suggest any actions; discuss with senior faculty. Suggest any new emphases. • discuss analysis of skills results with advisory committee and with faculty; review course coverage and intern experiences. Review instructional approaches and mtls. Make needed changes. • ditto with feedback from students, grads and employers. Changes needed? • review attrition data with dept. chrprsn., dean and admissions person/committee. Take needed actions.

Figure 6.7. Sample work sheet for an outcome goal of a social work program.

steering committee to the program or process work groups, which are or will be considering the matters in question.

Another reason for displaying such goals and process information in the way shown in figures 6.6 and 6.7 is to force the outcomes work group to relate goals to outcome study steps and then to the suggestions for improvement.

Additional Sources of Help

Outcomes work-group members may want to augment their own thinking about what studies to conduct by examining some of the literature on outcomes studies and by considering the outcomes taxonomy and list of suggested outcomes measures produced by the National Center for Higher Education Management Systems (Lenning, 1977). Also see appendix A of this book and the work by Winter et al. (1981).

Caveat: Remember that no one method or taxonomy or ready-made set of questionnaires or data schemes is totally appropriate as is for your college, university, or program. The outcomes methods must fit your goals and your outcomes plan. The existing schemes and systems may or may not be appropriate. For instance, some outcomes classification structures do not emphasize or may not even include community service goals. Some of the commercially available instruments do not contain enough items that will secure useful feedback to the college or program. Select the ideas, items, and parts of schemes that will help you conduct the studies and build the useful outcomes structure you want. Build the rest as you see fit.

Input, Environment, Program, and Process Studies

Having discussed the vital activities of goals clarification and the study of goal achievement, I will describe some of the activities and approaches to be used throughout the rest of the active phase of the study process—that is, the activities conducted by individuals and work groups that have to do with delineating and analyzing the input, environment, and process dimensions of the institution or the program. These dimensions can be viewed diagrammatically in the systems and flow models presented in chapter 3 and in the diagram of the entire self-study process in chapter 4 (see figure 4.1). This

section is devoted to these activities with the exception that the use of instruments will be treated in a separate following section.

The relative emphasis placed upon input, environment, or process matters or problems in a self-study is dictated by the study design. As indicated at the beginning of this chapter, studying such matters as program and procedural effectiveness, and human, fiscal, and physical resources requires describing things and gathering and analyzing facts and opinions. Those individuals or work groups assigned to study "the students," "the faculty," "the program," "academic services," "students services," and the like ought to review the sections at the beginning of this chapter on starting points for discussion. Unless the task given to a work group is to solve a previously identified problem, the work group will want to gather (or have presented to them by the staff) descriptive materials about the area to be studied, read any previous relevant studies, interview the key professionals involved, interact with any established advisory group to the program or area in question, review the goals of the program, ask for any initial data required, and prepare to ascertain any operating or other problems.

Once the initial description is intact and the units' goals are identified, work-group members will want to suggest to the steering group any items it would like included in information collection schemes so that student, staff, alumni, or community members may offer opinions about effectiveness of the program or process under study and make suggestions to the work group. These types of information, form the basis of the discussion in the work group about whether the program or service is operating effectively, or whether, for instance, some aspect of an input characteristic such as staff or financial resources is appropriate, adequate, or effective.

The job of the work group does not end when it has described and then collected and analyzed data on the strengths and problems or opportunities of the unit or area in question. The group must formulate recommendations for improvement or development. These recommendations should start the process of change by including tasks, assignments, timetable, governance approval steps, and so on. Finally, the group must either conduct hearings and/or develop written procedures for responding to the draft of the materials it has produced or it must help the steering committee conduct such discussions of the entire document for the college or program. The steering group may decide to edit or alter somewhat the report submitted, or it may ask for more information or additional study, discussion, and/or written material from the work group.

One final procedural reminder for work groups should be noted—particularly by the leader of the group. The quality of the product produced by the group—good analysis, a useful report, and improvement-oriented suggestions—will depend on the leadership provided in managing the process in light of the nature of the task, data, and other resources available and the progress made by other work groups (see chapter 3). The skills of the leader in motivating the group members, in employing useful developmental communication schemes when searching for new insights, in scheduling the work, in handling assignments and obtaining needed resources (funds, data, consultants), and in providing useful information and psychological rewards as the task progresses will make the difference between a mediocre process and a truly useful, first-rate job.

Instruments for Data Collection

The use of instruments in self-study processes is a subject that deserves special attention because of the unique assistance instruments can provide in a well-designed and carefully managed process and because of the potential dangers and problems associated with their use. The ability to gather fairly systematically facts and opinions from relatively large numbers of individuals is the substantial advantage of using instruments in a self-study. The indirect involvement of individuals who may not otherwise be actively engaged in the study can even begin the process of gaining commitment to resulting changes if the survey is done well and if the complete results are shared with the respondents soon afterward.

The disadvantages of using instruments are several and the extent to which they are felt depends greatly on the sophistication of the instrument designers and those who propose their use, and on the setting at the institution. A poorly designed instrument, used at the wrong moment with an unreceptive audience, will yield little or no useful information and it may damage the sense of community and morale at the institution involved. In brief, the following are potential problem areas in the use of instruments:

1. *Instruments take time and expertise to develop.* Commercially available instruments, therefore, are relatively expensive to use because the developers must recover their investment, which is often quite substantial. They are in business to make a reasonable profit and must recover funds for further instrument development. Locally produced instruments are of little value if they are not carefully developed. Even though one is not seeking statistically significant results of absolute proofs in a self-study process, the language must be unambiguous and the response must be reasonably high to any instrument. One must also be assured of at least face validity; that

is, the questions must generally yield the information intended. Pretesting any "homegrown" instrument is a must on a few respondents of the type who will eventually respond in order to check wording, terminology, the time it takes to use, and general understanding. The development of any questionnaire on campus for use in a study process should definitely be overseen by the institutional research office or a psychology or statistics group. It is, of course, a simple enough matter to gather a few facts from twenty departments or from ten counselors using a simple set of questions in a memo. But it is quite another thing to develop a fifty-item follow-up questionnaire to a thousand graduates or a faculty survey eliciting facts and opinions for use by three different work groups and two administrative offices.

2. *The instrument sometimes becomes the focus.* This writer has visited too many campuses (and encountered too many research processes) in which the leader(s) described the self-study as synonymous with an instrument used—say, a goals inventory or a delphi technique. Instruments are tools. They are procedures used to attempt to achieve the intentions of a study or to answer research questions. They are not the study. They should be chosen to meet a need for data, as perceived by the study participants. One must avoid becoming fascinated with an available instrument because others have used it or because someone on the campus thinks it would be nice to use.

3. *Sophistication, coordination, and good judgment are required.* Most self-study processes now employ both locally produced and commercially available instruments. The wise study designers carefully choose the type they need, and prepare the respondents to be approached. They tap professional advice in formulating and administering instruments and in analyzing the data, and they spread the use of desired data collection sorties over a long enough period of time so the respondents are not swamped with questionnaires or other requests for data.

In the remainder of this section, a brief survey of types of possible instruments will be presented and sources of information about them will be indicated. A few examples will be provided in order to highlight some interesting aspects or uses. Readers must contact the producer of the instrument to receive complete sample copies and explanatory information.

General Types

Two useful general taxonomies of instruments were produced in the late 1970s. First, Mary Jo Clark at the Educational Testing Service presented

	Input	Process	Outcomes
Institutional	• High school student surveys • Employer market surveys • Basic skill tests	• Student reactions to services • Surveys about environment and functioning	• Basic skill and general education tests • General alumni surveys
Program	• Market surveys • Student career interest surveys	• Student reactions to the program • Faculty reactions to program • Employer's reactions	• Knowledge exams • Skill, proficiency, or certification tests • Employer surveys
Course	• Cognitive style instruments • Diagnostic exams	• Student reactions to teaching and courses • Faculty peer reactions	• Proficiency tests • Reactions of employers or subsequent teachers

Figure 6.8. A scheme, with some examples, for classifying instruments for use in self-studies.

a general scheme for classifying formal instruments in April 1978. Basically, Clark reasoned that one can think of two axes and distribute the available instruments within the matrix provided by the two scales—one that describes the level of use within the institution and one that describes the point in the total institutional process (see figure 6.8, wherein this writer has added examples to the Clark matrix). This conceptualization is useful, particularly if one remembers that instruments can also be classified other ways: commercially available formal instruments versus "homegrown" varieties; and those that yield group-reliable data versus those that produce data that are reliable for the individual respondent. The latter type, of course, is very expensive to develop and usually contains a large number of items.

Sources

It is possible to classify most available instruments using the Clark scheme. It is also possible to use the scheme presented by James Bess (1979). Bess's article, readily available in journal form, should be examined by self-study steering and other work groups because it lists about seventy available instruments that he has classified in six different categories: personality and attitude scales; curricular and pedogogical style preferences; omnibus instruments measuring a variety of variables; placement, guidance, and counseling instruments; diagnostic tests of academic and personal problems; and typical local data collection instruments. Most of the instruments noted by Bess are for use with students.

If one adds to the Bess list the instruments and general sources that provide expert help on matters of facilities, finances, libraries, general manage-

ment, student services, teaching, boards of trustees, and general outcomes, the landscape of available formal instruments will be pretty well described for any study group. The major producers of these types of instruments are listed in appendix B.

Examples of Instruments

Goals. Earlier in this chapter the use of the Institutional Goals Inventory (IGI) from the Educational Testing Service by a community college was described in some detail. The reader will remember that IGI measures the perceived degree to which general goal areas (and also specific local goals) are important and should be important at the institution. It is possible then to look at the absolute and relative levels of importance ascribed to a goal area, to compare perceptions among groups on the campus, to focus on the discrepancy between "is" and "should be" for each goal area, and to examine the rank order of those discrepancies. The IGI is an extremely useful instrument if the response rate is high. It can be used in goal clarification and as a starting point for discussion about discrepancies among areas and about priorities to be set for goals and the processes called for by the goals.

An example of rank order discrepancy data and corresponding plot is presented in figure 6.9 for a four-year private college. The highest rank order discrepancy items became the focus of work group discussion, as did the relatively low "is" levels of cultural aesthetic awareness and off-campus learning.

General Functioning. One of the most widely used instruments for study processes is the Institutional Functioning Inventory (IFI), also from the Educational Testing Service. This instrument measures the perceptions of respondents (faculty, administra-

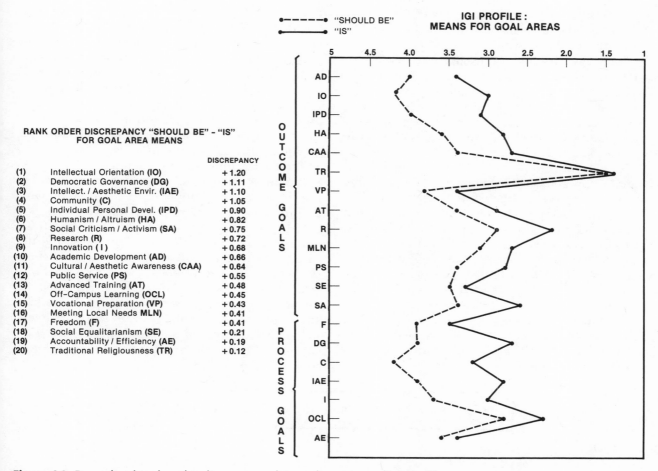

**RANK ORDER DISCREPANCY "SHOULD BE" – "IS"
FOR GOAL AREA MEANS**

		DISCREPANCY
(1)	Intellectual Orientation (IO)	+ 1.20
(2)	Democratic Governance (DG)	+ 1.11
(3)	Intellect. / Aesthetic Envir. (IAE)	+ 1.10
(4)	Community (C)	+ 1.05
(5)	Individual Personal Devel. (IPD)	+ 0.90
(6)	Humanism / Altruism (HA)	+ 0.82
(7)	Social Criticism / Activism (SA)	+ 0.75
(8)	Research (R)	+ 0.72
(9)	Innovation (I)	+ 0.68
(10)	Academic Development (AD)	+ 0.66
(11)	Cultural / Aesthetic Awareness (CAA)	+ 0.64
(12)	Public Service (PS)	+ 0.55
(13)	Advanced Training (AT)	+ 0.48
(14)	Off–Campus Learning (OCL)	+ 0.45
(15)	Vocational Preparation (VP)	+ 0.43
(16)	Meeting Local Needs MLN)	+ 0.41
(17)	Freedom (F)	+ 0.41
(18)	Social Equalitarianism (SE)	+ 0.21
(19)	Accountability / Efficiency (AE)	+ 0.19
(20)	Traditional Religiousness (TR)	+ 0.12

Figure 6.9. Example of rank order discrepancy data and corresponding profile chart for goals inventory data at a four-year private college. From *Institutional Goals Inventory*. Copyright © 1972 by Educational Testing Service. All rights reserved. Used by permission.

tors, students, etc.) on eleven scales concerning the way in which the institution functions:

Intellectual/Aesthetic Extracurriculum (IAE)
Freedom (F)
Human Diversity (HD)
Commitment to Improve Society (IS)
Undergraduate Learning (UL)
Democratic Governance (DG)
Meeting Local Needs (MLN)
Self-Study/Planning (SP)
Advancing Knowledge (AK)
Curriculum Innovation (CI)
Institutional Esprit (IE)

The item structures are both graduated response scales and "agree," "disagree," "don't know" types. The data are presented as scale means by respondent group and can be plotted on a percentile ranking basis against all respondents from the college or against colleges of similar type. Different types of colleges do show dramatically different mean scale

scores for the scales. For instance, a public community college may show mean scale scores at the 10-20 percentile levels on the IAE, IS, and AK scales, with concurrent scores at the 90 percentile level for the DG, MLN, CI, and IE scales. In contrast, a religiously affiliated liberal arts college may score very low on the F, HD, MLN, and CI scales but relatively high on the UL, SP, and IE scales. The profiles obtained can be very useful starting points for work-group discussion. In figure 6.10, the profile for the composite respondent group at a four-year private college is pictured. The college in question compared the profiles for four subgroups (administrators, faculty, student government leaders, and chairpersons), and it compared the 1977 results with results from a 1974 administration of the IFI.

For a more specific measure of student perceptions of services, teaching, and so on, self-study work groups may wish to examine the ETS Student Reactions to College (SRC) instrument with versions available for four-year and two-year colleges, a similar instrument produced by the American College Testing (ACT) program, or the UCLA Higher Education Measurement and Evaluation Kit (see appendix B). These instruments or those that are composed locally have been effectively used with students by employing student-led distribution through dining or residence halls, by classroom use with the cooperation of faculty members in core or specially selected courses, or with senior students at class meetings or via the registrar's office as they file graduation applications.

Alumni Follow-up Studies. Many of the institutions and programs that conduct self-studies use one or another form of an alumni follow-up survey. Most institutions devise their own questionnaire, but general questionnaires are beginning to be commercially available. One is available through The National Center for Higher Education Management Systems (NCHEMS) in Boulder, Colorado, and the College Entrance Examination Board, which also provides instruments for entering students, continuing students, former students, program completers, and graduating students. Another system of follow-up services is being marketed by the American College Testing Program.

With the NCHEMS and ACT instruments, it is possible to add local items to create at least some feedback possibilities for specific local services, programs, and courses. Many institutions that use the NCHEMS general data systems undoubtedly will want to consider the NCHEMS questionnnaires.

When building an alumni questionnaire at your own college, remember the following guidelines:

1. It is just as valuable to receive information *from* graduates as it is to receive information about them. Seek their reactions and suggestions.

2. Sample many or all recent graduates from the last five years. Their opinions will be most relevant to improving the current programs.

3. Use some in-depth case studies, particularly for feedback about job skills, training needs, and the like. Telephone interviews can also be used effectively for such attempts.

4. Alumni response rates can be enhanced by "talking up" alumni surveys and working with students before they graduate and by mailing surveys to parents' homes at holiday time if graduates' current addresses are unavailable. Although most institutions expect to get few responses to alumni

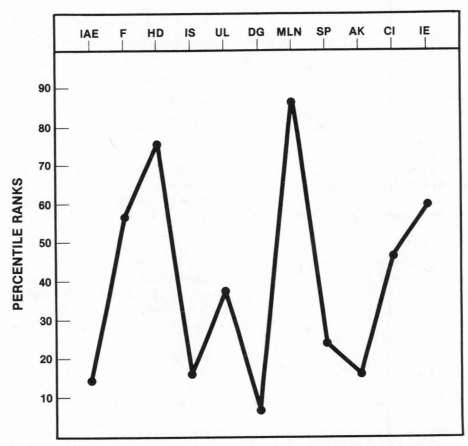

Figure 6.10. IFI profile for a four-year private college. The percentile scales are the standard ETS distribution of faculty means for thirty-seven comparison-group institutions. From *Institutional Functioning Inventory.* Copyright © 1968 by Educational Testing Service. All rights reserved. Used by permission.

questionnaires, the last two this writer worked with received between 65 and 70 percent response. Anonymity must be assured, reasons for seeking graduates' help must be given, and they should be promised and given a copy of the results. Publication of the survey in the alumni magazine is an ideal format for informing graduates.

5. Remember—one wants useful information, not fodder for bragging about graduates. The latter is expensive and shaky. What you want is solid information about needs graduates perceive and suggestions for course and services improvement. With the data about perceptions of goals fulfillment or patterns of activity, look for patterns of unfulfilled expectations. That is where the work needs to be done.

When constructing the actual questionnaire, one can count on getting some generally useful information if the following categories are included:

1. *Background characteristics* about the respondent for cross-tabulation (dates of attendance, status, graduation specifics, major, sex, grade average at graduation). Use checklists.
2. *General activities since graduation.* Relate these to the goals and purposes of the college. Use some checklists.
3. *Opinions regarding the extent to which the college is achieving its goals.*
4. *Opinion about impact of college on the graduate.* Relate these opinions to college goals and perceived job skills needed, and include basic and higher-order skills.
5. *Suggestions for improving the college.*
6. Give room for *General Comments.*
7. *Thank them. Send or publish the results.*

Appendix C contains examples of alumni follow-up questionnaires. The first one is a departmental (or program level) alumni follow-up of doctoral and masters degree graduates over the preceeding ten years. It was pretested, and sent out with a stamped, self-addressed envelope; one postcard follow-up was mailed. A 65 percent response rate was achieved. The data were tabulated and cross-tabulated using data processing techniques. A useful set of tables and corresponding comments were presented to a self-study work group.

The second questionnaire is the one used by Mercy College in their 1977 self-study.

References

"Academic Competencies as Defined in New Project of College Board." *The Chronicle of Higher Education*, 30 September 1981, p. 6.

Andrews, Grover J., et al. *Assessing Nontraditional Educa-tion.* Washington, DC: Council on Postsecondary Accreditation, 1978.

Baird, Leonard; Hartnett, Rodney; et al. *Understanding Student and Faculty Life: Using Campus Surveys to Improve Academic Decision Making.* San Francisco: Jossey-Bass, 1980.

Bess, James L. "Classroom Management Decisions Using Student Data: Designing an Information System." *The Journal of Higher Education*, May/June 1979, pp. 256-79.

Bowen, Howard R. "Goals, Outcomes and Academic Evaluations." In *Evaluating Educational Quality.* Washington, DC: Council on Postsecondary Accreditation, 1979.

Breen, Paul. "76 Career-related Liberal Arts Skills." *AAHE Bulletin*, October, 1981, p. 9.

Campbell. "On the Nature of Organizational Effectiveness." (See refs. for Chap. 3.)

Casserly, M. *Self-Study and Planned Change in Academic Libraries.* Ph.D. Dissertation, Rutgers University, 1983.

Educational Testing Service. "Institutional Goals Inventory, Specimen Set." Princeton, NJ: ETS.

Fiske, Edward B. "Harvard Tightens Up Curriculum; Ends General Education Program." *The New York Times*, 3 May 1978.

Fordyce and Weil. *Managing with People* (Chap. 4).

Forrest, A. "Competency Based Assessment in Postsecondary Education: Some Issues and Answers." *North Central Association Quarterly*, Fall 1977, pp. 322-26.

Frances, Carol, and Coldren, Sharon I., eds. *Assessing Financial Health.* New Directions for Higher Education Series, no. 26. San Francisco: Jossey-Bass, 1979.

Griffin, G., and Burks, D. R. *Appraising Administrative Operations: A Guide for Universities and Colleges.* Berkeley: University of California, 1976.

Harpel, R. L. "Planning, Budgeting, and Evaluation in Student Affairs Programs: A Manual for Administrators." *NASPA Journal*, Summer 1976, pp. i-xx.

Hartnett, Rodney. "Problems with the Comparative Assessment of Student Outcomes in Higher Education." Paper presented at the meeting of the Association for Institutional Research, May 1974, Washington, DC.

Kania, A. *The Development of a Model Set of Regional Accreditation Standards for Academic Libraries.* Ed.D. Dissertation, Rutgers University, 1983.

Johnson, Edward R. "Academic Library Planning, Self-Study and Management Review." *Journal of Library Administration*, vol. 2 (1982), nos. 2–4.

Kells. "Institutional Accreditation" (chap. 3).

Kells and Kirkwood. "Institutional Self-Evaluation Processes" (chap. 2).

Koerner, James D. "Preserving the Status Quo: Academia's Hidden Cartel." *Change*, March/April 1971, pp. 50-54.

Lenning, Oscar T. *The Outcomes Structure: An Overview and Procedures for Applying It in Postsecondary Education Institutions.* Boulder, CO: National Center for Higher Education Management Systems, 1977.

Micek, Sidney S., and Walhaus, Robert A. *An Introduction to the Identification and Uses of Higher Education Outcomes Information.* Boulder, CO: Western Interstate Commission on Higher Education, 1973.

Miller, Richard I. *The Assessment of College Performance.* San Francisco: Jossey-Bass, 1979.

Peterson, Richard E. "The Institutional Goals Inventory in Contemporary Context." In *Using Goals in Research and Planning*, edited by R. Fenske. New Directions for Institutional Research Series, no. 19. San Francisco: Jossey-Bass, 1978.

Romney, Leonard C. *Measures of Institutional Goal Achievement.* Boulder, CO: National Center for Higher Education Management Systems, 1978. (P.O. Drawer P, Boulder CO 80302; paperback, $6.00.)

Romney, Leonard C., and Bogen, Gerald K. "Institutional Goals: Proceed with Caution." In *Using Goals in Research and Planning*, edited by R. Fenske. New Directions for Institutional Research Series, no. 19. San Francisco: Jossey-Bass, 1978.

State University of New York. *Student Affairs Planning and Evaluation Guidelines.* Albany, June 1977.

The University of the State of New York. *A Handbook for Self-Assessment for Colleges and Universities*, Albany, 1979.

Washington State Student Services Commission. *A Manual for Student Services.* Seattle: Washington State Board for Community College Education, 1977.

Winter, David G.; McClelland, David C.; and Stewart, Abigail J. *A New Case for the Liberal Arts.* San Francisco: Jossey-Bass, 1981.

7

Program or Departmental Self-Study

For Independent and Accreditation-related Settings

In the ideal circumstance, the self-evaluating (Wildavsky, 1972) or the truly healthy (Huse, 1975) organization conducts useful self-study and planned change at all of its levels and in all of its constituent parts on a continuous basis. With an eye on the overarching organizational intentions, capacities, and resources, individual department or program directors manage the efforts of their unit with due consideration to and periodic beneficial assistance from the study of goals, the solution of operational problems, and the assessment of the results of the efforts of the unit. However, in higher education organizations the evidence of ongoing useful self-analysis is still relatively small, and this lack is most seriously felt at the departmental or program level. For it is here in American colleges that most—perhaps 80% for larger institutions—of the decisions which directly affect students, learning, research, and service are made. This level of importance has not been matched with a corresponding emphasis on the effective selection and training of managers at the program level. For over a decade pleas have been made for increased efforts to train college and university department heads, directors, chairpersons, or managers, but until lately, little response has come from either institution heads or departmental leaders. For an excellent discussion of this condition and for a marvelous new management training resource, see the work by Allan Tucker (1981).

So it is little wonder that one finds relatively little useful self-study at the program level across all fields at American institutions. That does not mean that no self-study efforts are conducted at this level or that none are useful. Far from it. But successful efforts have been limited to certain fields where common efforts and guidance are available and to specific settings and instances. Two influences have created some change in this circumstance. The first is the increased use, particularly by large research universities, of cyclical department reviews—usually occurring in a five-year cycle and involving at least a descriptive study by the local unit and a team of visitors from sister departments at noncompeting but similar institutions. This custom has existed at some universities for at least two decades and has been propelled by the growth of state coordinating agencies, by the cost–price squeeze, by changing student demographics, and by the public pressure for accountability.

The second influence, of longer standing than the first, is the presence of specialized accreditation in some twoscore or more disciplines. These processes touch almost two-thirds of the US nonprofit institutions and perhaps 10 percent of those which are profit-seeking. Some large universities and heavily career- or profession-oriented colleges are extensively involved with them (Kells and Parrish, 1979). As pointed out earlier in this book, most of the specialized accreditation agencies have insisted for some time that the programs they review conduct self-study, but only recently has this activity been more than a descriptive question-and-answer exercise concerning the agency standards for a handful of the agencies. Many specialized accrediting agencies now take self-study very seriously (see Zimmerman, 1974 and French and Elkins, 1979) and that is one of the reasons for devoting this chapter to the study of departmental or program self-assessment efforts.

Conceptual and Contextual Issues

Several important issues and dimensions should be addressed before the mechanics of self-study at the program level are discussed. From this point forward we will use the term program to mean department, program, or other similar unit. We must first address the nature or structure of the program in a systems sense and how the elements in the structure are related. Then the specific aspects of the context in which the program exists will be explored, for they have an important effect on the design of self-study efforts. Design issues, expectations for program level studies, and a general self-study flow model will then be presented.

It is important to note that program level self-study efforts should really be discussed in two groups—those which are conducted without stimulus from an accrediting agency, and those which are so stimulated. The initial discussion of context, concepts, and procedures applies generally to both situations. The last part of this chapter contains materials and suggestions specifically related to studies conducted in relation to an accreditation action.

The System

The general context for program self-study and some of the challenges to be surmounted in doing it well are depicted in figure 7.1. In this simple linear systems model one can readily see that the flow of students, professionals, and resources into and through the system is affected by the same external forces which act on the whole institution; however, some may be weaker or stronger in impact on the program in question. The program is also heavily influenced by its setting *within* the institution, in terms of stated intentions (goals), resource availability, access to services including information, and other factors. One could argue, of course, that program self-study, if it is to be useful and improvement-oriented, should not be attempted unless an institutionwide review has recently been conducted or at least initiated, since judgments about *institutional* intentions, resources, services, and expecta-

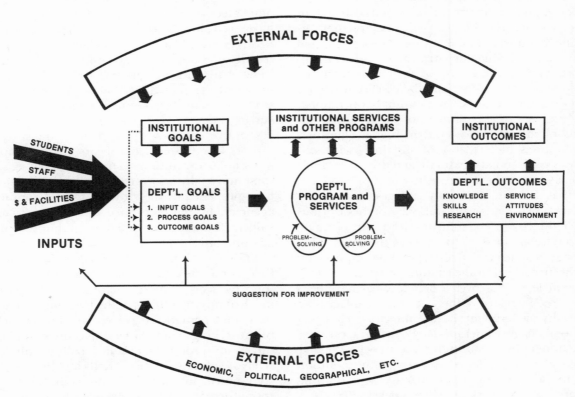

Figure 7.1. The general linear systems model of a program (or department) with some aspects of a self-study process indicated.

tions of the program could change. An integrated cycle of study initiated at the institutionwide level, overlapping perhaps with program studies initiated slightly after the larger study, would be ideal. But if this is not possible, program reviews can be carried out fairly usefully in reasonably stable institutions even if the larger institutional context has not been reviewed for a while. All of the potential benefits of a program self-study—which are not different in their basic character from those described in chapter 3—may not be realized in such "go it alone" studies, but since self-study *should* be cyclical, the unrealized potential can probably be achieved in the next cycle, unless the whole institution still has not conducted its review.

The Barriers

While the general organizational setting provides some complications for program studies, there are several other barriers as well to useful study. First, most program units are isolated in several ways. They are more or less isolated from institutional power centers, a fact that affects the likelihood of achieving certain changes which the study may call for. They are usually also isolated from data and particularly from the ability to get useful data (information), a fact that, unless remedied, can severely limit the capacity to study the program. They are often small in size, a fact that usually determines the number of persons available to conduct the study. The program members are often conditioned by the conventional wisdom in the field, a kind of guild effect, which unless surmounted can seriously limit the range of interpretation of data, the options considered, and the like. Similarly, program professionals, who understandably focus on the specifics of their discipline, courses, workload, and the like, often "cannot see the forest for the trees." They usually know little of the potentially useful curricular and procedural dimensions of related fields; they often have a limited perspective on campuswide issues; they eschew both administrative matters and parameters and methods of planning, and often know little about methods for assessing and changing programs such as their own. Finally, as indicated at the start of this chapter, the program director, so important in designing, organizing and completing self-study or planning efforts, is likely to have limited managerial experience and to be unaware of the ways and means with respect to these matters. Fortunate is the program with a strong leader who is knowledgeable both about the discipline and about getting things done through the agency of other people in a complex organization.

Some of the special circumstances of a program (as opposed to an institutional) setting are quite helpful to self-study efforts. First, of course, there is usually intense interest in the program and its students on the part of the professionals who will conduct the study. Strong orientation and pride regarding the discipline—often barriers to useful involvement at the institutional level—are potentially helpful motivators at the program level. The possibility of useful student involvement is greater at the program level and the possibility for implementing change *during* the study is at least potentially greater in such studies. The other side of the size issue, the possibility of thoroughly studying a program because it is small enough to be studied, is a great advantage. Finally, program members are more likely to feel satisfied after a useful study, because they can see the results of their efforts.

The Intentions

Program self-study should seek to achieve the same basic things that institutional efforts do—clarified stated intentions (goals), improvement in the program, a better system of ongoing study (data and analytical capacity and the inclination to use it) and planning. Secondary benefits should be sought as well—a report that can be useful in several settings, some increased leadership capacity and awareness of management issues, some reworked procedures, and, if outsiders are involved, perhaps direct benefits from visitors. Increased awareness and perhaps status in the field, and other benefits perhaps associated with accreditation status, can also occur.

It is probably fair to say that with a few notable exceptions the second and third of the basic intentions (improvement and a better, ongoing study capacity) have resulted far less frequently from program self-studies than many have hoped for. These vital dimensions have not often been realized through the generally descriptive preparation for "outside" visitors in either university-mandated or in specialized accreditation program reviews. Anxiety over the results of the external review, fear of retrenchment, or other political dimensions have sapped many of the efforts to date. This predicament will be explored in the last two sections of this chapter and it is treated extensively and usefully in the article by Arns and Poland (1980). Where improvement in the program and the instructional efforts have occurred as a result of study efforts, the processes have been extremely well led and they have been internally motivated, "quiet," relatively "private," unpoliticized events. Cycles of such study and planning efforts would benefit *any* organization.

There are some additional, more situation-specific

expectations that we should hold for program self-study processes. The study process should reduce the isolation of the program, its professionals, and its students in the university or college. The program should be better understood and appreciated by those in the administration of the institution and by other professionals in the larger system. Data services and useful information should be more available to the program, and any gap between program goals and institutional goals should be narrowed. Finally programmatic leadership and general esprit should be enhanced, and the willingness to work together to recognize and solve problems should increase. The program should be healthier in an organizational as well as a disciplinary sense.

General Procedures for Program Self-Study

In addition to the general steps recommended for institutionwide self-study—a prestudy preparation and design step, an organization phase, the actual study phase, and the use of strategies to implement the recommended changes, including the use of visitors (see chapter 3)—several special activities, distributed appropriately across the aforementioned phases, must be attempted in order to achieve the intentions and surmount the barriers noted above.

First, if possible, the program should initiate its study at a time that will permit maximum awareness of and assistance from the institutional context. Such situations might exist during or just after an institutionwide study or planning effort. During such efforts, the attention of the top leaders is focused on study efforts; access to data is enhanced; willingness to consider boundary issues and other intramural concerns is generally increased; institutional research opportunities are greater; and willingness to consider changes if not alternative futures is usually strong. At the minimum, the institutional goals and resources which are the starting points for program review should be portrayed in greater relief and in more reliable ways during such periods.

Second, it is very important that the program director secure a measure of interest, if not positive support, from the campus leadership for an improvement-oriented study of the program. This support should take the form of access to data, help for the study, and a willingness to review and use the results of the study. If possible, the commitment of central administration should be expressed in ways which would insure participation in or at least useful inputs from and reactions to the study effort from administrators and perhaps from faculty *outside* the program. This will help to reduce

isolation and to produce reactions which can place the program self-analysis in a larger context. If well done it can reduce provincialism and produce better results and more confidence or perhaps less self-congratulation—common tendencies among program faculties.

Third, it is particularly important at the program level that the mechanics of self-study not be overwhelming. Design is critical. Size is often a problem, and faculty members should not be subjected to endless meetings in a committee-heavy scheme. Leadership, judgement, and timing are very important. The simplest scheme possible which permits the program faculty to review the program (goals, data about students, services, courses, problems, and results) and to discover needs for improvement and ways to improve should be used. The interactions should be more sequential than concurrent, carefully timed to the availability of information and assistance, adequately staffed, and more intensive than extended. A sequence of well-led, properly designed, and carefully timed and staffed one- and two-day work sessions can be far more productive at the program level than a group of year-long committee efforts.

Finally, the possibility for travel away from the campus and visitors to the program site during the study effort should be considered. The staff members must discover what their problems are and what the possibilities for change may be by using data about their own program and its apparent results and by viewing similar situations elsewhere. The participants must be able to interact with new ideas, which they may, of course, reject. But the stimulation of such interactions often fires the consideration of new ways of doing well or even better the business of the program.

A Useful Model

The scheme presented in figure 7.2 represents the general steps and relationships between them in a model program self-study process. Several general characteristics of such a model are worthy of note. They arise from the fact that most programs are relatively small organizational units and the professionals are very busy with teaching, advising, regular committee work within the program and without, and often with heavy research and/or community service, extension, or other professional activities. Therefore, the keys to successful study effort at the program level are *design, leadership,* and *staff work.*

Design is even more important in program self-study than in institutional-level study, since it often must focus on complex curricular, instructional,

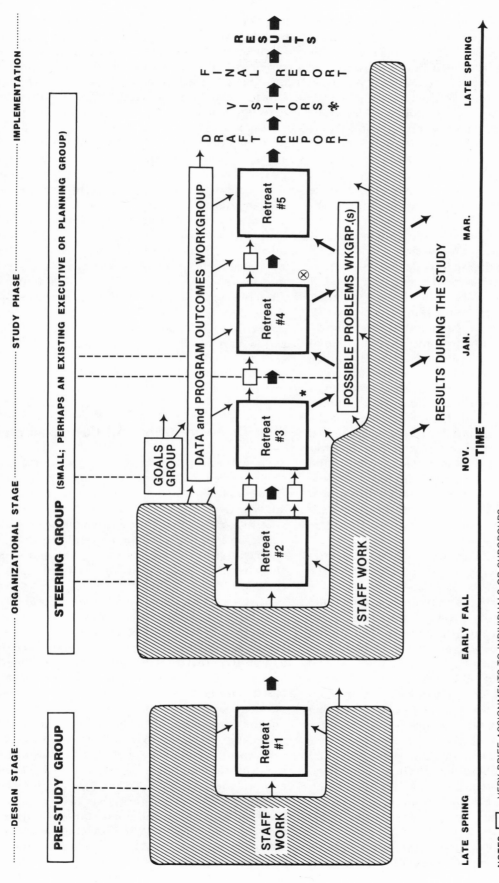

Figure 7.2. Flow diagram of a model self-study process at the program level.

NOTES: ☐ = VERY BRIEF ASSIGNMENTS TO INDIVIDUALS OR SUBGROUPS

✱ = A GOOD TIME TO VISIT OTHER PLACES

⊗ = A GOOD TIME TO HOST VISITOR(s) OR CONSULTANT(s)

✤ = A GOOD TIME FOR ANY FORMAL VISITING TEAM

and student issues in the absence of a large, well-organized data base and of adequate regular professorial and administrative staff help; and moreover it must make do with a limited group of faculty or other primary professionals as the focal point for study activity. Therefore, *the design must make the effort as efficient as possible.* Usually very few committees are employed. The program professionals are brought together only when the right information is available to address real and important questions. This design is accomplished by using a *sequence* of activities and by employing *adequate preparation* prior to *carefully led, intensive work sessions.*

The program leader must secure from the natural leaders within the program the necessary backing, help with data and other staff work, and willingness to direct the activities that are agreed upon. The staff work can, of course, take many forms. In larger programs where permanent administrative assistants or other regularly assigned staff exist, professional priorities must be realigned and an orientation provided so these people can work with campus-wide staff in order to prepare the data and historical analyses, to collect written policies and procedures, and even to draft propositions for consideration by program professionals at the various stages of the study. In smaller programs, borrowed or reassigned temporary help, faculty on partial release from teaching duties, part-time graduate assistants, and plain overload activity by the chairperson are the sources of the critically important staff help required for the study effort. Even though such measures seem a bit unfair, one must remember that the alternative to the mode being suggested—an unassisted, unrealistically large covey of additional, simultaneously employed work groups, which must discover the data and often all of the basic questions—is rarely useful, often destructive of morale, and sometimes harmful to the regular program activities and to any hope of subsequent effective study or planning efforts. Good staff work, on the other hand, can accomplish wonders.

The reader should also note that two types of group activities are used in the model. The first consists of a few small work groups—a small steering effort which can be a two- or three-person executive group; a temporary group of senior people to review stated intentions (goals); a small, staff-assisted group to advise the staff about data, to design any data-gathering instruments, and to consider program outcomes; and any needed work group to address specific issues, problems, or other needs discovered during the study.

The second type of activity is a sequence of brief, properly designed and staffed programwide retreats or work sessions. These are held at important stages of the study in order to secure some participation of all program members, to discover issues, to consider important, well-honed sets of data on the program, to stimulate interest in any specific work-group efforts, and to lay the groundwork for the acceptance of recommended changes in the program, away from telephones, piles of work, and other familiar distractions, at a neutral, comfortable, but not necessarily expensive, on- or off-campus site. They can be most useful if they are of sufficient length to explore thoroughly issues which are carefully selected and prepared for study. One- to three-day retreats conducted at the campus center or continuing education facility where participants can be comfortable are often appropriate. Such sessions, when provided with generous schedules that include time for informal conversation, recreation, and the like, are often remembered as the turning point in a study or curriculum review process.

Year-long self-studies often use lengthier retreats at the start of the process to encourage informal activities, and subsequently more structured, intensive schedules ("bring sandwiches in and let's wrap this up by three-thirty").

Specific Suggestions and Case Examples

We will now proceed to discuss each of the major stages in the program self-study model presented in figure 7.2 and to provide some examples of materials and full case experiences.

Design Stage. In addition to what has been stated about the design of a program self-study both in this chapter and in chapter 4, several of the more subtle elements and program-specific aspects must be considered.

At this organizational level more informality is possible, and more comfortable direct conversation about the real needs of the program can usually be part of the design stage. If the program director or a carefully chosen program member can convene and lead a series of thoughtful conversations which are based in part on previous reports by outside agencies or other internal records, a useful design might emerge. The questions to be answered include the following: "What are our primary program needs, concerns, or unknown dimensions?" "Who within the institution and the program can help us most to explore these issues?" "What external forces are affecting us?" "What timetable makes the most sense, given our situation and the other aspects of the next academic year?" "What basic information are we likely to need?" "What comparable programs elsewhere should we visit or otherwise consider?"

"Who can assist us with our information and other staff needs?" "What are the political dimensions of our program's present existence?" "What is the best use we can make of these factors?" "What outsiders might assist us and in what ways?" "What additional expertise do we need?" As these questions and others are explored over several sessions, the nature of, sequence of and leadership for the study should (probably will) evolve easily and naturally. The conversations should be open, developmental in nature, and increasingly informed by facts about and experiences in the program.

One of the activities that should surely go on among some or all of the program faculty members during the design stage of a self-study process is conversation about ways of looking at organizational entities like theirs. A good way to stimulate discussion is for the group designing the study to select a few articles and perhaps a book or two which could be basic "required" readings for the first stage of the study. Several excellent pieces come to mind in this regard. With respect to the administrative procedures and services of a program or department, the ideal book is Allan Tucker's *Chairing the Academic Department* (1981). It is thorough and an excellent starting point for discussion about any program. It is also a wonderful basic tool for training chairpersons or potential chairs. For a general overview of issues at the program or departmental level, one might consider the book by Dressel, Johnson, and Marcus (1970). For those who know they will be considering curriculum issues very heavily, the essay by Lynn Wood and Barbara Gross Davis entitled "Designing and Evaluating Higher Education Curricula" (1978) is a good starting point. Essays or articles provided by the national association of the particular discipline are, of course, good starting points for faculty members. With respect to meeting student needs, particularly with respect to noncognitive (affective) development, one might use *The Modern American College* by Chickering et al. (1981), which contains general and discipline-specific essays. It might be a good idea as well to ask a student services professional or someone from the academic planning or institutional research office to sit in on early discussions and suggest some materials.

The study should include approaches specific to the program. Graduate programs should review the materials prepared under the Graduate Program Assessment Service of the Educational Testing Service. Programs preparing professionals ought to review Barbara Andrews's essay entitled "Can Professional Competence Be Measured?" (1980) and recent materials from the professional agency with which it is most closely affiliated. Finally, some state

boards, regents, coordinating agencies, and university central planning offices have fairly thorough (although not necessarily improvement-oriented) lists of departmental criteria and checklists or report outlines which can be reviewed as a starting point by program studiers.

Once everyone has reviewed some common materials and the planners of the study have had some first thoughts about a possible design, and once the necessary funds, backing, and staff assistance are in hand, the ideas should be presented at a program-wide meeting or retreat (number 1 in the model) to elicit any other ideas, to orient the staff, to gain commitment to the study through participation in the design step, and to introduce the possibility that study may actually yield some welcome results.

Organizing and Getting Started

If the design stage and retreat go well, the resulting design should be summarized concisely and distributed to those to be involved outside the program and to all staff members within it. Then the process can begin. Beginning usually means a heavy dose of staff work before any work group is formed—other than perhaps a data subgroup, if one is used. Few departments have available in a usable form all the necessary data about students, courses, staff, funds, equipment, facilities, and the like which should be available before anyone meets to discuss the issues. The steering group or coordinator should have the basic data assembled in large part before any group meets. Inferred goal analysis, which any goals subgroup may wish to discuss, may require such information (see chapter 6). Once basic data documents and descriptions are available (see final paragraphs of chapter 5) the steering group should then empower a small, carefully chosen subgroup to review the stated intentions (goals) of the program.

Working With Program Goals

The group asked to review the program goals should usually be composed of senior people with enough breadth and depth of experience to be able to consider some extremely important and complex matters. They must be able to interpret the trends in the field, the expectations of the institution with regard to stated program intentions, and the collective attitude about issues such as causality—that is, whether there is a need to state intentions (goals) so that one may subsequently assess some cognitive and other student outcomes. The group must consider the nature of the educational environment desired by most of the staff and the complex relationship of program inputs to likely outputs, measurable or not. Surely some of these things are "prescribed" by the norms in most fields, but any given program may wish to challenge or depart significantly from the conventional wisdom.

As suggested in chapter 6 in the section on institutional or collegewide goals, the amount of work to be done depends on the perception of the group about the adequacy of the present goals, the length of time since they were last reviewed, the degree of consensus on them, their completeness (with respect to the tasks presently attempted or intended), their clarity (with respect to usefulness for evaluation of progress in achieving them), and the perceived and correctly noted priority among them. As indicated also in chapter 6, it is possible to involve the staff in an exercise to assess anonymously the consensus on priority and completeness of the program goals. The same technique and type of instrument (commercially available or "home-grown") goals inventory used at the institutional level can be used at the program level.

The biggest needs with respect to goals review at the program level, as I see them, are (1) to augment the program goal statement to include goals regarding *input* (who is sought to teach and who should come to the program to learn), *process* (the environment to be created and maintained, the attitudes and values to be rewarded, the proper way to relate to the institutional context), and *outcome* (the general and specific knowledge, the skills and attitudes sought or intended in graduates); (2) to indicate *where appropriate, and for internal purposes*, what *some* of the expected criterion (performance) levels for *groups* of graduates are with respect to the outcome goals; and (3) to create a sense of priority about what intentions are most important in the program. Two totally fictitious examples follow of program goal statements that illustrate some of these aspects.

Example: *Goal Statement for an American Studies Program*

The American Studies Program at Elite College is interdisciplinary and multidisciplinary in nature. It accepts students who are interested in the serious study of American culture at the baccalaureate and master's level. The program is conducted by a small staff of fulltime faculty with complementary backgrounds and interests presenting a wide range of courses and introducing faculty interests from other departments in the fields of art history, literature, crafts and folklore, history, architecture, music, economics, philosophy, anthropology, and political science. The unifying theme of the program is the study of culture, with particular emphasis upon material culture. The

primary focus of faculty efforts is the teaching function; all faculty are however expected to have an active scholarly life, and research and publications are encouraged—but not expected at the level usually found at research universities. Students are expected to demonstrate writing skills marked by integration of thought and by analysis as opposed to the regurgitation of facts.

The specific goals of the program are:

1. to educate students who will be prepared to go on to further study and to excellent performance in the same field or related fields, or to competent employment in a range of occupations including journalism, museum work, work at historical societies, libraries, and the like;
2. to produce graduates (a) who can aptly analyze cultural characteristics and who have a broad appreciation for the literary, historical, and other aspects of such settings (all students must pass a departmental examination on these matters before graduating); (b) who can express themselves clearly in written and oral modes; and (c) who can think critically and integratively about American and other cultures;
3. to attract and develop staff members with an interest in teaching in ways which foster the foregoing items;
4. to develop a program of scholarly activities which are appropriate to this setting, and which complement the needs of the Elite students;
5. to maintain an intellectual atmosphere which is typified and fostered by regular discussion of scholarly work, an active program of visitors and speakers, and a vigorous collaboration with staff members in other disciplines and in organizations outside Elite; and
6. to take the lead in fostering the consideration and preservation of the material cultures of this region of the state, and to collaborate with the State University in fostering interest in such matters statewide.

Example: *Goal Statement for a Social Work Program*

The Social Work Program at State College offers baccalaureate work to a wide range of students who wish to work as members of a team offering social services in a wide range of settings and/or who wish to go on to a graduate program at another institution. This institution welcomes students of many backgrounds, and it places great emphasis on the ability of its graduates to function *well* in the work setting. Therefore, in addition to the competencies and knowledge in the discipline, students must demonstrate fluency in language, writing, and analytical ability. The staff of the program are carefully selected professionals and teacher–scholars whose first interest is the State College students.

The specific program goals are:

1. to graduate students who can (a) function as com-

petent professionals in the field as members of a social science team, (b) write and speak well in their native language and present clearly their views on the subject matter of and conditions and context for social service work, (c) demonstrate adequate knowledge of social science principles and the four basic areas of professional and clinical practice embodied in the Social Work Assistants Examination (all students must take this exam; the program expects each group of graduates to average better than the 80th percentile), and (d) demonstrate adequate human relations and group skills;

2. to attract and develop a faculty with demonstrated professional abilities and experience, and interest and skill in teaching;

3. to develop an environment in which the freedom to teach and the freedom to learn are perceived by all;

4. to assist in the improvement of the social work field through selected scholarly activities, curriculum projects, training efforts, and research;

5. to play an important role in conjunction with the graduate program at State University in the continuing professional education of the social work professionals in the state; and

6. to have the professional staff actively participate in the development and governance of the program.

The Consideration of Outcomes (Goal Achievement)

The study of goal achievement is, of course, much more practical and potentially more useful at the program level then at the institutional level. Diagnostic assessment of expected results, whether in the educational product, the environment, or the expected functioning of the program (all of which may be directly stated or implied in the goals statement), is quite possible at the program level. And yet, not many programs usefully assess outcomes. As is described in detail in chapter 6, goal achievement studies conducted for purposes of improving the program can be planned and conducted without political repercussion and with definite benefit to the program and to its students, *if* (1) they are carefully developed with the stated intentions (goals) of the program as the guiding premise, with locally determined methods and criteria of acceptable performance, and (2) they are developed patiently over time by the program professionals themselves. The reader is referred to figure 6.7, in which the first goal of the social work program mentioned in the example above is completely explored in all its dimensions—explanations of how the program professionals seek to achieve the goal, how they assess the extent to which it is being achieved over time, and how they use the information they gain to improve the program.

In figure 7.3, goal number 5 of the American Studies Program (example above) is analyzed in the same way, and a plan for conducting and using goal achievement information is presented. The goal is a *process*-type goal, as opposed to the *outcome*-type

Program Goal	Related Program Activities	Outcome Measures	Use of Results
To maintain an intellectual atmosphere. . . .	• Faculty seminar on scholarly work (each faculty member presents once each year); Elite College faculty from other departments also invited to present their work. • Senior thesis projects. • Visiting Scholars program. • Program "journal" of faculty and student work. • Statewide material culture conference held at Elite every year. • State Folk Festival in collaboration with State U. • Professional-in-Residence Program with the State Library and State Museum. • Phi Beta Kappa and Sigma Xi participation. • Sabbatical leaves and faculty research grants.	• Results examined from Elite-wide functioning inventory...for American Studies faculty and students ...every 2 yrs.["intellectual atmosphere" scale; see chapter 6]. • Panel of visitors hosted every two years from American Studies Association and from State U. to examine the program and particularly student and faculty scholarly attitudes, capabilities and productivity. • Written evaluation by participants in the various programs and conferences. • Student survey results (seniors and graduates; items about intellectual life in the program).	• Discussion of all data (reactions and facts) at faculty retreat each year. • Results used to develop new research ideas, budget and grant requests, and seminar programs. • Results used in part to guide faculty hiring as positions become vacant. • Faculty personnel policies, evaluation schemes, and promotion procedures periodically examined in light of results. • Visitors' reports discussed with senior faculty and with the Dean of Elite. • Some results shared with other departments.

Figure 7.3. Example of a work sheet for a process-type goal for the American Studies Program at Elite College.

goal depicted in figure 6.7. The goal analyzed in figure 7.3 concerns the environment which the program hopes to create. It can be looked at usefully in an "outcomes" sense if one accepts the notion that "outcomes" equals performance related to stated goals and if one wants to conduct the analysis in order to improve the program.

The other example of outcome analysis technique presented in this book is the first item in appendix C. It is a detailed follow-up questionnaire related in part to the goals of a graduate program (items 13–16; 18; 21–25). The results were used in a major curriculum revision and rewriting of the goals for the program in question. Many other examples could be given. The shame is that not enough programs consider or conduct such analysis as part of self-study processes. Rather, most studies are primarily related to input dimensions and to reputation.

The Study of Process, Input, and Problems or Issues

At a program level, unless the program is very large, the heart of the self-study (that portion dealing with the students and their progress, the faculty resources, the curriculum or parts of it, the learning resources and services offered, and any of the needs for change and improvement in any of these aspects) can be conducted using a modified "committee of the whole" technique as opposed to reliance on a series of committees. This can work well if:

- the leadership is strong and sensitive to group dynamics
- the staff work is adequate and timely
- very brief assignments are made to knowledge-able productive individuals or small subgroups in order to explore issues, and to draft and present materials for consideration *prior* to the major meetings so that the work of the program faculty in concert can be productive
- the large, "in concert" meetings (or retreats) are brief, sequential, well timed, effectively planned (including a number of activities or modes), and held only when the preparation is adequate, the climate relatively stable, and the chance for progress reasonably high.

For a portrayal of this type of process see figure 7.2. If the program is very large, then the reliance on the total group is diminished in favor of an appropriate sequence of subgroup activities. In very large organizations, of course, only one or two "total group" activities may be possible or desirable in the course of a yearlong study. The reader is advised to consider the institutional models for self-study (see earlier chapters) in these instances, for the large programs probably have an infrastructure and set of functions and facilities equal to those of a small college.

The subjects to be addressed in the heart of the study via properly staffed retreats and/or by lengthier subcommittee activities depend, of course, on the nature of the program and the balance desired between comprehensiveness and concentration on a limited number of topics or problems. In some cases a systematic review (description and assessment) of goals, markets, students, staff, program, instruction, research, extension activities, learning resources, finances, facilities, and outcomes is conducted. In others the study may focus on one or more of these items, on a problem or problems of which the program faculty have been long aware, or on a problem which is identified when the initial display of data and perceptions is arrayed early in the study. In some studies, the overriding purpose is to "take stock" and then to handle the problems perceived in that process. In others, the purpose is to dream about the future of the curriculum based on a solid assessment of what has worked, is working, and might be possible in the years ahead. In some, it is to find a way to survive, and therefore the focus is on markets and strategic possibilities. In yet others, it may be to "plug some leaks," to seek coherence in a curriculum, or perhaps just to involve all of the staff in almost any common enterprise because "distance" must be bridged or morale enhanced. The design stage should have determined these things, and if it has, the breadth, depth, sequence, nature of topics and work groups, and data required then flow naturally from the intentions for the study. Study processes should not be identical, substantively and structurally, from program to program and from cycle to cycle in the same program.

In some instances, because of historical, political, internal, or external factors, there is no choice other than to design and conduct a full, comprehensive assessment of the program. That usually means hard work for all concerned and the topics flow perforce from the nature of the place. But design is still important. Rational sequence, staff work, and intensive activities combined with some larger work-group activity still are far more effective than a clutch of simultaneous committees meeting for a year or more.

As explained earlier, ample lists of questions, data elements and displays, and starting points for discussion by function and by program element are available from discipline associations, accrediting agencies, university planning offices, state coordinating boards, and the like. I will not attempt to list them all here. Most are obvious items; a few are appropriate in any given setting; and most are covered one way or another at a more general level in the examples of institutionwide tables of contents of study reports in appendix D. At the program level, of course, more focus can be placed on evidences of student learning, on details of program responses to student input characteristics, on program sequence and content, on the nature of course and program objectives, on the detailed responses of students to teaching, program offerings, advising, learning resources and services, and on the nature of any research and community service efforts. Issues can be seen more clearly than at the institutional level, and if the faculty leadership is strong and concerned about the welfare of the program and its students, the potential for improvement is great.

Reports, Visits by Outsiders, and Strategies for Change

For an exploration of these matters the reader is referred to chapters 8–10, which apply equally well to the program and the institutional levels.

In order to illuminate further some of the matters presented up to this point about program-level self-study, a case is next presented which focuses heavily on design and organizational considerations.

CASE: Departmental (Program) Self-Study at State University

The setting. The program is offered by a department with ten faculty members, one technician, a chairperson, and 1.5 secretaries. It offers instruction in a field for which there is no program-accrediting agency, but the program is reviewed in a State U. process every five years just prior to the major contact of the university with its regional accrediting agency. The internal review with its team of outside visitors, which the State U. chief administrators will select with some help from the program, is due in about eighteen months. The chairperson was involved in the previous self-study process, which unfortunately consisted mainly of filling out data sheets, sent by the planning office, that corresponded roughly to the regional accrediting agency standards, and then of discussing the report at two regular department meetings. No noticeable changes had occurred as a result of the previous process, save that the chairperson vowed to keep up-to-date records on all university-required statistics, some of which proved useful at budget time and in the periodic planning process run by the central staff of the university. The

chairperson felt that more involvement by faculty members would be beneficial and that a greater payoff should result from the next study.

Prestudy planning. The chairperson asked two faculty members and a senior student to join her at home for supper on a Friday night. After dinner, she engaged them in some searching discussion on the real needs of the department and of likely opportunities for benefit from a period of study that could precede the outside visit. An initial list of four or five possible needs was assembled; the items were other than the usual "more money, more time, and a reduced teaching load." The members suggested that the latest data sheets and an article on the design of useful study processes be distributed to each member of the department and to other students, and that the next department meeting be conducted by the chairperson in order to complete the agenda for study.

At the department meeting, scheduled so it could be daylong, the chairperson led participants through a wide-ranging discussion of needs and opportunities, used some work groups to look at specific questions, and then summarized the needs as follows:

1. The department does not gather enough useful feedback from its graduating students, from alumni, and from graduates in the labor force and in graduate school.
2. Multiyear planning, particularly of human and fiscal resources, is not adequate.
3. Articulation with "feeder" or potential "feeder" institutions is meager.
4. Course objectives and content must be reviewed for their consistency and agreement with institutional and departmental goals and for the avoidance of duplication.

The chairperson then asked the original small planning group to spend an afternoon with her to design the study process.

The design. The chairperson found that there was no possibility of merging the department's study with a larger institutionwide venture because none was scheduled for at least two years. She succeeded in extracting a promise for a half-time administrative assistant for nine months, to be loaned by the Office of Planning and Institutional Research—apparently a policy often followed at State U. to assist programs undertaking a study or planning process. The planning office also agreed that the self-study process being designed would, if useful, serve as the preparation for the next institutionwide accreditation review, with but a small progress report and updating of data to be required. Since the chairperson had been gathering data, the group agreed that she and the administrative assistant would compile the current data and descriptions of each function and aspect of the department to provide a context for the specific topics to be studied. They also would present to a small steering committee any apparent problem areas for preliminary review which they uncovered in the process of general data compilation and description of the students, staff, resources, programs, and services.

The steering group, which would coordinate the department's efforts over the next year, was essentially the original planning group, with the addition of one faculty member and the administrative assistant.

The following decisions were made about the process:

1. The steering group would lead the study effort and would arrange the consideration of the results of the work of any task groups at the regular department gatherings and at a retreat which they would plan for the semester break.
2. The chairperson would discuss the initial data and the design of the study with the Office of Planning and Research and with the dean of the college. She would make them aware of the tasks being undertaken as part of the study and the possible implications for the program.
3. The four specific tasks were organized by asking the three faculty members from the steering group each to head a task subgroup which would conduct its business over a three-month period commencing in each case when the appropriate data or necessary assistance became available. The chairperson agreed to lead the fourth effort—the multiyear resources planning group. It was to begin in midfall when help would be available from a budget-planning staff member on the central staff.

   The articulation group was to begin its work after admissions data had been compiled on past years and when an admissions expert was available for consultation. A program of written and personal contacts was to be developed and an analysis made of activities and program elements needed. The course review team was to begin compiling specific, heretofore unavailable materials on the department's thirty courses. The analysis of course objectives and content and their relationship to departmental goals was to be assisted by two visits from a consultant. The group slated to conduct student, alumni, and employer surveys in search of the desired feedback was to meet with institutional research staff members and to compile drafts of telephone surveys and questionnaires that maintained the upbeat tone of finding ways to improve the program.
4. All the work groups were asked to present any resource or other needs to the full steering group,

and all were asked to prepare draft reports as they completed their work and by the end of the nine-month period or before, if possible. The steering group was asked to organize the materials and recommendations for change to be presented to the full department for action in time for an invitational conference that the department would hold, with some of the steering group's results as background reading for the conference. Two-person teams consisting of a chairperson and faculty member from similar departments at area colleges would be invited to discuss course content, articulation practices, and recent feedback from graduates. The arrival of the chosen visitors would follow the conference. Discussion and implementation of recommendations would proceed during the second year of the study in light of all of the first year's experiences.

Some analysis. The department of State U. did quite well with its self-study design. Many of the desired attributes of self-study could be achieved under the plan—work with goals and outcomes, some internal motivation, positive leadership, an appropriate design, some problems assessed and potentially solved, some possibility for data and research systems in place for the future, and so on. The agenda established by departmental members rather than by an outside agency seemed to dominate; they tried to use available resources and the leverage that the outside visit and the invitational conference provided to the advantage of the self-study. Whether the design would yield adequate results would depend in part on the quality of the leadership in the steering and work groups. Whether or not progress capable of spurring its participants onward could be seen during the year of study would depend heavily on the attitudes of the faculty leaders. Such useful studies are difficult to conduct in small departmental units, but they can be successful if they are well led and realistically planned.

CASE: A Study To Improve an Administrative Function—A Program of Services to Foreign Students

All Too Typical University, hereafter referred to as ATTU, is part of the Usual State College system located near the West Coast of the U.S. It is one of the newer and smaller institutions in that system, having been opened in 1966 and now enrolling some 7,000 students with about 2,000 at the master's degree level. Many of these students are part-time, many are evening students who are employed full-time, and none live on campus. ATTU prides itself on its willingness to try innovative programs and its responsiveness to student needs.

Until 1976, the number of foreign students at ATTU was limited to about 50. In 1976 with the arrival of President Lester Gogonow and the appointment of Mr. I. Gettum as Acting Director of Admissions, this informal and unstated policy limitation was removed and ATTU began to admit larger, but still relatively modest, numbers of foreign students. At the same time, the number of immigrants, refugees, and other culturally diverse students increased substantially, so that in 1980 ATTU had a population of some 268 foreign students and 245 immigrants. At least these were the figures that Gettum used, but their accuracy was regularly questioned.

During this time of growth of the foreign student population, the policy of the University toward foreign students could be described as one of benign neglect. Foreign students were welcomed to the campus as sources of cultural and educational enrichment, but services for them were minimal or nonexistent. By the beginning of the last academic year, it became apparent that the University needed to take steps to provide better services and programs for foreign students. A part-time (0.50 FTE) faculty position of Foreign Student Adviser was authorized, but was not filled until the beginning of the spring term. An ad hoc International Education Committee of the Faculty Senate was formed and has devoted considerable attention to foreign students (in addition to other matters related to international education) during the current academic year. President Gogonow, who has always had an interest in and supported international education and foreign student programs, asked the Dean to prepare a report for him on the status of foreign students at ATTU.

Prestudy Activity. The dean, Dr. I. M. Spotless, met with Mr. Gettum and with the new part-time faculty foreign student advisor, Dr. Les Help, to discuss the situation. It was clear that among them they had relatively little and surely inadequate expertise to frame the proper questions for the inquiry which the president requested.

They agreed on several steps: (1) to attend a regional workshop being conducted by the National Association for Foreign Student Affairs (NAFSA); (2) to contact five or six area institutions to seek program information; (3) Gettum agreed to stop in at the NAFSA office to pick up materials when he would be in Washington the following week on other business; and (4) Spotless and Help would convene an ad hoc "bag lunch" discussion group of available foreign students to hear their assessment while Gettum was in Washington.

Gettum's visit to Washington was an eye-opener.

The following excerpt from his memo drafted on the plane on the way back to ATTU is indicative of the consciousness raising he experienced:

It appears that ATTU has backed into the international educational interchange business. Although we have very few US-born ATTU students going overseas each year (ten or less), this policy probably will accelerate as President Gogonow visits, consorts, and generally pushes international education. What we *do* have is a substantial population of local immigrant and non-immigrant foreign students who have special needs. Many persons at ATTU probably accept the notion that the admission of students who have some special needs carries with it the obligation to provide for those special needs. However, it appears that the administration has not realized the scope of the foreign student program and the extent of the special needs of these students. In considering services to foreign students, one must think not only of the identified 268 foreign students, but also of the 245 immigrants and other persons from diverse linguistic and cultural backgrounds, such as the Samoans and Filipinos in the community from which ATTU tries to draw its student body. Many of these students (and potential students) need the same kinds of services as foreign students, including specialized study in English as a second language and assistance in adjusting to a new culture and educational system. While the university might choose to curtail the admission of nonimmigrant foreign students in order to avoid having to provide these special services, it cannot and does not want to curtail the admission of local immigrants.

Meanwhile, Spotless and Help got an "earful" from the students and a few faculty members at the bag-lunch session. The foreign students described their feelings about the lack of services for them and of attention to their needs. Their grievances might be summarized by the following statements:

- Nobody in the administration understands foreign students or is able to represent their interests and needs.
- Foreign students need help in dealing with the Immigration and Naturalization Service and in knowing what is expected of them under the immigration regulations.
- Foreign students need help in cutting through the university bureaucracy and in understanding what is expected of them and what opportunities are available to them within the university and in the community.
- Long delays of from two weeks to two months in getting certificates of registration from the admissions office cause further delays in getting funds from home, extensions of passports, and other essentials.

- No one within the university has the responsibility for looking out for the welfare of the foreign students and seeing to it that their special needs are met.

Not articulated by the students, but stated clearly by several faculty members, was the need for additional resources to improve the English proficiency of students whose native language is not English. Another need articulated particularly by staff members was for rational and coherent policies and procedures regarding the admission and the later advising and care of foreign students, as there was confusion about present policies and procedures.

When Gettum arrived at ATTU he brought word of two other possible sources of help: a consultation service run by NAFSA and a program of self-regulation which had at its core a self-assessment component in light of the institution's intentions and a set of *Principles for International Education Interchange* (a copy of which had apparently been sent to ATTU and lost in the Administrative Tower. He brought another copy).

The three then met and decided to seek Gogonow's approval to take advantage of a consultant visit immediately, in order to raise as many questions as possible and in order to use an outsider for concentrated and systematic interviewing. The consultant could perhaps summarize much of this in a useful report at low cost. Gogonow agreed. He also agreed to read and think about the NAFSA principles.

Spotless moved to start the planning for a period of self-study by asking two concerned faculty members and one interested foreign student to join the three previously energized staff members as the design or "prestudy" planning group. He provided all with copies of the NAFSA *Principles* and their *Self-Study Guide*. They agreed to start reading and thinking and to be prepared to assist the consultant.

The consultant came, spent two days, talked with fourteen different administrators and faculty members, and had a two-hour session with over forty foreign and local immigrant students. The consultant's report proved to be a very useful thing—twenty single-spaced pages of commentary accompanied by description and recommendations about ATTU's apparent but unstated intentions; the implications of these; services present and probably needed; apparent problems; other areas needing study; and a good deal of personal advice. The planning group circulated the report widely and received within one week a commitment from President Gogonow to launch a yearlong study which he intended to have as part of the preparation for the next regional accreditation review due eighteen months hence. The critically important commitment had thus been made and the process of planning a study which could involve ATTU people in addressing the issues raised by the consultant and by a few at ATTU could begin—with ample reason to believe that the results would be heard at the highest levels and that many concerned would be willing to implement all or some of the results.

The General Design.   After two meetings the planning group, armed with the NAFSA *Principles* and the consultant's report, decided to organize the study as follows:

1. The steering group would be composed of the present planning group members minus the student, who wished to participate in a task group later in the study and who did not feel she could devote the time which the steering activities required. Also, Dean Spotless decided that his associate dean, Dr. Doital, would represent him on the steering group and would serve to recruit the necessary and appropriate academic folk for other assignments in the study process. Spotless hoped that Doital would evolve as overall foreign student coordinator on campus—although Dr. Help argued that he would naturally assume that role as foreign student advisor.

2. The group decided that President Gogonow and the board should begin the process by endorsing the NAFSA *Principles* in principle. Then any specific study group activity would follow a general data-gathering effort which Doital and the registrar, Noah Count, would organize. The group listed fifteen different tables of data which they thought would be needed in the study effort, at least at the start.

3. The effort to state ATTU's goals for international study was to be the first subgroup effort. It was helped by reference to NAFSA documents, by Dean Spotless's insistence that ATTU had to delimit its efforts carefully, and by reference to the statements of three area institutions that had recently reviewed their stated intentions for international activities.

4. The early reviews of the NAFSA *Principles* and the consultant's reports seemed to point to other central tasks for the study, namely, the examination of recommendations on advising, English language instruction, and admissions. A fourth concern, community program and services, would be addressed initially by a weekend retreat/seminar to

be planned with the help both of community leaders in area volunteer groups and of the immigrant groups. Additional work directions would emerge from this retreat.

5. The sequence initially decided on was data collection, then clarification of goals, then two simultaneous task groups—the Admissions Task Group and the English Language Diagnosis and Program Work Group. As these activities yielded results and as the issues became clarified, a third group, Foreign Student Advising, would begin its work. The community services retreat would be held during the last third of the effort.

As these work groups were planned and before they began their work, a survey of all foreign students, immigrant students, involved faculty members, and appropriate administrative officers was formulated and conducted to gather feedback on issues identified by the steering group, data about the respondents to supplement available data, and general reactions. These results were given to the work groups, and any follow-up interviews were scheduled by the group concerned.

6. A small group was set to work examining the issue of goal achievement. It was to be concerned with these questions: Were the goals/intentions that had been set forth for the educational interchange program at ATTU and for each service-oriented subunit being achieved? How would such determinations be made? What kinds of facts and systematically gathered opinions would be needed? A *plan* for ongoing analyses of these issues was to be the major item which the "achievements" group would formulate.

7. The steering group decided to monitor activities closely, to prevent the whole study or any of its parts from becoming too consuming, nonproductive, or duplicative. They decided that their initial NAFSA consultant should be invited back after the bulk of the work-group activity was completed and some draft reports were available. They planned to ask for two knowledgeable team members (to be suggested by NAFSA) to come as members of the regional accreditation team.

Results. Everything did not work out as planned, but many good things happened at ATTU as a result of the program self-study activities. The self-study effort had commitment from the top levels, was internally motivated, and was designed to meet local needs according to the conditions found at ATTU. As a result, ATTU adopted the NAFSA *Principles* and saw consensus emerge on eight or ten decided strengths and weaknesses of their programs. They approved a fairly useful statement

entitled ATTU Commitments and Intentions for International Educational Interchange. Several new part-time staff assignments were made at ATTU as a result of the program, a commitment many felt was inadequate. But all were guaranteed NAFSA professional development experiences at ATTU expense. A new Senate Council on International Interchange was approved and set forth to monitor progress, and to receive yearly data and biannual survey responses about adequacy of services for foreign students and immigrants at ATTU. A new consortium membership for overseas study was arranged so that ATTU students could go overseas with a solid program in which ATTU staff had confidence. Finally, the study process bridged the gap between the administrative staff members and ATTU faculty members. It reduced harmful program isolation.

More remains to be done, but the ATTU program had a good, much-needed first study experience. It is hoped that the next attempt at self-study, to begin in four years, will move things forward even more decisively.

PROGRAM SELF-STUDIES RELATED TO SPECIALIZED ACCREDITATION

While internally motivated, periodic self-study conducted as part of the usual management cycle of a program and not related to any outside agency is the ideal situation, the vast majority of program self-study attempts *are* made in response to the request of such an agency. Most are related to a particular kind of agency—the specialized, or, as it is sometimes called, program accrediting agency. The basic nature and description of such agencies are presented in chapter 2. What will be explored here are the possibilities for conducting useful program self-study processes as part of an accreditation review. In order to do this we must start with the context.

The fifty or so recognized specialized accrediting agencies vary greatly in sponsorship, size of accrediting activity and executive staff, and nature and extent of services available to the college- or university-based program in an accrediting relationship (COPA, 1980; Glidden, 1983). All, however, operate nationally; most are reviewed periodically by The Council on Postsecondary Accreditation, which requires that programs conduct a self-study process in light of the standards of the agency as part of the accreditation process (COPA, 1981). The specific context for self-study in such a relationship has both helpful and less-than-advantageous aspects that affect the design of any study process seeking to achieve the attributes proposed and discussed in this book.

The Context for Study

First, it must be duly recognized that specialized accrediting agencies perform a very important self-regulatory function for a wide array of disciplines and professional training programs. Tensions exist between these agencies (as well as the professions that spawned them) and the postsecondary institutions that house the accredited or potentially accreditable programs (Glidden, 1983). This tension is important, and in need of attention and perhaps some redress in the balance of power (Kells, 1980), *but* such redress is second in order of priority to the basic worth of the self-regulatory activity provided by most of the specialized accrediting agencies. This activity provides great support for many academic programs in the form of guidance, common standards, and professional and curriculum development opportunities. It assists students and the general public in identifying worthy programs, and it assists business and the professions in identifying those who have graduated from such programs (Assembly of Specialized Accrediting Bodies, 1981).

Programs which seek to conduct self-study processes in this setting have the advantage of detailed standards and criteria to use. Many of the agencies have self-study guidelines and some conduct training sessions. While few can afford to send staff members to visit campus sites to assist with curriculum development or self-study, some do schedule consultation visits for specific programs, and annual or regional meetings are used as opportunities to discuss agency standards and self-study methods. Finally, some of the agencies are actively pursuing validity studies for their standards. Even more important from the standpoint of useful self-assessment, several are actively engaged in detailed analysis of the nature of good professional and practice in their field. Some are developing competency exams based on these studies, which could be used diagnostically to benefit students and to improve the programs which yielded the outcomes (Schiller, 1973; American Association of Collegiate Schools of Business, 1980; Jacobson, 1981; Fiske, 1981). These agencies and some of their sponsoring professional groups are being assisted by foundation grants and by the Council on Occupational and Professional Assessment at the Educational Testing Service (Goleman, 1981; "Consortium of Medical Schools. . ," 1977; Council on Occupational and Professional Assessment, 1976).

All of the foregoing notwithstanding, it is not an easy matter to conduct a useful self-study process when the program concerned is working with a specialized accrediting agency. Several difficulties exist—matters that can be dealt with in most instances. To begin with, except in the case where the specialized program is a freestanding school of some size and organizational complexity (such as a medical school or school of theology, podiatry, or optometry), specialized programs conducting an accreditation self-study must deal with the matters put forth in the first part of this chapter—organizational isolation, small size, and leadership needs. In addition, the accreditation relationship usually brings one or more of the following complications:

1. *Anxiety*—Once a program has decided that it wants or needs accreditation, it often has trouble persuading staff members to recognize faults and to pursue solutions to acknowledged problems as part of "self-study" conducted for an accrediting agency. The inspection motif and accountability intention of the process tend to dampen analytical activities and efforts to improve.

2. *Newness of Self-Study Intention in Such Settings*—It is only in the last ten years that substantial progress has been made across the spread of specialized agencies in establishing the expectation for serious analytical self-study activity. It was not until 1981 that COPA firmly established that all agencies must require such activity as part of the accreditation process in order to receive or retain recognition as an approved agency.

3. *Lack of Expertise and Assistance*—Because of the newness of the effort, specialized agency staff members, many of them inundated with a vast array of other activities and relatively few of them with experience and expertise in organizational analysis and development, have only recently begun to enhance the services available to member programs with respect to self-assessment methods. Ideally, of course, assistance with self-study should be given on site, a difficult matter for many of the agencies that operate on a limited budget and for a dispersed nationwide clientele. The next best method is a well-planned self-study workshop with hands-on experience, case materials, and instruction in the matters discussed in this book. Some agencies are beginning to prepare more useful written materials, and jointly administered regional self-study workshops are a possibility some have discussed.

4. *Lack of a Usable Outcomes Focus*—Ironically, in the setting where some reliance on performance-based assessment is most desirable, most possible, and potentially most useful, there has been relatively little progress. The potential for internal diagnostic use of detailed, grouped outcome data (knowledge gained, skills acquired, and the like) in order to improve programs as part of self-study activities is

largely unfulfilled at this point. This writer has reviewed the standards, self-study guidelines, and resulting self-study reports for many of the agencies. Although some agencies require programs to state behavioral course or program objectives, few expect diagnostic analysis of the corresponding performance data. Reports of visiting accrediting teams and self-study reports (dutifully organized on the basis of the accrediting standards) seldom discuss these matters. This is all the more distressing since at least one-half of the fields with which specialized accrediting deals employ certification, licensing, or other examinations which could provide part of the basis for such analyses. Even if the exams are not as valid or reliable as leaders in these fields would desire, they should be used and improved as a central dimension in the self-study process. Doing so would enhance and inform efforts to improve such exams and the agency standards which relate to them.

5. *The Centrality and Dominance of the Accreditation Standards*—It is entirely understandable that the consensual if not predictively valid standards (Kells, 1980; Friedrich, 1980) used by specialized accrediting agencies are the central focus of the entire activity. The primary purpose of the exercise is to identify programs which meet the standards. Therefore, improvement of programs is a recognized but secondary intention (Assembly of Specialized Accrediting Bodies, 1981). Accordingly, the usual result of study processes in this setting is the production of a descriptive, question-and-answer type of report rather than an analytical one. Any program which seeks to conduct an *internally* focused, improvement-oriented self-study must cope thoroughly and responsibly with the standards orientation of the process as put forth by the agencies.

6. *Concerns about Costs, Duplication of Activities, and Institutional Prerogatives*—This is one of the hottest issues in the accreditation scene. Many institutions feel that specialized agencies have too much power and that they inflict costly, duplicative processes on institutions, yet yield relatively minor benefits to the institutions concerned (Kells, 1980; Pigge, 1979; O'Neill and Heaney, 1982; Northwest Association, 1982; Warren, 1980). On campuses where these feelings are strongly held, and these include most of the large universities with multiple accreditation relationships and most of the accredited specialized programs, it is often difficult to stimulate interest in a self-study process.

Coping with the Context

It is quite possible to have a productive self-study experience from the perspectives both of program improvement and of the benefits of accredited status.

To do so requires that plans be carefully drawn and steps be taken to *make* it happen. In addition to the steps suggested earlier in this chapter that every program-level study should consider (integration with institutionwide study efforts, use of extra-program collaborators, enhanced access to data, heavy use of staff work and some use of brief, intensive, properly sequenced activities), the accreditation-related study must employ some additional strategies and tactics.

First, in order to enhance support for the effort and to dispel ill feeling about outside agencies on the part of collegewide leaders, *it is wise to seek ways in which the impending review can be integrated with any regular institutional cycle of study and planning and with other agency reviews.* There is the potential for real savings in time and funds if outside reviews can be arranged, perhaps clustered, into useful cycles which can share much common data, be served by at least some common committee and other study efforts, result in at least some common elements for study reports, and perhaps be served by joint or concurrent visits of outsiders. This would generally enhance the regular study and management cycle of the *institution*, as opposed to timetables decided independently for many different reasons by the various accrediting commissions or their staff members. (For more on this subject see Kells, 1980; Northwest Association, 1982; O'Neill and Heaney, 1982, 1982a: and chapters 8 and 9.

For various reasons, many program directors would rather have their programs evaluated independently—not as part of any joint or concurrent study or visit. Some seem to be afraid to question the accreditation agency about the cycle or timing of the visit. Some have argued that they want the undivided attention of local officials when the team visits, perhaps to gain increased leverage, possible resources, and the like. These are understandable but shortsighted reactions. The more time and energy consumed in externally-oriented accreditation reviews, the more the institution is weakened, and the less control it will have of its management processes. The more fragmented its study and planning efforts, the less data will be available in the long run for any given use (because of wasteful duplication), and the more frustrated and less tolerant the institutional leaders will be regarding the program interests. It makes more sense for all concerned to achieve accredited status where desired by focusing most efficiently and effectively on program reviews in a logical, institution-based sequence, so that the program, the accrediting agency, and the institution can benefit from the process. *This does not mean that ailing or seriously deficient programs should not be addressed when the outside agency and the university feel it is needed.* Nor does it mean that program leaders need be denied the attention they deserve from university officials during and after the study or visit. Indeed, a rational, sensible, internally generated review cycle is likely to focus even more attention and resources on any given program than is an ad hoc, politically motivated, or entirely externally determined cycle. Thus program leaders should look for collaborative opportunities, discuss them with institutionwide officials, and seek reasonable accommodation in timing and other dimensions from the accrediting agencies. More assistance, more useful data, and an economical, amicable, and fruitful study and external review are likely to result.

Second, program leaders ought to *seize or create opportunities* through the aegis of the accrediting agency involved or through other auspices *to engage in training opportunities for the program staff* concerning evaluation, self-study, use of program data, and the like. They should seek and use agency materials and other general materials (see first section of this chapter); pose questions of the agency staff; ask for suggestions about other comparable programs that have faced similar situations or conducted similar studies. Most of the specialized program studies I have reviewed have been conducted in isolation, and consequently they missed most of the opportunities for benefit from a study process. Nearly all have been responses to an external agency, resulting in the preparation of a report with little benefit in terms of organization development. One can make the processes more useful by *asking more of them and of the agencies which request them.*

Third—and this follows naturally from the previous point—*the program director must lead the way to create an internal motivation for the study.* If busy program professionals are going to spend time, energy, and program and institutional funds conducting a study, more than accredited status should result. The place ought to be better as a result of the process. The next items on the agenda of program needs ought to be addressed—not set aside because it is time to get reaccredited. In the case example presented earlier in this chapter, the department chairperson at State U. wanted specific results from her next study and made them happen.

Fourth, *the design* dimensions put forth earlier in this chapter for program-level studies *must be augmented in order to accommodate and benefit from the presence of the accreditation standards.* They are very important and should be used as one (but *not the only*) focus of the study. In figure 4.4 specific flow diagrams are presented which accommodate this important dimension without making it the total focus on the study. This focus is again discussed in the case example which follows. It is very

important, of course, that in any internally motivated study the program leaders include in the design the seeds for change or, as we have called them in this book, the *strategies* for change (see chapters 4 and 10). The selection of the working-group members, the interest and support of extraprogram institutional leaders, the promotion and acceptance of change *during* as well as after the study, the open use of the report, and the schedule and mechanism for follow-up of recommended actions are all important and must be included in the design.

Fifth, *the accreditation standards must be used creatively and augmented if necessary.* In figure 7.4 some examples of specialized accreditation standards (here termed "essentials" or "criteria") are presented. Some agency standards are quite specific. Some have quantitative criterion levels indicated. However, many are more general in nature and require qualitative judgment by the program professionals and any subsequent group of external reviewers. With some agencies, a full, complementary set of self-study guidelines are provided. Such guidelines usually direct the program studiers to ask questions like these: "Does it work?" "How do you study the effectiveness of this service or other dimension?" (or "What evidence do you have that this aspect functions well?") "How do you use this evidence to improve the function (course or service)?" If, however, the guidelines are somewhat general, those conducting the self-study process should *add these questions* to each standard *and then seek the answers.* Similarly, if the accreditation standards do not explicitly call for "outcomes" or goal achievement studies, if they do not expect diagnostic use of performance data such as results of licensing or certification exams for groups of students, then again the study group should *add these dimensions* so that something useful can result from the study of educational outcomes of the program. As discussed in chapter 6 and earlier in this chapter, such studies can be conducted usefully, controlled internally, and then used externally if one chooses to do so. Some agencies are beginning to explore the use of such studies (American Assembly of Collegiate Schools of Business, 1980; Schuller, 1973), and the COPA criteria for accrediting agencies now expect agencies to enact such stated expectations for institutions and programs. Until all do so and until assistance is provided to programs in this regard, they must proceed as best they can.

Finally, the programs conducting accreditation-related self-studies should *plan for and then create useful self-study reports and visits by accreditation teams.* This procedure is explained in some detail in chapters 8 and 9, but let it suffice to say at this point that the report should be brief enough to be read in

From the "Criteria and Guidelines" of the Council of Podiatric Education (August, 1980, p. 10)

> 2. *Clinical Competency Evaluation. The college shall present to the Council on Podiatry Education evidence of a comprehensive evaluation of the student's competency based on appropriate methodologies to measure the clinical competency of each student.*
>
> 3. *Faculty. The clinical faculty shall be sufficient in number to assure adequate supervision of students and quality care to patients.*
>
> Clinical faculty should have pursued advanced study beyond the professional degree and should be eligible for membership in a professional specialty organization.
>
> 4. *Director. The clinical program shall be under the direction of a podiatrist employed on a full-time basis.*
>
> The podiatrist responsible for the clinical program should meet the college's definition of full-time faculty.

●

From the "Essentials and Guidelines of an Accredited Educational Program for the Radiographer" (Allied Health Education Directory, AMA, p. 205)

D. Library

The library shall contain adequate up-to-date scientific books, periodicals and other reference material related to the curriculum and profession.

Holdings
The library owned and maintained by the program sponsor should contain enough printed and other media holdings to accommodate required study, to promote independent study and research, and to aid faculty in delivering and improving the program. Clinical education centers should provide access to reference materials to support the clinical assignments; these and/or supplementary materials may be supplied by the sponsoring institution. A list of holdings at the sponsoring institution and at the clinical education center should be available to students and staff.
Availability
Library holdings should be reasonably accessible with regard to location and hours of operation. Security and circulation of library holdings should be assigned to an appropriate individual.

●

From the "Essentials and Guidelines of an Accredited Educational Program for the "Occupational Therapist" (Allied Health Education Directory, p. 175)

A. Director of Educational Program

The director must be employed at least one year in advance of the date when students will be enrolled in the professional program for the purpose of curriculum planning, faculty recruitment, field placement development and related administrative responsibilities.

1. *Qualifications*

The director of the educational program shall be a registered occupational therapist with a minimum of five years of relevant professional occupational therapy experience including teaching, direct service and administration. The director must hold the masters or doctoral degree except when special professional experiences can be considered the equivalent by the educational institution.

"Relevant professional occupational therapy experience" should be interpreted as experience evaluated in relation to the responsibilities and focus of the position being filled.

●

Figure 7.4. Selected examples of specialized accrediting agency standards and self-study guidelines.

> From the "Essentials and Guidelines of an Accredited Educational Program for the Medical Laboratory Technician (Associate Degree)" (Allied Health Education Directory, p. 142)
>
> ## VI. PROGRAM EVALUATION
> 28. The effectiveness of the educational program must be documented through periodic review of all aspects of the program.
>   a. *Significant aspects may be assessed through questionnaires, surveys, interviews or other means with faculty, students, graduates of the program, and employers of graduates.*
>   b. *Review of program objectives, means of implementation, and levels of effectiveness should also involve appropriate individuals who are not affiliated with the program. The self-evaluation document prepared for accreditation purposes is recommended for use in monitoring program effectiveness.*
> 29. Records of scores on external certifying examination(s) of graduates from the three preceeding years must be considered in the self-evaluation review.
>   *Such data constitute an important but not the only means of monitoring effectiveness. When examination scores are used for this purpose, identification of individual students must be avoided, in accordance with requirements of privacy laws.*

Figure 7.4. (continued)

a sitting and it should be clearly written in a form that is useful. Analysis should balance the description and provide the fuel for healthy needed change. Such care is consistent with thorough, responsible reaction to the need of the accreditation agency to review the program standard by standard. The report can be organized on the basis of the standards and still be brief, analytical, and change-oriented (prospective or post hoc). It also can be organized (I argue) in any way the institution chooses, as long as a clear, useful, index tells agency users how to find adequate response to each agency standard. Some of my colleagues would add, "*Whose* report is this, anyway?" Indeed, it should bear the true likeness of the group that generated it.

The team visit can be planned to be more useful than an accreditation team visit often is. If the self-study has been useful, the team should be asked to respond to unresolved issues, in addition to completing their necessary and thorough analysis standard by standard. If the visit can be joint or concurrent with that of other agencies, the potential exists (too often unrealized in such joint visits) for additional cross-disciplinary, synergistic payoff. At the minimum, the institutional accreditation agency should be asked through the specialized agency to add a "generalist" evaluator who can range widely during the visit and help to put things in perspective with respect to governance, finance, and larger academic and administrative issues.

Those considering the design of an accreditation-related self-study process for a department or program within a university should examine the case entitled "Department (Program) Study at State U." presented in the first section of this chapter. Reread the case, inserting "previous accreditation review" in the first paragraph (the "previous process" with which the chairperson had not been satisfied), and realize that she and her colleagues chose a modification of the second variation of the study model presented in figure 4.4 ("The One-Step"), in which the steering group reviewed the accreditation standards in light of the data she had been collecting. The rest applies fully and is worthy of review.

Another case is explored in order to consider a second type of accreditation—related setting.

CASE STUDY: Self-Study For Icandoit Health School: A Freestanding Health-Related, Professional School Attempting to Relate To Two Accrediting Agencies

The setting: Icandoit is located in a large metropolitan area and provides doctoral-level training in a health specialty, conducts research both basic and applied, and runs a modern clinical facility which provides care to thousands of people per year. It is accredited by both the specialized accrediting agency in its field and the regional institutional agency, and it is approved and periodically reviewed by the state education department. It is to be reviewed by the specialized accrediting agency in nine months and the regional agency in twelve to eighteen months.

Icandoit completed a master planning exercise in the recent past, but the dean and the president felt that neither the faculty nor the board of trustees participated adequately in the process. The former did not seem to see the implications for some of the program dimensions and the latter was perceived as not facing the financial planning and fund-raising realities for the next five to ten years.

Prestudy activities. The dean attended a self-study workshop conducted by the regional agency. He became convinced that the next study exercise had to be much more productive and less wasteful of time and effort than previous efforts had been. He organized a four-person ad hoc group to help him design an exercise that would make sense for Icandoit *and* get it reaccredited by both agencies. The members of the group met twice to review the previous planning experience and the recent data that the dean had assembled about finances, enrollment, student characteristics, and the like. They concluded that four issues had to be addressed thoroughly in the next study and that it was imperative to get faculty and board interest, participation, and commitment. The issues were: (1) an in-depth review of certain aspects of clinical training; (2) financial planning and development; (3) student and administrative services; and (4) an aspect of the general curriculum that needed work. They were reasonably sure that most would agree with these priorities, but decided to explore them with the full professional staff in an "orientation day" work session at the start of the study. They knew that Icandoit met most of the other accreditation standards of both agencies. Facilities and staff qualifications were first-rate, and the school's reputation in the field was excellent.

The dean got the backing of the president with respect to the aforementioned matters and obtained permission to discuss a common self-study document and a concurrent, if not joint, visit with the two agencies. The specialized agency agreed to a three-month shift which would permit a joint visit with the regional agency in twelve months. The state coordinating agency agreed to send a visitor to accompany the agency team and thereby satisfy its regular five-year review requirement a year and a half earlier. This made sense to the Icandoit leaders. As they saw it, a twelve-month study could meet Icandoit's needs, provided the campus citizens participated fruitfully.

The design. The planners decided to use the process presented in figure 7.5. They agreed to remain as the steering group, with the dean as chair.

They planned to open the year with a presentation to the full staff and a member or two of the board of trustees at the orientation day proceedings. The staff would spend the afternoon in group activities to begin the review of specialized agency standards and to list Icandoit's strengths and weaknesses in ways that preserved confidentiality and provided priority lists in both areas. The dean and his assistant would "staff" the study—provide descriptions, assemble data, and work with a consultant with skills in survey methodology. It was agreed that an analysis of grouped data on licensing examinations and a major alumni follow-up study would be essential. The planners decided to handle the rest of the review of accreditation standards for both agencies by a combination of work (for a brief period of thirty days) done by natural departmental or office work groups, and by a major schoolwide work group. These groups would compile reactions, evidence, and the like and submit their findings to the steering group and the staff for digestion and compilation on a computer-based text editor. Four (or more, if the faculty thought it necessary) work groups ("A" to "D") would tackle the major focuses of this study, that is, the major problems that the steering group saw Icandoit facing. They planned a "twist" to get the board members involved. A board retreat would be used after the first stages of the study so that a consultant could be hosted when the motivations of task groups and the up-to-date results of the study were presented. The hope was to get participation by board members in some of the work and to prime them for the results of the study. The professional staff would convene for a half-day workshop at the same time to hear survey results and discuss the task subjects. Other consultants would visit as needed during the group work, and all group work would conclude in time for the dean and the steering group to extract a useful report from their materials. The study report would accompany the Icandoit Master Plan and, of course, be properly indexed with respect to the accreditation standards of each agency.

Results. Most things worked well for the Icandoit study. The board did get involved and made some firm financial plans. The accrediting agencies cooperated, although some team visitors grumbled about the nature of the report (a circumstance which most at Icandoit ignored). One of the two curriculum task groups made substantial progress; the other floundered, but got some good suggestions from two team visitors who took a real interest in the Icandoit curriculum. The dean was heard to explain, "All in all, I'd give the whole thing an A-minus, without grade inflation."

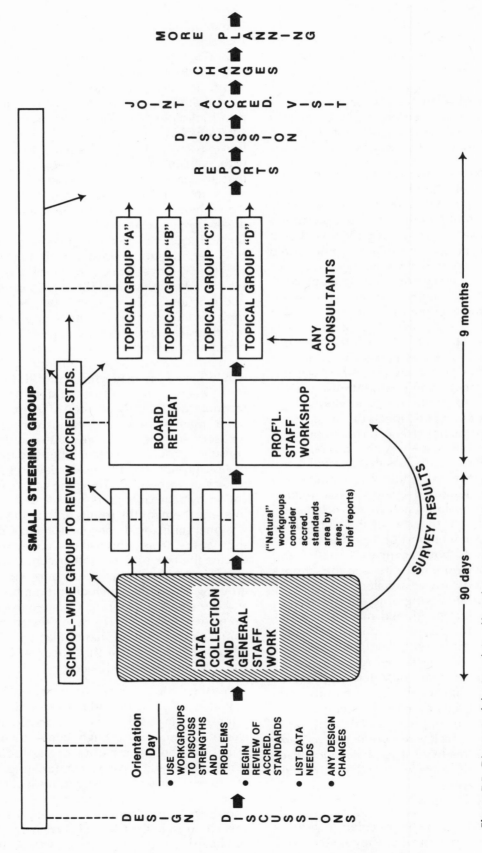

Figure 7.5. Diagram of the Icandoit self-study process.

References

AACSB. "Accreditation Research Report: Report of Phase I" (chap. 2).

American Medical Association. *Allied Health Education Directory*, 10th ed. Chicago, 1981.

Andrews, Barbara J. "Can Professional Competencies Be Measured?" In *New Directions for Program Evaluation*, edited by Edward H. Loveland. San Francisco: Jossey-Bass, 1980. Vol. 6: *Measuring the Hard to Measure*, pp . 39–52.

Arns, Robert, and Poland, William. "Changing the University Through Program Review." *Journal of Higher Education*, May / June, 1980, pp. 268–284.

Assembly of Specialized Accrediting Bodies of the Council on Postsecondary Accreditation. "Quality Assurance in Professional Education." Washington, DC, 1981.

Chickering, Arthur, et al. *The Modern American College*. San Francisco: Jossey-Bass, 1981.

"Consortium of Medical Schools to Test Applicants for Diagnostic and Patient Skills." *ETS Developments*, Spring 1977, p. 2.

Council on Postsecondary Accreditation. *A Guide to Recognized Accrediting Agencies, 1980–82*.

Council on Postsecondary Accreditation. "Provisions and Procedures for Becoming Recognized as an Accrediting Agency." Washington, DC, 1981.

Cronbach, Lee J., et al. *Toward Reform of Program Evaluation*. San Francisco: Jossey-Bass, 1970.

Fiske, Edward B. "Changes in the Offing for the New Law School Test." *New York Times*, 29 September 1981, p. C1.

French, Ruth, and Elkins, Carol M. "An Evaluation of the Self-Study Process." *American Journal of Medical Technology*, Vol. 45, 1979.

Friedrich, L. W. "Assessing the Validity and Reliability of Standards" (chap. 2).

Glidden, Robert. "Specialized Accreditation: The Agency Perspective" (chap. 2).

Goleman, Daniel. "The New Competency Tests: Matching the Right People to the Right Jobs." *Psychology Today*, January 1981, pp. 35–46.

Huse, Edgar F. *Organization Development and Change* (chap. 1).

Jacobson, Robert. "Laywers' Group Softens Proposed Requirement That Law Schools Teach Specific Skills." *The Chronicle of Higher Education*, 1 June 1981, p. 4.

Kells, H. R. "Proliferation and Agency Effectiveness in Accreditation: An Institutional Bill of Rights." *Current Issues in Higher Education*, no. 2 (1980), pp. 19–32.

Kells, H. R., and Parrish, Richard. *Multiple Accreditation Relationships* (chap. 2).

Northwest Association of Schools and Colleges. "Resolution Relating to the Coordination of Specialized Accreditation." *Newsletter*, Winter 1982, pp. 12–15.

O'Neill, Thomas, and Heaney, Robert. "Accreditation in Higher Education: Institutional Stance; Active or Reactive?" Washington, DC: Association of Academic Health Centers, 1982.

O'Neill, Thomas, and Heaney, Robert, "Taking the Initiative in Accreditation." *Educational Record*, Fall 1982a, pp. 57–60.

Pigge, Fred T. "Opinions About Accreditation and Interagency Cooperation: A Nationwide Survey." Washington, DC: Council on Postsecondary Accreditation, 1979.

Schuller, David, et al. "The Assessment of Readiness for the Practice of Professional Ministry" (chap. 2).

Tucker, Allan. *Chairing the Academic Department*. Washington, DC: American Council on Education, 1981.

Warren, Jonathan. "Is Accrediting Worth Its Cost?" *AAHE Bulletin*, no. 7 (1980), pp. 11–15.

Wildavsky, Aaron. "The Self-Evaluating Organization" (chap. 3).

Wood, Lynn, and Davis, Barbara Gross. "Designing and Evaluating Higher Education Curricula." AAHE/ERIC Higher Education Research Report, no. 8. Washington, DC: AAHE, 1978.

Zimmerman, Thomas F. "Self-Study—A Vital Component of Accreditation." *Journal of Allied Health*, Spring 1974, pp. 110–113.

PART THREE

Completing a Process

. . . the ways in which the most important outcomes of the self-study process—improvement, a useful report, and a better system of ongoing study—can be achieved at an institution or in a program.

8

Preparing a Useful Report

In part 3 of this book, we will examine the ways in which the most important outcomes of the self-study process—improvement, a useful report, and a better system of ongoing study—can be achieved at an institution or in a program. In chapter 8, the preparation of a useful report will be the subject.

Along with the absence of prestudy planning and design, and an orientation toward description rather than analysis and improvement, the prevalent weaknesses in self-study processes include the nature of the report prepared. At the worst, a report reflects a total preoccupation with the preparation of it—no study process is evident; just an activity to prepare a report. As one might expect, this malady is a concomitant of self-studies that are externally motivated. Somehow, the participants feel that they must produce a report to satisfy an outside agency, and they do not even seem to "see" their own institutions as they do it. Lesser variants of the problem have faults in common with processes other than self-study. One is the massive tome syndrome. Perpetrators of this attack upon the paper mills of America believe that they will score points in proportion to the weight of the document. A too-long report may also be the result of an ineffective steering group—one unable or unwilling to cull, select, and edit as needed to achieve the goal of the process. The consequence in any case is a document not unlike many unsuccessful master plan documents being used as bookends and doorstops—covered with dust, hard to lift, and unread by intended audiences.

Desirable Attributes

It is easy to sound syrupy when describing the desired attributes of a report that results from a self-study process, but certain qualities really do make a very large difference in the extent to which a report is useful. Clearly only part of the impact of such a process is expressed through the report, and some changes should have occurred before the report was written; the process of discussion is also valuable. The report, however, conveys most of the messages, and it ought to be well done.

The desired attributes of a self-study report include the following:

1. *The report should be clearly written and well organized.* Readability is a very important attribute to strive for. It may make the essential difference for some readers. Some people discard or strongly discount a poorly written report.
2. *The report should be concise.* Bulky reports are often a problem for large institutions, but a self-study report longer than 200 pages is too fatiguing for the reader. A good size is 100 back-to-back, single-spaced pages *or fewer*.

3. *The report should be focused on key issues.* The important items should not be buried in masses of description or dozens of tables.

4. *The report should be a frank and balanced view of the institution or program.* Both strengths and areas for improvement (and strategies for required change) should be included.

5. *The report should be useful for several audiences.* A point often forgotten: A report that describes an institution and its strengths and opportunities has multiple uses. If well written, the report could conceivably be used with the board of trustees, with potential donors, with state agencies, with all staff members and student leaders, with community leaders, and with one or more accrediting agencies.

6. *If the report is to be used for accreditation purposes, it should include systematic reference to how the standards of the agency are met* by the institution and how the definition of an accredited institution is met.

The self-study report should be used to educate constituencies and potential members of such groups. It should raise questions, provoke discussion, and inform visitors or newcomers of key issues. It should be able to build interest and morale and it should provide a written record of the process, which forms the base for planning. Finally, the report should list the things the institution or program should achieve or change in the next two or three years. Ideally, it also should indicate the strategies necessary to accomplish the changes, record the roles expected of individuals and groups, and suggest a timetable and a mechanism to assure that it all happens.

Suggestions for Producing a Useful Report

Several suggestions should be considered by the steering group of any self-study process if they wish to achieve the attributes mentioned above.

First, the steering group members must play a large role in assuring that a useful report is produced. As indicated earlier, they must exercise the option to produce an integrated report with the desired attributes, rather than a collection of work-group reports and compilations or data loosely organized with a few introductory comments and transitional sentences. They must authorize the writing of one report, using one writer who begins with the work-group reports, position papers, and the like, and if necessary using an editor who can

help assure readability. Culling, selecting, adding, and polishing—even major rewriting—are often required.

Second, the quality of the report and certainly its acceptability will be enhanced if a set of serious, well-staffed, and well-advertised hearings are held on the documents or its parts (see figure 4.1). Draft materials can also be circulated and can be put in the library or in other central locations for use by campus citizens. It is extremely helpful if the chief executive officer and other campus leaders let it be known that they will attend the hearings and will read any comments submitted as they prepare to receive and approve the final document.

Third, it is very important to strike a balance between the need for supporting data, descriptions, and other documents, and the need to produce a concise, readable report. Use appendixes and refer to other materials which are appended to the report. Use necessary, readable tables in the text, but have all other supportive data on file and accessible as needed. Do not repeat descriptions of programs, facilities, and services that can be found in catalogs, master plan documents, and other materials, all of which can be listed in the appendix and supporting materials and can be available to interested parties.

Fourth, to emphasize the key issues and any important strengths or opportunities for improvement, summarize these at the end of each section in which they first appear; recapitulate all such important points in a final section, which also can contain the commitment to, and schedules and strategies for, change.

Fifth, as indicated previously, a computer-based word processor with text-editing capabilities is a great help in projects like these. It obviates the need for multiple retyping of textual materials, charts, and minutes, and cuts the time involved to a fraction of that involved in manual systems.

Finally, the steering group should draw up a work plan to guide the production of the first draft materials. The following pages (figure 8.1) show a sample work plan for the production of a report of a selected topics self-study. The work plan includes the intended structure of the report (the forerunner to a table of contents), a list of assignments and important steps to be taken, and a list of suggested dates by which the draft materials should be submitted for each part of the report. Of course, the draft of some of the major subsections would probably be compiled by the specific work group concerned, which would also schedule due dates for the subelements in that section. The example given is for a report resulting from a study process not strongly tied to accreditation standards; but the same work plan concept can be used for accreditation-related studies.

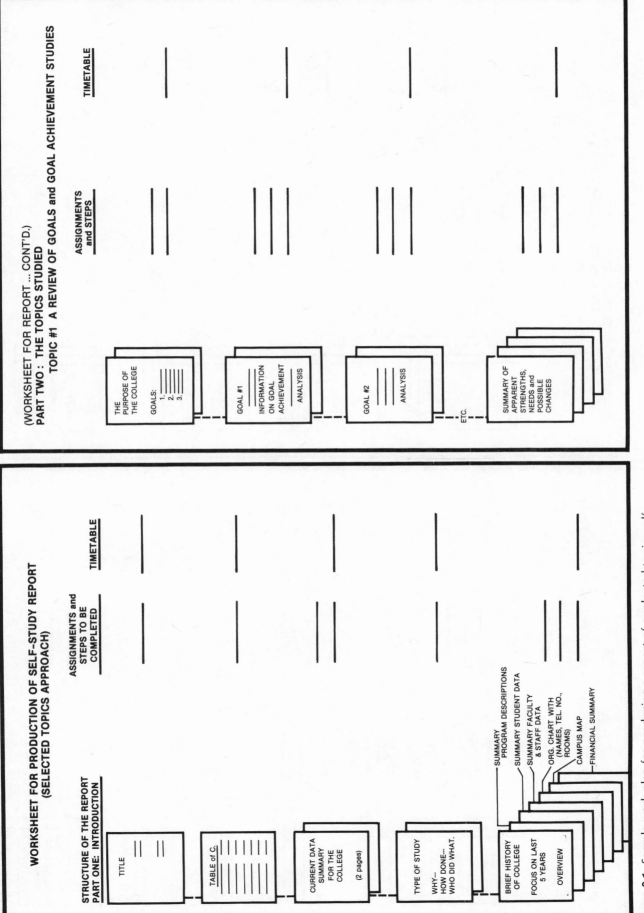

Figure 8.1. Sample work plan for producing a report of a selected topics self-study.

Figure 8.1 Sample work plan (continued)

PART THREE: OVERALL STUDY

ASSIGNMENTS and STEPS   **TIMETABLE**

SUMMARY OF STRENGTHS AND
AREAS FOR IMPROVEMENT
BY TOPIC.

AGENDA FOR
CHANGE

   HOW?
   WHAT?
   BY WHOM?
   WHEN?

APPENDICES

- LATEST AUDIT
- RECENT CONSULTANT REPORTS ON GRAD. PROGRAMS
- DATA NOT INCLUDED IN TEXT
- LIST OF DOCUMENTS AVAILABLE ON CAMPUS

SPECIAL NOTES

EXPECTED SIZE : 80 – 90 SINGLE SPACED, BACK TO
BACK PRINTING, SPIRAL BOUND,
NICE COVER.

DISTRIBUTION : TO ALL FACULTY, STAFF, STUDENT
LEADERS, BOARD MEMBERS, LIBRARY;
SUMMARY TO HOUSE ORGAN,
ALUMNI MAGAZINE AND STUDENT
NEWSPAPER.

EXTRA COPIES TO DEVELOPMENT
OFFICE, FOR STATE BOARD, AND
ACCREDITING AGENCIES.

TOPIC #4 THE LEARNING RESOURCES CENTER

ASSIGNMENTS and STEPS   **TIMETABLE**

LRC:
- AN OVERVIEW
- RELATIONSHIP TO INSTRUCTION
- ON CAMPUS ACCESS &
- MATERIALS OFF CAMPUS ACCESS

- HISTORY
- DESCRIPTION (DATA, STAFFING, COLLECTIONS)
- HOW STUDIED

COLLECTION BUILDING

EFFECTIVENESS

ANALYSIS OF STRENGTHS AND WEAKNESSES

PLANS FOR FURTHER DEVELOPMENT AND IMPROVEMENT

Figure 8.1. Sample work plan (continued)

Sample Organization Schemes

Tables of contents and other explanatory materials for self-study reports and the processes that yielded them are presented in appendix D. The first of these details the process and report of the Brookdale Community College self-study, totally organized around the goals for the college, and the extent to which these goals are being achieved. The second is the outline for the report of John F. Kennedy University in California; that report is oriented primarily toward the standards of the Western Association of Schools and Colleges Accrediting Commission for Senior Colleges and Universities. The third presents a more traditional outline from a comprehensive self-study at the University of Southern California. The fourth is the outline of a report of a current special self-study approach at the University of California, Riverside. The fifth outline is from a special-emphasis self-study at North Country Community College in Saranac Lake, N.Y.

These outlines are not presented as models. Several could focus more on goal achievement and on change strategies. However, they are fairly typical of organizing constructs used in self-study reports.

The vast majority of self-study reports related to specialized accreditation are directly organized according to accreditation standards, guidelines, or criteria of the agency. Other organizational constructs—such as those aligned with the nature of the program, its specific goals, or a theme or set of problems—are also possible, which through the use of careful and complete indexing schemes can relate the content to the accreditation standards, can meet the agency's needs, and in fact are often of more use to the institution.

In those instances (and they are *far* too few in number as I can see it) when an institution has had the foresight and good judgment to conduct a common self-study effort for two or more accrediting agencies, the report should not be a barrier to the effort. It is quite possible to compose a modular report with a general data section which includes the organizational setting and the like, and two or more sections concerning the specific materials required by any given agency, with any or all of it available as needed. As the agencies cooperate more and as common data needs are defined, this type of cooperative report will become the usual mode. It makes much sense.

9

Using Results, Peers, and Accrediting Agencies

Some readers may find the language in this chapter title a bit severe—*using* rather than, say, *working with*. It is not intended to be severe; just accurate. The institution or program that is serious about useful self-assessment and the implementation of the results of such assessment—that is, one that engages in an internally motivated process—must *use* its results, *use* peers, and *use* any agency with which it works if it is to achieve optimal results. Those institutions engaged in externally motivated, status-oriented, or otherwise reactive processes will not have many results to use, will probably host peers who may or may not be of any use to the institution, and may be left with an empty feeling after a polite, somewhat frustrating, if not humiliating, interaction with an agency. In this chapter, we will examine some of the ways results, peers, and accrediting agencies can be used to institutional advantage.

Using Results

In preparation for writing this section of the chapter, I reread most of Jack Lindquist's useful and important book, *Strategies for Change* (1978). It has helped me translate and understand my ten years of experience with over 300 institutions that were attempting some kind of study or planning process. Lindquist's proposals for adaptive institutional development and change are founded upon the work

of Ronald Havelock, Arthur Chickering, and others and developed during the 1970s in the Strategies for Change and Knowledge Development Project. I would suggest that any self-study coordinator or institutional leader seriously interested in planned change ought to read Lindquist's book. My experiences, also in the 1970s, have independently corroborated the major elements in the Lindquist formulation: interpersonal and informational linkages to stimulate the creation of new models and the perceived need for change; openness to new ideas; effective leadership and process "initiation"; the creation of "ownership" of any new ideas; and the use of appropriate rewards (see figure 9.1). Basically, Lindquist contends that institutions and programs *can* change and develop if the five elements are present; proper leadership, new ideas which participants can discover or develop, ownership through participation, openness to solving problems, and rewards. This notion is strongly related to the change theories of Kurt Lewin (1947). Lewin argued that situations must be "unfrozen" by discovering the need to change (seeing the problems through new data, discovering new ideas); then change must be managed through strong leadership and effective participation; then the situation must be "refrozen" or stabilized so the work of the organization may proceed without anxiety or hindrance.

The self-study steering group interested in seeing change occur should have laid the groundwork for

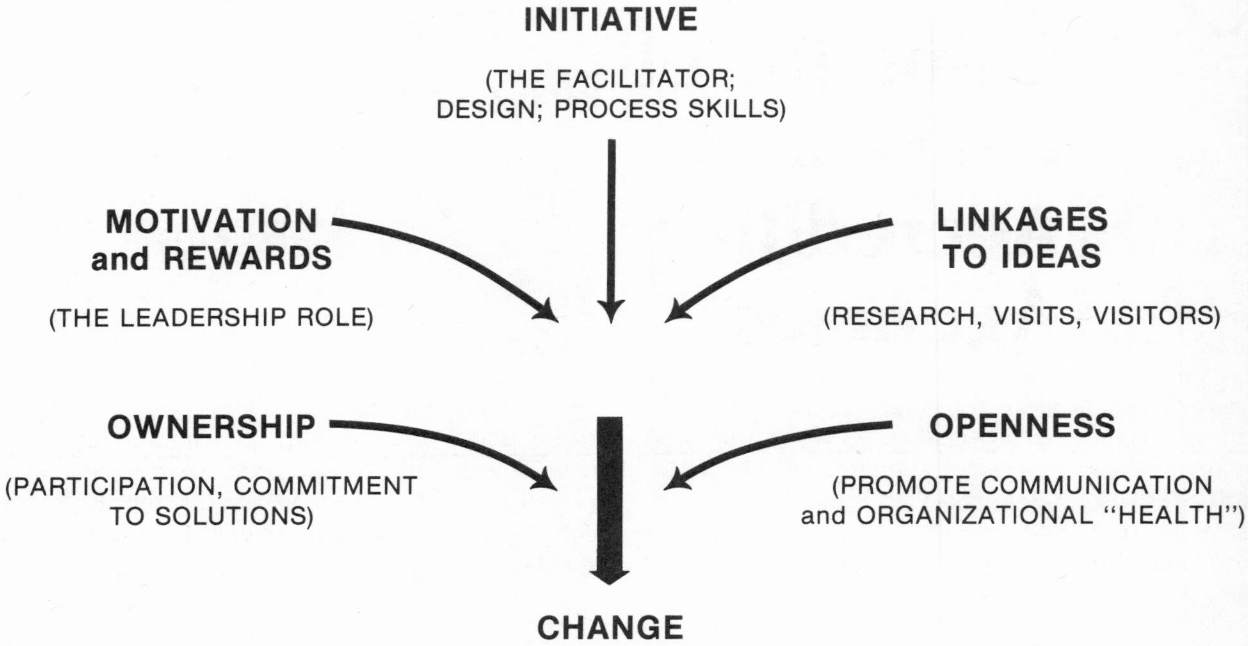

INITIATIVE

(THE FACILITATOR;
DESIGN; PROCESS SKILLS)

**MOTIVATION
and REWARDS**

(THE LEADERSHIP ROLE)

**LINKAGES
TO IDEAS**

(RESEARCH, VISITS, VISITORS)

OWNERSHIP

(PARTICIPATION, COMMITMENT
TO SOLUTIONS)

OPENNESS

(PROMOTE COMMUNICATION
and ORGANIZATIONAL "HEALTH")

CHANGE

Figure 9.1. Diagrammatic representation of Jack Lindquist's adaptive development strategy (Lindquist, 1978).

such positive results in the prestudy planning and design phases. The questions of internal motivation, active formal and informal leadership, the desire for change to occur during as well as after the study process, and the careful marshaling of human resources and involvement in order to create ownership of the results all should have been addressed.

More can be done to promote effective implementation of study results:

1. Publish the report and distribute it widely. If the self-study process has been open with active participation, discussion, and useful communication, then it will be hard for anyone to "bury" the report that results (Attempts to bury reports can and still do occur, despite the obvious negative impact on morale and the increased psychological distances created.) Instead of printing 50 copies, print 500 on inexpensive newsprint. Distribute the report to all staff members, student leaders, and board members. An open process should be followed by an open report.

2. Produce an agenda for action and include it in the published report. Also include recommendations for further study and by whom, items to be implemented by priority and by whom, and items that need consideration in the governance scheme and by whom. Suggest a continuing role for the steering group or another appropriate, mandated group in order to monitor progress and to provide continuing impetus. Those individuals and groups so (publicly) named will have little chance to avoid considering the agenda items, particularly if the executive leaders

and the faculty leaders have been involved in the study and want the agenda to be implemented.

3. Create overlap as early in the self-study process as possible between the study work groups and some of the regular governance work groups. This will reinforce the chance that recommendations will be considered and acted upon.

4. If the study report must be submitted to an outside agency, insist that the board of trustees and the chief executive endorse it in writing. This process is now required by the Western Association's Commission on Senior Institutions.

By implementing the prestudy and design suggestions and some of the items suggested above, the steering group is essentially creating "hooks" that can be used to integrate the results of the study process with the ongoing life of the institution. For years accrediting agencies have been asking for self-study processes. Those processes that have produced some useful suggestions for change and improvement have often left the recommendations on the doorstep of enactment. Sufficient momentum must be generated to overcome any inertia and fear of change. A process that results in recommendations but no action has failed.

For those institutions that are actively engaged in self-study processes associated with accrediting agencies, one other relatively recent change will assist the implementation process by providing some leverage. Institutional accrediting agencies now require a Progress Review Report five years after the accreditation review at the midpoint of the usual ten-year cycle. The institution is asked, among other things, to report progress on the consideration of key issues and recommendations from the self-study process. The agency reviews the report, usually using peer readers, and may ask for more information or schedule a special visit if no progress is seen. This accreditation step fits well with a useful cycle of study and planning (see chapter 10) and reinforces the points presented above.

Using Peers

All of the processes discussed in this book can and often do involve the use of peer visitors to a campus or program—consultants, teams of visitors engaged solely by the institution, and teams sent by accrediting or other agencies. All of these can be very useful if the motivation for the visit is appropriate and understood by both parties, if the participants are carefully chosen, and if the procedures employed are appropriate. Let us examine each of these situations.

Using Consultants

There was a time when consulting had a dubious reputation. Consultants were the people who, being more than five miles away from home, became experts or were brought in to add credence to the "party line" or the pet point of view. (Perhaps times were easier then and the dollar was freer.) Institutions demand and usually get much more from a consultant today, provided that some basic elements are understood and the match between institutional needs and consultant expertise is a good one. Consultants, or, more specifically, consulting needs, fall into two general types: subject matter consultation and process consultation. The subject matter consultant is the person with specific subject matter expertise or skills and adequate appropriate experience to propose specific answers to a problem, to test the effectiveness of a program, to design a needed element, or to give an expert opinion. The biology curriculum consultant, the structural stress engineer, the ceramics expert, or the reviewer of the English literature program are examples. The process consultant is entirely different. Such a person is engaged to assist a college or a program in finding the appropriate solution to their problem *themselves*. Process consultants have skills in group leadership, questioning, problem-solving techniques, change strategies, and the like. Both types of consultants are useful under certain circumstances. The value of the process consultant is in ascendancy at this point as institutions realize that if they can come up with

solutions themselves, carrying out the solution may be much more possible than seeking to adopt a solution proposed by an outsider.

To use consultants effectively, the institution or program must decide what it wants—subject matter advice or process advice. It may want both, simultaneously or in sequence. It may find some or all of the help it needs on its own or at a neighboring campus, or it may seek an outsider. Timing is important. A consultant may be needed to help formulate commitment to change or study, to help people to see the value of internal motivation, or to help with design. These would be early in a self-study process and finding someone with the adequate expertise or stature is vitally important. If someone is needed to assist with the work of a particular work group, problem, program, or service, adequate data must be available before the visitor comes. During the visit, people must be available to meet with him or her. After the consultant leaves, the results of the visit—oral and written—must be available and used. Finally, a consultant may help by reading and reacting to draft reports—commenting on completeness, frankness, strategies for and commitment to change, and suggesting the best way to present the results. However, using a consultant to write a self-study document is to waste the opportunity for involving people on the campus and gaining their commitment. To pass such an act off as *the* self-study process is folly. It also is an insult to the professional staff of the institution.

Using Teams of Visitors

Many institutions regularly undertake assessment processes that include visits by advisory boards for programs, or teams of evaluators, for each degree program. Graduate programs are a popular focus for such activities. It can be very fruitful to receive regular feedback from well-intentioned, informed, unbiased peers. However, many programs of regular, institutionally instigated visits are a dismal failure because several important elements are missing. Most commonly, these are as follows:

1. *Self-study does not precede the visit.* Brief visits by outsiders can be useful only if these complement self-assessment, adequate data collection, and presentation of systematic information on goals, objectives, process (programs, people, dollars, space, services, etc.), and outcomes. Not every visit must be preceded by a full study process; but to ask visitors to collect data and interview frantically as they try to piece together a picture of an institution or a program is an insult, and just foolish business.

2. *The purpose for the visit is misunderstood.* Such misunderstanding is usually at its worst in politicized, fragmented academic communities. In these situations, each faction sees the visitors differently and interprets their questions, schedule, comments, and report politically and often in a way harmful to the institution. Openness, clear communication, and sound leadership are needed to prevent or to at least minimize these conditions.

3. *The schedule permits little useful interaction.* Any group of visitors worthy of invitation should have a comfortable (as opposed to frantic) visit, and should be asked to take some time on campus during their visit to formulate some reactions and to discuss them with a group of local faculty and staff leaders. This interaction promotes understanding and adds clarity to the thoughts of and reports of the visitors. Too many institutions schedule visitors for many brief one-on-one interviews, running from breakfast until exhaustion with no time for thinking, rest, or interaction with groups. This kind of scheduling is less than useful.

4. *The nature of the report desired is not adequately clarified.* Teams of visitors can be asked to give an oral and/or written report. They can be asked to report certain things in writing in a public report and others in a private communiqué. They can be asked to be specific or general, analytical and/or synthetic, lengthy or brief. What is needed is a clear understanding before the visit of what is desired. Indeed, an institution with a program of regular visits should have a complete set of written guidelines for the visitors and the people to be visited, including the statement of desired study to be completed before the visit.

5. *A strong, experienced, sensitive chairperson for the team is not employed.* Making sure that team members' skills and time are used effectively to meet the goals intended for the visit is the job of the chairperson. Not everyone is able to handle a team of talented peer visitors. Care must be taken to choose a chairperson able to meet these challenges.

Once the foregoing elements are arranged, the institution leaders need only strive for openness for the visitors, treat them with respect and care, and engage them in discussing the life of the institution. Frankness and genuine appreciation for the visitors' effort will promote success for the visit.

Using Accreditation Evaluation Teams

All the caveats regarding routine assessment team visits apply to accreditation team visits as well, but even more care is needed if such visits are to be useful. Two factors further complicate the visits. The first is any apprehension visitors may create in their role of accreditor, or evaluator, or inspector. This apprehension is hard to dispel and perhaps cannot be dispelled because the accrediting agencies and their representatives do assess the extent to which agreed-upon standards appear to be met. The second complicating factor is the sometimes total lack of control the institution may have in selecting team members. It is not an isolated occurrence to have a positive, study-for-improvement attitude on a campus stifled by a rigid, poorly managed accrediting team experience. Both institution and agency have a function in achieving the desired, positive results of accreditation visits.

First, let us examine the nature of accrediting teams. Ideally, team members are chosen by the agency to visit the institution after a period of self-study to assist the institution and the agency in achieving the goals of the agency—stimulating improvement in institutions or programs and verifying that standards of good practice are met. Stimulating improvement is one important focus of institutional (regional) accrediting; conforming with standards is one important focus of specialized (program) accrediting. The institution or program may have the opportunity to suggest types of visitors, and usually has a limited veto power over persons suggested by the agency if possible conflict of interest or other serious problems are perceived. But the team is ordinarily drafted by the staff of the agency. At least one specialized agency allows the team chairperson to select the members. The possibility for bias, inconsistent coverage, or activity out of agreement with the general approach of the agency may be greater in such instances.

Team visit composition and management are people processes that have only recently begun to receive systematic study (Kells, 1979; Silvers, 1982; Robertson, 1982; and Cooney, 1983).

Methods of selection are only as good as the staff of the accrediting agencies involved. Institutional accrediting agencies seek to provide a team that reflects the nature of the institution, the nature of the self-study and the key issues inherent in it, and the need of the agency to assess achievement of stated institutional goals and agency standards. The institutional accrediting team sizes vary from region to region, although they generally correspond with institutional size (Kells, 1979). The members usually receive one day of orientation/training run by the agency, and the team leader usually makes a one-day preliminary visit to the campus. In one region, the team chairperson has usually also worked with the institution as a consultant.

For specialized accreditation, many of the same procedures are used. However, the focus of the team activities is much narrower and on a much greater level of detail—specifically on the program and related services in question. In some instances, the specialized agency may include a member of its own staff on the teams; and in other instances, the chairpersons are drawn from a specially designated pool of experts who play a substantial role in policy formulation and team member selection.

From the agencies' point of view, the success of an accreditation team visit probably rests on the quality of team construction, the role of the team chairperson, the usefulness of the self-study report, and the presence of a confident, knowledgeable cadre of leaders on the campus who can make the most of the visit. The same elements are important from the point of view of the institution, but some specific steps can be taken to increase the likelihood of a useful team visit. The following items should be considered.

First, the institution or program leaders should see the team visit as an opportunity for relatively inexpensive consultation and they should be proactive, not reactive, about team construction. They should carefully consider the timing of the visit and request a change (indeed, press for a change) if there is good reason to think that a six-month or a year's advance or delay would be more productive. Institution or program leaders should remember their needs and agenda and should suggest types of expertise needed on the team. They should help the agency staff members design the team.

Next, the institution should insist on a timely preliminary visit by the team chairperson—after the draft self-study report is prepared but soon enough before the visit if more work is needed. Institution leaders should make the visit a useful one. Frankness should be the style. The team chairperson should learn everything possible about the institution during the day's visit so he or she can play a role in augmenting the team, if needed, adequately orient the team, and decide on primary team visit assignments. The institution representatives should help the chairperson design the team visit. This institutional participation may not be comfortable for older, experienced chairpersons, but it is appropriate if the visit is to meet agency and institutional needs. Talented chairpersons know such sharing is wise. Institutional leaders should make sure the team chairperson understands the nature of the self-study process, its major findings, and the locally perceived needs, problems, and opportunities.

Finally, institutional or program leaders should probably raise questions for the team, and present these through the chairperson. What is it that the institution would like to solve? What is the team's opinion on issues A and B? The object should be to promote as much dialogue as possible.

A few thoughts about a useful visit merit noting.

The effectiveness of the visit will be increased if the institution sends the self-study report and any needed catalogs, books, and so on to team members four to six weeks before the visit. The team chairperson should insist that team members come prepared. He or she should test that preparedness in a private team meeting upon members' arrival and should send home anyone not prepared to engage in full and fruitful discussion with the host institution. The day of the team's arrival should include a relatively brief "mixer" during which visitors are introduced and key institutional representatives are identified, and at which the chief executive officer and the team chairperson indicate briefly the procedures to be used, the services available to the visitors, and their goals for the visit. The team's planning session and then at least two days of individual and group meeting should ensue. Also included may be examination of facilities and records and some class visits in specialized or departmental team visits. The worth of a few class visits during an institution-level visit is very small; however, such visits may be quite useful in specialized, program-level visits.

The team should be asked to cover as much ground as possible at the institution. Individual members can work alone; two, three, or more members can undertake activities together; and team members can be available for a specified time to chat with anyone desiring to talk with them.

A useful visit may also include a seminar on a topic or problem presented in the self-study report. It surely will include a visit with key trustees, all the major executive staff members, faculty leaders, committee members, student leaders, and other members of the academic community. It must include a session on the last day during which all or most of the major impressions of the team are shared with campus leaders. The visit should finish with the production of a team report that meets agency and institutional needs and that is shared first with institution representatives so they can check the facts. These representatives should also formally respond to the report before it is sent to the accrediting commission or other accrediting group.

Accreditation team members should be helpful and sensitive, but responsible. Institutional leaders should be confident and frank, and should expect fair, helpful reactions from the team. A visit reflecting these attitudes can happen. When it does, it complements a good self-study process.

Using Accrediting Agencies

Too many postsecondary institutions and program leaders within them have been fearful of accrediting agencies, or at least have accorded them a level of deference that far exceeds reasonable respect and common courtesy. The nature of the attention varies with the primary motivation of the campus leader involved. If the leader, who may be a department chairperson, believes that accreditation itself is the vital commodity for reasons of student placement, status, or leverage in the competition for resources, the medium of interaction can become the message and any interest in improving the program or other benefits of interaction with accrediting team members or agency services can be swept aside or never perceived at all. Such programs and their leaders may actually receive harmful, prescriptive treatment from some agencies because they permit—even invite— total focus upon the inspection function of accreditation. The agencies, we must remember, have, in a technical sense, a limited ability to conduct such specific inspections since the standards of the agencies for the most part have not been validated in a predictive sense. Rather, the standards are the best statement of currently perceived good practice written by experienced practitioners of good will. If one permits these standards to become the total focus of any interaction with an accrediting agency, the result can often be inconsistent and troubling. At the least, the results of such a narrow interaction between an accrediting agency and an institution or program can be of limited value compared with a "partnership" that combines the use of standards with service to improve that which is the focus of active, frank self-study processes.

The posture that is more effective for working with accrediting agencies has several elements. First, institutions and programs should be participating in validation studies of agency standards for some accrediting agencies and otherwise supporting their work. If the accreditation standards are improved through the efforts of member institutions, then the accrediting process will improve and the institutions will benefit. An institution deserves what it gets if it insists on seeking accreditation from an agency whose standards are unclear, incomplete, inappropriate, or unsatisfactory in any way. For an institution to state dissatisfaction takes courage, but the negative consequences possible from proceeding without attempting to reach some agreement on usable standards or investing the time needed to effect changes in the agency are quite serious. The institutions should insist that accrediting agencies focus appropriately on self-study processes as a part of the accrediting process. (Some agencies have a long way to go in this regard.) The provision by accrediting agencies of other services to improve programs at institutions (consultants, workshops, data banks, training materials, etc.) and the proper training of agency staff members and evaluation team members should be sought by institutions.

Using accrediting agencies in a given interaction is a subject that has been addressed at length by Robert Kirkwood (1978). The first consideration should be the nature of self-study. It is possible to include a review of agency standards in most self-study designs, which can be compatible with an institution-centered process. Institution leaders should design the process to meet institution needs, seeking accrediting agency assistance and concurrence, but insisting that institution needs be the primary consideration. Too often, institutions permit the agency to dictate their process, thereby expending resources on unnecessary, usually duplicative, exercises. Be congenial, but be assertive. Challenge the agency to do its job and meet your needs.

This same approach should be applied to producing agency-mandated reports. Most accrediting agencies should be forced to bend more to meet institutional needs in this area. To insist, as most agencies do, that their special data forms must be filled out is bad enough, but to call that a self-study process is ludicrous. Some agencies, however, are beginning to consider common terminology and data needs. They are also considering the possibility of reviewing data from U.S. Department of Health, Education, and Welfare HEGIS forms and other available sources, rather than insisting that institutions fill in separate documents of use only to one agency. The lack of an "industry standard" for data and terminology is a serious problem that only institutions can remedy by insisting on change.

Institutions must also be assertive in multiple accreditation relationships. They should request the use of common self-study reports, instead of totally separate ones for each agency, and joint or concurrent team visits for various accreditation processes (see chapters 7 and 8). This area is now receiving some study in the literature (Kells and Parrish, 1979; Kells, 1980; O'Neill and Heaney, 1982; Pigge, 1979) and some attention from key interagency tasks forces sponsored by the Council on Postsecondary Accreditation in Washington. In one region of the country, the regional accrediting commission has received from the accreditation liaison officers on more than 100 campuses of all sizes and purposes a resolution requesting an integrated policy of coordination for multiple accreditation relationships not unlike the recommendations made in the Bill of Rights put forth by this author in 1980 (Northwest Association, 1982). Presently, agency duplication, and its impact on institutions, though not fully measured, is substantial. While only 10 percent of American institutions have more than five relationships (Kells and Parrish, 1979), the cost to a struggling institution of one relationship may be large. The cost of two or three often is a burden. Joint self-study reports (at least in part), joint or concurrent team visits, and flexibility in scheduling to permit it, are reasonable accrediting agency responses. Institutions should insist on them.

Finally, institutions must remember that there is a code of good practice, nationally recognized, in accrediting. It calls for appeal procedures, due process, trained personnel, and the like. The statement is issued by COPA and institutions should be aware of it, just as they are aware of agency standards. Accrediting agencies, for instance, employ team visits as part of a process. The team is not the accrediting body. The institution, if it disagrees with the team conclusions, should confidently and in an informed and nondefensive way respond to the accrediting body. The response must be considered by the agency commission in making its decision.

All the foregoing points may seem negative and combative. Their purpose is to wake up some institutional leaders, many of whom have not exercised their responsibilites to participate in and improve accrediting activities. Accreditation can be a very useful process. The agencies are reviewed by COPA and the U.S. Office of Education to acquire their status. But they must be worked with and brought to full potential. Institutions must use them effectively if they are to benefit from the interactions.

References

Cooney, Robert. "The Training of Evaluation Team Members: Toward a Theory and a Model Design." Doctoral Dissertation, Rutgers University (in progress).

Kells, H. R. "The People of Institutional Accreditation" (chap. 2).

Kells, H. R. "Proliferation and Agency Effectiveness in Accreditation" (chap. 7).

Kells and Parrish. *Multiple Accreditation Relationships* (chap. 2).

Kirkwood, Robert. "Institutional Responsibilities in Accreditation."

Lewin, Kurt. "Frontiers in Group Dynamics" (chap. 1).

Lindquist, Jack. *Strategies for Change* (chap. 1).

O'Neill, Thomas, and Heaney, Robert. "Accreditation in Higher Education: Institutional Stance Active or Reactive?" (chap. 7).

Pigge, Fred L. *Opinions About Accreditation and Interagency Cooperation: A Nationwide Survey.* Washington, DC: Council on Postsecondary Accreditation, 1979.

Robertson, Mary Patricia. "A Study of the Characteristics of Specialized Accreditation Teams for Community Colleges." Ed.D. Dissertation, Rutgers University, 1983.

Silvers, Philip. "An Assessment of Evaluation Teams in Regional Accreditation of Baccalaureate-Granting Institutions". Doctoral Dissertation, University of Arizona, 1982.

10 Enhancing the Study/Planning Cycle

In this final chapter, we will examine the larger context for self-study processes, the relationship of self-study to planning, some ways to enhance a useful self-study/planning cycle, and the likelihood that systematic study and planned change can become an institutional way of life.

Let us begin by recounting the major aspects of the self-study scheme presented in this book. First, we have developed quite fully the notion that self-study is an important element of the management process of postsecondary institutions, and that it can be a fruitful exercise if it is carefully planned, designed in light of local circumstances, conducted for internal, improvement-oriented purposes, and well led and sensitively conducted. These primary considerations are founded on the results of research about many self-study processes and enhanced by the analysis of several hundred firsthand experiences with institutions conducting such processes. We have also developed quite fully a set of intentions for and desired attributes of self-study processes. The likelihood of achieving these was promoted by a detailed discussion and an integrated step-by-step regimen of design, organizational, and process steps for self-study. Finally, the ways of implementing useful results and the ways of working successfully with peer visitors and accrediting agencies were explored. Throughout the book, the notions of design, openness, involvement, internal orientation, and assertive self-determination have been stressed.

Some Remaining Problems

While the quality of self-study efforts has improved considerably over the last decade, some problems remain—even if most of the attitudes and schemes recommended in this book are adopted. Two are of particular importance.

The first remaining problem is the lack of a critical mass of ongoing institutional research or study capacity at virtually all postsecondary institutions. The model for self-study described in this book provides the ability to help institutions improve in rough proportion to the presence or absence of basic study capacity. Only so much new data collection, analysis, and the like can go on in any given process. Until institutions enhance and sustain a capacity for assessing goal achievement, inputs, and processes, each concentrated period of self-study—with all of its positive potential for change and development—will be sapped by the need to start with much basic study that ought to be ongoing, increasingly sophisticated, and useful to daily management and academic processes. Most current self-study reports that I read—and I see many each year—still conclude that much basic institutional research is needed at the institution. Like a family outing rich with planned recreational activities that degenerates into a prolonged hunt for firewood and gasoline for the return trip, such study processes have not achieved their goals in part because the fuel for the process was in short supply.

This problem was confirmed during an extensive retrospective analysis of self-study processes (Kells and Kirkwood, 1978). The inescapable conclusion of this research was that continuous, broadly conceived institutional research is not as highly developed as people had assumed—certainly not sufficiently developed that institutions may begin concentrated self-study processes with an adequate base of useful information about goals, programs, students, processes, resources, and goal achievement. The research showed clearly that those institutions that conducted goal achievement studies—particularly those that studied student development—during a self-study process were usually the institutions that perceived that the process had been useful. Usually, such outcomes studies were not a regular part of the institutional regimen and had to be conducted specially for the self-study. *There is a pressing need for investment at postsecondary institutions in ongoing study capacity.*

The second major problem in self-studies is re-lated to the first. It is the relatively low level of momentum for improved management and programs that results from or is evident after self-study processes. Despite the fact that self-study is and should be part of the ongoing cyclical management process, such processes remain isolated events in the continuum of activities at virtually all postsecondary institutions. A large commitment to self-study—sometimes leaving a healthy legacy of suggestions and even some change resulting, sometimes not—occurs about every ten years. In more progressive institutions, these processes are alternated at five-year intervals with some sort of planning effort (see figure 10.1, ''Usual Situation''). But most of the legacy of self-study and planning is lost. Some changes may result, but many ideas are lost in committee, buried in reports, or not recognized as important to consider amid the frantic day-to-day activities of contemporary institutional life. What is worse, the study process does not form the basis of a complementary planning process. The data and ideas on strengths and weaknesses are too old to use by the time the planning process starts. That process must

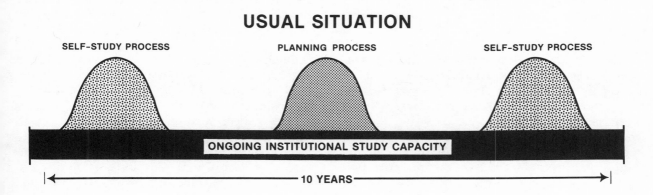

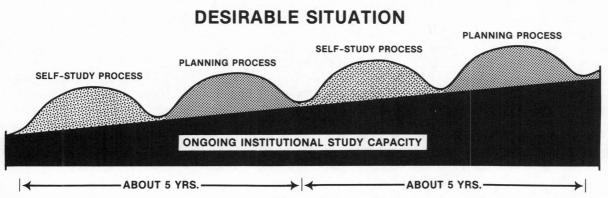

Fig. 10.1. The usual versus the desirable self-study/planning cycle at postsecondary institutions.

generate the new data and ideas before planners can turn to the major agenda. Finally, and equally discouraging, the momentum toward ongoing study capacity dissipates in the lull between the processes. Once the pressure is off, the need is forgotten. Thus, one of the key goals of self-study is not achieved. No additional, useful ongoing study capacity is added to the institution.

Enhancing the Study/Planning Cycle—Making Systematic Study and Planned Change an Institutional Way of Life

In figure 10.1, under "Desirable Situation" is depicted a workable, useful study/planning cycle for postsecondary institutions. The intention is to reverse the usual self-study situation. Self-study should yield improvement and it should form the basis of a planning process that follows on its heels. Study and planning, then implementation and more study and planning, should be part of ongoing management. They should not be seen as special or externally related events. *Accrediting agencies should not be the prodders for study, as, unfortunately, state coordinating boards are for planning processes. These activities should flow naturally and continuously; the leaders of the institution should make them happen.*

I am not calling for a total, comprehensive self-study process and a total, comprehensive planning process in each five-year period, although first attempts of each kind, and perhaps second, probably ought to be major endeavors. Subsequent cycles would not require comprehensive ventures because recent studies will have created useful data and resulting changes in some parts of the enterprise, particularly if, as is shown in figure 10.1, the ongoing study capacity in the form of institutional research into inputs, goals, programs, processes, resources, and outcomes is enhanced with each cycle.

Effective self-study is not enough. An enhanced, complementary study/planning cycle ought to be a way of life at postsecondary institutions. The benefits will be manifold. A study/planning cycle is compatible with the tenets of the organization development movement and with the concepts espoused by Lindquist (1978) in his adaptive development strategy.

Making It Happen

Saying that self-study and planned change ought to be an institutional way of life rather than isolated, peripheral, and periodic is one thing. Making it happen is quite another—as many institutions and programs have discovered. And, of course, at the center of the matter are fundamental attitudes about how things ought to run (for instance, rationally rather than the impressionistically), about roles and relationships in an organization (such as executive power and roles in policy making, or programmatic scope of institutions in a system), about preferred governance style or mix of models (autocracy, organized anarchy, collegiality, and political struggle) and about degrees of freedom (*knowing* the facts might limit options considerably).

My thesis is that regardless of the particular leadership style, governance mix, or organizational arrangement, the program or institution involved will be able to function more effectively if its intentions are clearer, if the average professional's knowledge of how well the place functions is greater, if the distance between personal and institutional intentions is relatively narrow, and if more often than not the members of the group are inclined to face problems as practical matters to be solved together. Even if these circumstances exist, the burden of creating a system to foster such behavior nevertheless falls on the *leaders;* and if the leaders are not inclined to function in an informed, open, relatively rational, "healthy" climate, then the benefits of participative study and planned change will not be realized. After all, the results of such studies must be infused into the budgetary, personnel, resource allocation, and programmatic dimensions of the unit—activities largely controlled by the leaders. Thus, new behaviors must be rewarded by the leadership or they will cease; ideas must be used and fed or they will wither away.

The hope of this author is that faculty and administrative leaders of programs and institutions will become convinced through external forces and "grapevine" influences that self-study for purposes of improvement is desirable; certainly better than wasteful, externally directed responses; less costly, and more productive. Once the door is opened to consider the possibility of a more useful type of study, then study efforts can be designed to yield positive results, to touch lives in a new way, and to *start a cycle* that will gain momentum and begin to invade the major administrative and other work of the institution. At this point the leaders must *decide to adopt the cycle of study and planning as a central framework* or it will fall away as just another "paste-on" attempt which clutters the life of the organization.

The following are useful questions and considerations:

1. Will the board of trustees be expected (*helped?*) to ask the executive staff periodically about the

achievement of stated institutional or program goals? Will they expect to have clear, well prepared, informed, and timely studies which put forth policy choices for them to make? Will they expect, in a regular cycle, a summary "audit" on each major aspect of the institution? Will they expect planning to be regular, effective, and based on previous studies of what works well?

2. Will the executive staff create and *use* an institutional research function and basic data base to inform their planning, their program reviews, and their resource allocations? Will the research function be included as a full member of the management team? Will it be guided and staffed to conduct regular studies on inputs, goals, process, and goal achievement? Will the results be used in the budget cycle and in decision-making? Most institutional research efforts in American institutions are very limited, are "captured" by a single office, and focus on only some of the basic elements discussed throughout this book. They do not provide the ongoing solid, well-maintained data base which fuels cyclical study and planning. They do only part, often very little, of the job which would permit ongoing study and planning. So choices must be made here and resources and talent invested, or the desired end will not be reached.

3. Faculty leaders must make choices, too. Just as faculty all over the country are beginning to use (some to demand) office computers to manipulate and store information, to edit manuscripts and the like, they must expect that the managers will do the same. They must come to meetings prepared to discuss choices and policies based in part on common, useful information now regularly available. Where the managers are less well informed, faculty should suggest strongly that they increase their knowledge. The faculty must also suggest that study efforts and committee work be streamlined, effective, and received in regular cycles—not confounded, discontinuous, duplicated, and generally chaotic as is often the case. I am convinced that part of the reason why faculty members despise administrative work and "committees" is that they see it as a poorly done and wasteful effort which leads nowhere.

4. The inevitable and various studies and planning ventures ought to be integrated as far as possible. In order to simplify, clarify, and make study cycles more effective and tolerable (if not fully acceptable to all), the leaders must distill the various requests, perceived needs, and demands from inside and outside the institution into *one cycle.* Accreditation requests, state board demands, master planning efforts, and the like can after a cycle or two of careful trial be effectively coordinated. They can be put on *one data base* built over, say, one five-year

cycle and considering all of the needs for self-study, planning, and external review. The time schedules for all of the requested study and planning efforts can then be juggled, stretched, pulled, or fought out into a single coherent scheme (see figure 10.1). This action will strengthen the institution's position and make it more effective in all of its management functions. The average faculty member and staff assistant will breathe more easily as well. The various mandatory study tasks will be more predictable, under greater control, probably somewhat less politicized, and certainly easier to accomplish. The smaller benefits in such a situation are important, too. To have a single data set that is accessible and reliable is a great help; not to have to create it anew and with a different twist twice a year is a positive joy. It is also a joy to be able to respond thus to an outside agency: "Here is our statement of intentions, our current plan, our tabulation of 'x' or 'y.' It is well done, and is the basis of all our regular decisions; it represents what we are willing to submit to outside agencies." Such a statement would dispense with most of the separate and multiple responses institutions now make to outside agencies.

5. Finally, the institution that decides to invest in a single cycle of ongoing study and planning as a central focus of its managerial way of life will want to conduct a regular program of staff development seminars and workshops so all of its officers and staff members can know the system, and help to build and improve it as a team effort. A program of this kind will enhance the ability to conduct other efforts well—among them, self-study efforts. The cycle will then be complete.

One example of an institution that has carried out some of the above ideas quite well is a public major university center—State University of New York at Binghamton. This institution was able to use recently the results of its regular cycle of study and planning to satisfy the need for the regional accrediting agency. No new self-study was required. A team of nationally prominent visitors were able to conduct the accreditation review because the following materials were available:

1. a recently completed review of the undergraduate curriculum—the second in ten years;
2. evidence of several successive cycles of five-year reviews and external visitors for each graduate program;
3. the report from a thorough internal and external review of the nonacademic administrative function—the second in a series;
4. the second successive self-study effort for the student services.

All of these studies together with the current master

plan (four-year cycles conducted for over twenty years)—in a state where master planning is serious business—were locally initiated on a regular basis. The visiting team's report is published and available to attest to this situation. Clearly, then, institutions can make ongoing study and planning a way of life. They must only *decide* to do it, and to *use* the results.

Common Elements in Self-Study and Planning

The more experience we gain with effective processes on self-study and planning, the more it becomes clear that certain elements are common to the two processes. Certainly, some of the desired attributes and effective approaches are common. Planning processes have been the subject of much interest in the 1970s and they have received considerable attention in the literature (Richardson, 1977; Halstead, 1979). In a retrospective study of ten cases of successful and unsuccessful planning efforts, this author found that some of the causes of failure in academic planning are the same as those for self-study processes. Both self-study and planning are "people" processes. Both require commitment from top leadership, a good design, goals for the process, good group skills and activities, sensitive use of human resources, good staff work, and commitment and strategies to use the results. The planning process also requires a good base of information and a list of strengths and weaknesses—the results of self-study (Kells, 1977).

Some Suggestions

I would now extend the previous analysis to state that both self-study and academic planning processes, particularly as conducted in an integrated study/planning cycle, should also contain the following desirable attributes:

1. Much more attention to group skills, group leadership, problem-solving techniques, and other tools for working effectively with people;
2. A much stronger ongoing institutional research base;
3. More staff assistance to work groups;
4. A different pace and basic design. They should be conducted more frequently, with sharper focus (less comprehensive, on the average) and a more limited scope. Such efforts should prove to be more useful.
5. More integration between the study and planning phases. More interdependence and continuity are desirable. The self-study process should not be terminated until the first stages of the planning process are begun.

I am fully convinced that self-study processes can be effectively used as a base for solid planning, as well as a generator of change and improvement on the campus and a spur to increased ongoing study capacity. I hope that this volume has assisted individuals and institutions in their effort to conduct processes that accomplish these things. Readers are invited to share their experiences and thoughts with the author. Future editions of this book will include more materials and ideas from those who have recently conducted self-study processes and wish to share with others what they have learned.

References

Halsted, D. Kent, ed. *Higher Education Planning: A Bibliographic Handbook*. HEW/NIE/Education Policy and Organization Group. Washington, DC: Government Printing Office, 1979.

Kells, H. R. "Academic Planning: An Analysis of Case Experiences in the Collegiate Setting" (chap. 1).

Kells and Kirkwood. "Analysis of a Major Body of Institutional Research Studies" (chap. 1).

Lindquist. *Strategies for Change* (chap.1).

Richardson, Richard C., Jr.; Gardner, Roy E.; and Pierce, Ann. "The Need for Institutional Planning." *Research Currents*, September 1977, pp. 3-6.

APPENDIX A

Outcomes Taxonomy and List of Outcome Measures

Produced by the
National Center for
Higher Education Management
Systems (NCHEMS)

Reproduced with permission from Oscar T. Lenning, *The Outcomes Structure: An Overview and Procedures for Analyzing It In Postsecondary Education Institutions* (Boulder, CO; NCHEMS, 1977).

CODED LISTING OF THE SECOND- AND THIRD-LEVEL SUBCATEGORIES
FOR EACH FIRST-LEVEL CATEGORY OF THE TYPE-OF-OUTCOME DIMENSION[a]

Category Code Number	Entity Being Maintained or Changed	Category Code Number	Entity Being Maintained or Changed
1000	***ECONOMIC OUTCOMES***	**2000**	***HUMAN CHARACTERISTIC OUTCOMES*** (continued)
		2760	Power and/or Authority
1100	Economic Access and Independence Outcomes	2770	Job, School, or Life Success
1110	Economic Access	2780	Other Status, Recognition, and Certification Outcomes
1120	Economic Flexibility, Adaptability, and Security	2800	Social Activities and Roles
1130	Income and Standard of Living	2810	Adjustment to Retirement
1200	Economic Resources and Costs	2820	Affiliations
1210	Economic Costs and Efficiency	2830	Avocational and Social Activities and Roles
1220	Economic Resources (including employees)	2840	Career and Vocational Activities and Roles
1300	Economic Production	2850	Citizenship Activities and Roles
1310	Economic Productivity and Production	2860	Family Activities and Roles
1320	Economic Services Provided	2870	Friendships and Relationships
		2880	Other Activity and Role Outcomes
1400	Other Economic Outcomes	2900	Other Human Characteristic Outcomes

Category Code Number	Entity Being Maintained or Changed	Category Code Number	Entity Being Maintained or Changed
2000	***HUMAN CHARACTERISTIC OUTCOMES***	**3000**	***KNOWLEDGE, TECHNOLOGY, AND ART FORM OUTCOMES***
2100	Aspirations	3100	General Knowledge and Understanding
2110	Desires, Aims, and Goals	3110	Knowledge and Understanding of General Facts and Terminology
2120	Dislikes, Likes, and Interests		
2130	Motivation or Drive Level	3120	Knowledge and Understanding of General Processes
2140	Other Aspirational Outcomes	3130	Knowledge and Understanding of General Theory
2200	Competence and Skills	3140	Other General Knowledge and Understanding
2210	Academic Skills	3200	Specialized Knowledge and Understanding
2220	Citizenship and Family Membership Skills	3210	Knowledge and Understanding of Specialized Facts and Terminology
2230	Creativity Skills		
2240	Expression and Communication Skills	3220	Knowledge and Understanding of Specialized Processes
2250	Intellectual Skills		
2260	Interpersonal, Leadership, and Organizational Skills	3230	Knowledge and Understanding of Specialized Theory
2270	Occupational and Employability Skills	3240	Other Specialized Knowledge and Understanding
2280	Physical and Motor Skills	3300	Research and Scholarship
2290	Other Skill Outcomes	3310	Research and Scholarship Knowledge and Understanding
2300	Morale, Satisfaction, and Affective Characteristics		
2310	Attitudes and Values	3320	Research and Scholarship Products
2320	Beliefs, Commitments, and Philosophy of Life	3400	Art Forms and Works
2330	Feelings and Emotions	3410	Architecture
2340	Mores, Customs, and Standards of Conduct	3420	Dance
2350	Other Affective Outcomes	3430	Debate and Oratory
2400	Perceptual Characteristics	3440	Drama
2410	Perceptual Awareness and Sensitivity	3450	Literature and Writing
2420	Perception of Self	3460	Music
2430	Perception of Others	3470	Painting, Drawing, and Photography
2440	Perception of Things	3480	Sculpture
2450	Other Perceptual Outcomes	3490	Other Fine Arts
2500	Personality and Personal Coping Characteristics	3500	Other Knowledge, Technology, and Art Form Outcomes
2510	Adventurousness and Initiative		
2520	Autonomy and Independence	**4000**	***RESOURCE AND SERVICE PROVISION OUTCOMES***
2530	Dependability and Responsibility		
2540	Dogmatic/Open-Minded, Authoritarian/Democratic	4100	Provision of Facilities and Events
2550	Flexibility and Adaptability	4110	Provision of Facilities
2560	Habits	4120	Provision or Sponsorship of Events
2570	Psychological Functioning		
2580	Tolerance and Persistence	4200	Provision of Direct Services
2590	Other Personality and Personal Coping Outcomes	4210	Teaching
		4220	Advisory and Analytic Assistance
2600	Physical and Physiological Characteristics	4230	Treatment, Care, and Referral Services
2610	Physical Fitness and Traits	4240	Provision of Other Services
2620	Physiological Health		
2630	Other Physical or Physiological Outcomes	4300	Other Resource and Service Provision Outcomes
2700	Status, Recognition, and Certification	**5000**	***OTHER MAINTENANCE AND CHANGE OUTCOMES***
2710	Completion or Achievement Award		
2720	Credit Recognition	5100	Aesthetic-Cultural Activities, Traditions, and Conditions
2730	Image, Reputation, or Status	5200	Organizational Format, Activity, and Operation
2740	Licensing and Certification		
2750	Obtaining a Job or Admission to a Follow-up Program	5300	Other Maintenance and Change

[a] The fourth-level categories, into which any of the categories listed here can be divided, are "maintenance" (a fourth digit of "1") and "change" (a fourth digit of "2").

Category Code Number	1000 ECONOMIC OUTCOMES*	
1100	*Economic Access and Independence Outcomes*—Outcomes that relate to the entrance into, obtainability, flexibility, and levels and amounts of monetary or pecuniary situations, conditions, and characteristics.	
	(Categories)	**(Examples of Outcome Measures or Indicators)**
1110	*Economic Access*—The amount of openness or ease of admittance to economic opportunities, advancement.	Percentage of students obtaining their first full-time job in the field of their choice within a specified time after graduation. The number of alternatives for an entry level job open to minority group graduates compared to minority group nongraduates.
1120	*Economic Flexibility, Adaptability, and Security*—The amounts of self-sufficiency, liberty, frugality, thrift, self-government, confidence, certainty, safeguards, stability, and adjustment that are exhibited in economic matters.	Geographic mobility of college graduates compared to those not attending college. Self-report of college graduates about the economic security for them and their families, and the contribution of college to this.
1130	*Income and Standard of Living*—Amount of profits, return on investment, necessities and comforts of life, wealth, and other signs of economic "well-being" that are obtained or possessed. Included is direct support provided to individuals and the community through local purchases by the educational institution and through staff salaries and wages.	Amount of annual and lifetime earnings of those attending college compared to those not attending college. Average student and/or former student reported scores on scales measuring perceptions and evaluations of their current and desired socio-economic level.
1200	*Economic Resources and Costs*—Outcomes that relate to the amount and type of material, energy, effort, people, organization, and other economic assets that are available or that are expended in economic activities and production.	
	(Categories)	**(Examples of Outcome Measures or Indicators)**
1210	*Economic Costs and Efficiency*—The amounts of sacrifice, effort, expenditure, and waste present in economic activities and production.	The absenteeism and tardiness on-the-job of college graduates as compared to nonstudents. The number of firms that use the college degree as an inexpensive screening device that allows them to hire qualified employees at minimum initial cost to the firm.
1220	*Economic Resources (including employees)*—The assets available that can aid economic production, distribution, and gain.	Percentage of college graduates employed in management positions within a specified time after graduation. Average number of patents and/or copyrights received per student, former student, and/or faculty member.
1300	*Economic Production*—Outcomes that relate to the creation of goods, services, and economic value.	
	(Categories)	**(Examples of Outcome Measures or Indicators)**
1310	*Economic Productivity and Production*—The value of goods and services that are created or produced by and within specific enterprises of "audiences" or clients of the educational institution, and especially in relation to the resources expended in the enterprise.	Percentage of college graduates who can adequately do their personal typing and complete their own income tax forms as a result of having attended college. Expert judges' ratings of the amount of increased worker production and higher worker motivation that results from having attended college.
1320	*Economic Services Provided*—Amount and type of direct-assistance activities provided by the educational institution or its subunits in the economic area.	Dollar amount of goods and services bought in the local community by the institution, its staff, and its students. Number of hours of consultation in the business area provided to area companies and institutions by the university's college of business.
1400	*Other Economic Outcomes*—An example would be that a company with a large payroll located in this community rather than another similar community because there is a more prestigious college here.	
	*Many of the subcategories for this category were suggested by the economic outputs classification developed by Goodman (1971).	

Category Code Number	2000 HUMAN CHARACTERISTIC OUTCOMES	
2100	*Aspirations*—Levels, patterns, and directions (in persons, groups, organizations, or communities) of interests, desires, drives, ambitions, goals, and intentions.	
	(Categories)	(Examples of Outcome Measures of Indicators)
2110	*Desires, Aims, or Goals*—Places, conditions, things, or other ends that individuals and/or groups crave, toward which they have ambition, or that they intend to reach because of importance to them.	Changes in observed desires from college entrance to graduation. Changes in the reported aspirations for graduate school as a class proceeds through undergraduate school. Self-report of changes in goals and aspirations as a result of college.
2120	*Dislikes, Likes, and Interests*—The persons or types of persons, objects, content areas, occupations and other things and situations for which there is a preference or antipathy.	The reported likes and dislikes of persons before college as compared to after graduation, and comparison with such change over the same period of time for those the same age not attending college. Score or change in score on an interest inventory, e.g., Strong Vocational Interest Blank, Kuder General Interest Survey, Kuder Occupational Interest Survey, ACT Interest Inventory.* Self-report of changes in interests as a result of college.
2130	*Motivation or Drive Level*—The intensity of striving toward a goal that is elicited by a need or other stimulus.	Score or change in score on an instrument that measures "need for achievement" or "achievement motivation," e.g., the Strong Vocational Interest Blank Academic Achievement Scale, the College Student Questionnaire Motivation for Grades Scale, the California Psychological Inventory Achievement Scales, Personal Value Inventory. Self-report of changes in motivation level as a result of college.
2140	*Other Aspirational Outcomes*	
2200	*Competence and Skills*—Levels, patterns, and direction of ability, capability, proficiency, and talent of different kinds.	
	(Categories)	(Examples of Outcome Measures or Indicators)
2210	*Academic Skills*—The amount of ability or competence in taking tests, earning good grades, persisting in college, etc. without regard to the amount of cognitive learning that has taken place.	Grades earned when the effect of ability, motivation, and other such factors have been controlled. Persistence in college when the effects of ability, motivation, and other such factors have been cancelled out. Score or change in score on a test of study skills, e.g., Brown-Holtzman Survey of Study Habits and Attitudes, Comprehensive Test of Basic Study Skills.
2220	*Citizenship and Family Membership Skills*—The ability or competence to perform relative to the rights, duties, and privileges of a member of a family, community, state or nation; for example, competence in managing family finances, being an effective consumer, and evaluating political issues.	Self-report of abilities pertaining specifically to citizenship and home membership that college accentuated. Evaluation by others of citizenship and home membership skills mastery exhibited. Score or change in score on the Vineland Social Maturity Scales.
	*As an example, one could at graduation compare interest test scores of college students to a group of their high school classmates not attending college who had similar interests in high school. As another example, one could look at interest test change scores for college students, adjusted for initial level.	

Category Code Number	2000 HUMAN CHARACTERISTIC OUTCOMES (continued)	
2230	*Creativity Skills*—The amount of ability or competence in designing, producing, or otherwise bringing into existence original perspectives, explanations, and implementations.	Score or change in score on a test that measures originality and creative ability, e.g., Minnesota Test of Creative Thinking, Test of Creative Ability, Guilford's Alternate Uses Test, Sixteen Personality Factors Questionnaire Creativity Scale. Evaluation by judges of creative ability demonstrated in a building or forming task.
2240	*Expression and Communication Skills*—The amount of ability or competence in conveying information, attitudes, or emotions on a one-to-one basis and/or to large or small groups or populations, by whatever media, in order to inform, challenge, uplift, and/or persuade, etc., and in receiving and interpreting such communications—through reading, writing, speaking, listening, touching, body movement, silence, and cultural arts like acting, painting, sculpturing, singing, playing musical instruments, etc.	Score or change in score on tests that measure the ability to communicate or express oneself. Judges' rating in a debate or speech contest. Judges' rating of expression in a music, art, or ballet contest.
2250	*Intellectual Skills*—The amount of ability or competence in formulating and analyzing problems, comprehending and understanding, synthesizing information, evaluating information, implementing a solution to a problem, and in locating, retaining, and filtering relevant knowledge.	Score or change in score on a test that measures ability to analyze and solve problems and to make inferences, e.g., California Test of Mental Maturity, Watson-Glazer Critical Thinking Appraisal, California Psychological Inventory Intellectual Efficiency Scale. Self-report of changes in analytical ability as a result of college.
2260	*Interpersonal, Leadership, and Organizational Skills*—The amount of ability or competence in effectively living and interacting with others, social organizing, being a congenial friend and companion, establishing courses of action for others, and influencing others to follow.	Leadership awards. Self perceptions and evaluation of interpersonal and leadership ability. Perceptions by judges of interpersonal and leadership skills. Score or change in score on a test that measures leadership and interpersonal ability, e.g., California Psychological Inventory Leadership Scale, Chapin Social Insight Scale.
2270	*Occupational Skills*—The amount of ability or competence in the special, unique skills required by particular occupations, and in seeking, gaining, and maintaining a particular level and kind of employment.	Spatial relations test scores for someone who is, or is going to be, an artist. Demonstrated ability in writing FORTRAN or COBOL for someone who is, or is going to be, a computer programmer. Score or change in score on the Bennett Mechanical Comprehension Test.
2280	*Physical and Motor Skills*—The ability or competence in tasks requiring physical coordination, dexterity, manipulation, and other muscular or motor skills.	Score or change in score on tests that measure motor skills, e.g., Crissey Dexterity Test, Minnesota Rate of Manipulation Test. Judges' scores on skill events in athletic competition such as gymnastics, diving, and figure skating.
2290	*Other Skill Outcomes*—Examples are the ability to teach effectively, to handle one's leisure, etc.	
2300	*Morale, Satisfaction, and Affective Characteristics*—Levels, patterns, and directions of characteristics typified by emotion.	
2310	(Categories) *Attitudes*—The disposition or tendency to respond either positively or negatively to particular persons or types of persons, things, situations, etc. It is a predisposition to act in a certain way. AND *Values*—A strong preference based on a conception of what is desirable, important, and worthy of esteem. Values affect an individual's actions and thoughts toward others.	(Examples of Outcome Measures or Indicators) Score or change in score on an attitude scale, e.g., Thurstone and Chave's Scale for Measuring Attitudes Toward the Church, College Student Questionnaire Part I, Adorno Ethnocentrism Scale, Shaw and Wright Scales for the Measurement of Attitudes. Self-report of one's attitudes and the effect of college on them. Score or change in score on an instrument that assesses values, e.g., Alport-Vernon-Lindsey Study of Values, Differential Value Profile, Work Values Inventory. Self-report of one's values and the effect of college on helping to clarify them.

Category Code Number	2000 HUMAN CHARACTERISTIC OUTCOMES (continued)	
2320	*Beliefs, Commitments, and Philosophy of Life*—The acceptance and internalization of particular propositions or declarations; the particular things that one is convinced are true. The held view of what "man" is, the purposes and reasons for a person's existence, and the system of principles and laws that should govern his/her thought, morals, character, and conduct or behavior. Included is the promotion of and the adherence to the conventions, practices, and teachings of religious organizations or sects.	Score or change in score on instruments that assess beliefs, e.g., Harvey's Conceptual Systems Test, Inventory of Beliefs. Self-report of one's beliefs and commitments and the effect of college on them. The membership and participation in, and support of, a particular religious organization or cause prior to as compared with after college. Self-report of one's philosophy of life and the effect of college on clarifying and organizing it.
2330	*Feelings and Emotions*—The disposition or tendency to respond or not respond subjectively to stimuli and the ability to control or not control such expressions, i.e., feelings of anguish or distress, anticipation, anxiety, concern, contentment, empathy, excitement, fear, frustration, happiness and joy, humor, lethargy, love, pleasure, satisfaction, sorrow, etc.	Openness and acceptance of feelings before college compared to after college. Development of an *appreciation* of different cultures and a wide range of human values as a result of college. Greater reported satisfaction with life as a result of college.
2340	*Mores, Customs, and Standards of Conduct*—Social and cultural practices, rules, and conventions designed to guide personal and corporate behavior. They have strong ethical or moral significance according to tradition and are enforced by social disapproval of violations.	Self-report of the effect of college on assimilation or internalization of the customs of community or society. Score or change in score on the California Psychological Inventory Socialization Scale. The adherence to particular mores or social customs prior to college as compared to after college. The amount of subjectivity and emotion guiding one's standards of conduct prior to college as compared to after college.
2350	*Other Affective Outcomes*	
2400	*Perceptual Characteristics*—Levels, patterns, and directions of consciousness, awareness, and sensitivity exhibited, and the view(s) or concept(s) of self, others, surroundings, events, ideas, etc.	
	(Categories)	(Examples of Outcome Measures or Indicators)
2410	*Perceptual Awareness and Sensitivity*—The amount of consciousness or awareness of, or sensitivity to, stimuli that are exhibited by individuals or groups.	Increased sensitivity to needs and emotional cues provided by others. Increased alertness to the opportunities confronting one.
2420	*Perception of Self*—The view held about oneself; the characteristics that are perceived, i.e., self concept.	Development of positive self-regard and self-confidence as a result of college. Score or change in score on a self-concept scale, e.g., Adjective Check List, California Psychological Inventory Self Acceptance Scale, Tennessee Self Concept Scale.
2430	*Perception of Others*—The manner in which other individuals and particular groups of others are viewed or perceived; the characteristics that are perceived.	Reports by observers about how a person's respect for others has changed as a result of college. Self-report of how one's view of others has changed as a result of college.
2440	*Perception of Things*—The view one holds (i.e., the characteristics noted) of ideas or other things being examined with the physical senses.	Increased respect for the ideas of others as result of college. Movement as a result of college experiences from seeing things as all "black and white" to complex "grays."
2450	*Other Perceptual Outcomes*	

Category Code Number	2000 HUMAN CHARACTERISTIC OUTCOMES (continued)	
2500	*Personality and Personal Coping Characteristics*—Levels, patterns, and directions of human conditions, factors, and traits related specifically to the mind and mental processes (other than skills, knowledge, and understanding).	
	(Categories)	(Examples of Outcome Measures or Indicators)
2510	*Adventurousness and Initiative*—Willingness to take chances and risks; how daring an individual is; willingness to take a stand or speak out; willingness and capacity to initiate personal action or to become actively involved.	Reports by impartial observers of changes in initiative that seem to have resulted from college attendance. Self-report of the effect of college on one's willingness to take a chance, e.g., to take an educated guess on an exam. The frequency that one exhibits speaking out on issues as the college career progresses.
2520	*Autonomy and Independence*—The amount of freedom from control and influence of others that is exhibited.	Score or change in score on personality scales that measure autonomy and independence, e.g., Sixteen Personality Factors Questionnaire Group-Dependent vs. Self-Sufficient Scale, Edwards Personality Inventory Independent in His Opinions Scale, College Student Questionnaire Independence Scales, Omnibus Personality Inventory Autonomy Scale. Self-report of willingness to volunteer or "stand up for one's rights" and the effect of college attendance on such willingness.
2530	*Dependability and Responsibility*—The amount of reliability, trustworthiness, and accountability for own behavior that is exhibited.	Reports by observers of changes in dependability and responsibility that have occurred during college. Score or change in score on scales that measure dependability and responsibility, e.g., California Psychological Inventory Responsibility Scale, Edwards Personality Inventory Assumes Responsibility Scale, Sixteen Personality Factors Questionnaire Expedient vs. Conscientious Scale.
2540	*Dogmatism, Authoritarianism, and Open-Mindedness*—The amount of open-mindedness, assertiveness, unassertiveness, and/or unquestioning obedience to authority that is exhibited.	Reports of expert observers about changes in open-mindedness that have taken place during college. Score or change in score on a scale that measures dogmatism and/or authoritarianism, e.g., Rokeach Dogmatism Scale, California Psychological Inventory Dominance Scale, Omnibus Personality Inventory Religious Orientation Scale.
2550	*Flexibility and Adaptability*—The amount of adjustment to new and changing situations and circumstances that is exhibited.	Score or change in score on a scale that measures flexibility, e.g., California Psychological Inventory Flexibility Scale, Omnibus Personality Inventory Practical Outlook Scale, Sixteen Personality Factors Questionnaire Practical vs. Imaginative Scale. Reports by observers of changes in adaptability and flexibility that have occurred during college. Self-report of the effect of college on adaptability and flexibility.
2560	*Habits*—The tendency to perform certain actions or to behave in characteristic, automatic ways.	Observations by others of changes in habit orientation that have occurred during attendance. Self-report of changes in habits that have resulted from college.
2570	*Psychological Functioning*—The amount of psychological adjustment, contact with reality, self-understanding, and self-actualization (optimum self-realization) that is exhibited.	The amount of realization of one's actual strengths and weaknesses, and of what is reality. Score or changes in score on an instrument that measures psychological adjustment, e.g., Minnesota Multiphasic Personality Inventory, Sixteen Personality Factors Questionnaire, Moody Problem Check List. Reports by expert observers about changes in the psychological functioning of individuals that have occurred during college attendance.

Category Code Number	2000 HUMAN CHARACTERISTIC OUTCOMES (continued)	
2580	*Tolerance and Persistence*—The amount of endurance, tenacity, forbearance, patience, and restraint that is exhibited.	Observations by others of changes in tolerance and persistence during college. Score or changes in score on an instrument that measures tolerance and persistence, e.g., Edwards Personality Inventory Persistence Scale, California Psychological Inventory Tolerance Scale.
2590	*Other Personality and Personal Coping Outcomes*	
2600	*Physical and Physiological Characteristics*—Levels, patterns, and directions of human body traits and processes (other than skill functioning).	
	(Categories)	(Examples of Outcome Measures or Indicators)
2610	*Physical Fitness and Traits*—Physical and physiological characteristics such as toughness, endurance, strength, speed, flexibility or dexterity, physical energy, muscular control, size, vocal characteristics, etc.	Score or change in score on physical fitness tests, e.g., AAHPER Youth Fitness Tests, Basic Fitness Tests. Self-report of "feeling in better physical shape" as a result of college.
2620	*Physiological Health*—The physical well-being of individuals; how well the system of normal bodily operations is functioning.	Medical doctor's health physical examination report at college entrance compared to at college graduation. Self-report of the effect of college attendance on how well alumni take care of their bodies.
2630	*Other Physical or Physiological Outcomes*	
2700	*Status, Recognition, and Certification*—Levels, patterns, and direction concerning recognition of accomplishments, power, prestige, reputation, etc.	
	(Categories)	(Examples of Outcome Measures or Indicators)
2710	*Completion or Achievement Award*—A certificate, diploma, or some other award for having completed a course or program, for some demonstrated proficiency, or for accomplishment of some type.	An honorary degree. Graduation diploma. Alumni achievement award. Sales award or a job promotion. Danforth Fellowship Award. Being named a Rhodes Scholar.
2720	*Credit Recognition*—Formal or informal acknowledgement of work completed or of confidence, trust, approval, etc.	Graduate school grades. Credit hours given for completing a course. By-line credit for a movie, play, book, or article. Financial credit rating issued by a bank or credit bureau.
2730	*Image, Reputation, or Status*—The amount of fame, distinction, respect, and standing in the eyes or the profession, the community, or some other group.	Being on the social register. Being listed in *Who's Who*. Oral and written acknowledgements from others. Being interviewed by the press, radio, or TV. Writing an autobiography that is published or having a biography written about you.
2740	*Licensing and Certification*—Formal written authority that a person or firm is qualified and has met the test to practice some skill or speciality occupation.	Entry into the state bar. Passing a cosmetology licensing exam. Being a certified public accountant. An insurance company that has been licensed to sell in a state.

Category Code Number	2000 HUMAN CHARACTERISTIC OUTCOMES (continued)	
2750	*Obtaining a Job or Admission to a Follow-Up Program*—Success in being selected for a postgraduate employment position or a special educational program at a higher level.	Entrance to a university after graduation from a community college. Entrance to law, medical, or graduate school. Being selected by the civil service. Being selected for a company executive position. Being hired in the special field for which the training applied.
2760 2770	*Power and/or Authority*—The amount of acknowledged authorization or ability to influence, command, enforce obedience, or set policy as a right of rank, position, delegated jurisdiction, skill, strength, wealth, etc.	Appointment or election to a position of authority. Earning promotion to a position of authority. Influencing important community or public decisions. Getting acknowledged credit for the important job having gotten done.
	Job, School, or Life Success—Evidence of success in one's occupation or career, in graduate or professional school, or in some other aspect of one's life that is covered in any of the above categories.	Self report of success in career. Teacher's rating of success in graduate school. Employer's rating of overall on-the-job performance.
2780	*Other Status, Recognition, and Certification Outcomes*	
2800	*Social Activities and Roles*—Levels, patterns, and directions of social functions assumed and carried out.	
	(Categories)	(Examples of Outcome Measures or Indicators)
2810	*Adjustment to Retirement*—Altering self and lifestyle to meet the needs and adapt to the limitations of the retirement years.	Percentage of college educated retirees reporting productive retirement years compared to reports of those who never attended college. Self-report of the effect of having attended college on the retirement years.
2820	*Affiliations*—Finding appropriate organizations and institutions to join and associate with, and being accepted by them.	Number of affiliations and changes in affiliations for college graduates as compared to those never attending college. Self-report of the effect of having attended college on the affiliations sought and on the affiliations won.
2830	*Avocational and Social Activities and Roles*—Finding, pursuing, and achieving rewarding nonwork activities, hobbies, and parts to play in society, and exhibiting that pattern of behavior that is expected of persons having the status that has been earned.	The social roles and avocations of college graduates as compared to those who never attended college. Self-report of the effect of having attended college on the avocational and social roles sought, and on those practiced.
2840	*Career and Vocational Activities and Roles*—Exhibiting the patterns of behavior expected and/or that are needed for the part in the "world of work" that has been accepted or entered into.	The career roles of college graduates as compared to those who never attended college. Reports of employers concerning the advancement and roles of college trained employees versus the advancement and occupational roles of those who never attended college.
2850	*Citizenship Activities and Roles*—Facilitating and contributing to governmental functions and to the overall well-being of individuals, the community, and larger society.	Percent voting in a municipal or state election. Financial and other contributions given to service organizations. Percent running for public office or campaigning for someone who is.

Category Code Number	2000 HUMAN CHARACTERISTIC OUTCOMES (continued)	
2860	*Family Activities and Roles*—Contributing to and facilitating family functions, i.e., parent roles, sibling roles, son/daughter roles, etc.	The family roles of college graduates as compared to those who never attended college. Self-report of effect of the college on the roles played in one's family.
2870	*Friendships and Relationships*—Socially interacting with and entering into and sustaining intimate, in-depth, and satisfying associations with others.	Characteristics of friends and relationships of college educated people versus those never attending college. Self-report of the effect of college on friendships and social relationships.
2880	*Other Activity and Role Outcomes*	
2900	*Other Human Characteristic Outcomes*	

Category Code Number	3000 KNOWLEDGE, TECHNOLOGY, AND ART FORM OUTCOMES	
3100	*General Knowledge and Understanding**—Familiarity with, analysis and comprehension of, and application of facts and principles across broad areas of study—*breadth* of knowledge and understanding—as a result of dissemination through educational teaching-learning activities.	
	(Categories)	(Examples of Outcome Measures or Indicators)
3110	*Knowledge and Understanding of General Facts and Terminology*—Knowing about and understanding, and having an adequate vocabulary to be able to describe, the reality, existence, and circumstances of particular sensory (observed, heard, felt, etc.) phenomena, objects, people, products, events, conditions, etc., or components thereof.	Students' scores or changes in score on standardized or classroom tests that measure knowledge and understanding of general terminology and/or facts. For example, the Miller Analogies Test focuses entirely on knowledge and understanding of general terminology, and tests like the College Level Examination Program (CLEP) or the Graduate Record Exam (GRE) general exam include coverage of general terminology and facts. Students' self-report of knowledge and understanding about general terminology and facts.
3120	*Knowledge and Understanding of General Processes*—Knowing about and understanding customs, rules and standards for judgments, guidelines, processes, methods, procedures, techniques, trends, and other ways of applying and making use of terminology and facts.	Students' scores or changes in score on standardized or classroom tests measuring comprehension of general conventions, processes, and methodologies. Students' grades in a general application survey course.
3130	*Knowledge and Understanding of General Theory*—Knowing about and understanding principles and generalizations, theoretical formulations, hypotheses, supposition, conjecture, etc.	Students' scores or changes in score on standardized or classroom tests measuring comprehension of general theories in a broad field of study. Students' grades in a general survey course on theories of philosophy.
3140	*Other General Knowledge and Understanding.*	
3200	*Specialized Knowledge and Understanding**—Familiarity with, analysis and comprehension of, and application of facts and principles in particular specialized fields of study—depth of knowledge and understanding—as a result of dissemination through educational teaching/learning activities.	
	(Categories)	(Examples of Outcome Measures or Indicators)
3210	*Knowledge and Understanding of Specialized Facts and Terminology*—Knowing about and understanding, and having an adequate vocabulary to be able to describe the reality, existence, and circumstances of particular sensory (observed, heard, felt, etc.) phenomena, objects, people, products, events, conditions, etc., or components thereof.	Students' scores or changes in score on standardized or classroom tests that measure knowledge and understanding in a narrow, specialized area of study. Professional certification and licensing exams usually focus on this type of knowledge, as do tests like the College Level Examination Program (CLEP) subject exams or the Graduate Record Exam (GRE) area exams. Students' self-report of knowledge and understanding about specialized terminology and facts.
3220	*Knowledge and Understanding of Specialized Processes*—Knowing about and understanding customs, rules and standards for judgments, guidelines, processes, methods, procedures, techniques, trends, and other ways of applying and making use of terminology and facts.	Students' scores or changes in score on standardized or classroom tests measuring comprehension of conventions, processes, methodologies, and techniques unique to particular specialized professions or disciplines. Students' grades in a specialized professional course or program.
3230	*Knowledge and Understanding of Specialized Theory*—Knowing about and understanding principles and generalizations, theoretical formulations, hypotheses, supposition, conjecture, etc.	Students' scores or changes in score on standardized or classroom tests measuring comprehension of specialized theoretical formulations and models. Students' grades in a course that goes into depth about one or more theories or models unique to a specialized discipline or profession.
3240	*Other Specialized Knowledge and Understanding*	
3300	*Research and Scholarship*—Knowledge and understanding, techniques, and physical products resulting from basic and applied research and scholarship.	

*The subcategories used for this category came from Bloom (1956).

Category Code Number	3000 KNOWLEDGE, TECHNOLOGY, AND ART FORM OUTCOMES (continued)	
	(Categories)	(Examples of Outcome Measures or Indicators)
3310	*Research and Scholarship Knowledge and Understanding*—The discovery, development, preservation, and professional dissemination of knowledge and understanding resulting from activities conducted in basic and applied research and scholarship.	Average number of basic research publications, applied research publications, textbooks, or monographs, etc., per student, former student, and/or faculty member over a specific period of time. Number of faculty members and/or former students in the sciences listed in *American Men of Science*.
3320	*Research and Scholarship Products*—Applied techniques (for example, a new therapy treatment in the field of medicine or a new technique in the field of music) and physical products (for example, a new or refined serum) developed from basic and/or applied research and scholarship.	Average number of patents and/or copyrights received per student, former student, and/or faculty member over a given period of time. Average number of awards and citations received per student, former student, and/or faculty member (over a given period of time) for discovery or development of technological products.
3400	*Art Forms and Works*—Reproducing and preserving existing artistic forms and works, and developing new or revised artistic forms and works.	
	(Categories)	(Examples of Outcome Measures or Indicators)
3410	*Architecture*—Outcomes involving the design for construction of buildings, landscape, living complexes, etc.	Number of architectural works completed by students, former students, and/or faculty. Number of awards and other recognitions received for architectural works on the campus commissioned by campus officials.
3420	*Dance*—Outcomes involving preservation or development of forms, works, and performances in the art of dance.	Number of former students receiving recognition for performances in this area. Number of students involved in dance auditions and public performances.
3430	*Debate and Oratory*—Outcomes involving preservation or development of forms and performances in the oratory arts.	Competition record over a period of years of the college's debate team. The average number of graduates each year who go on to some kind of oratorical career.
3440	*Drama*—Outcomes involving the preservation or development of forms, works, and performances in the professional and amateur theatrical arts.	The number of students who enter a professional acting career, and the number acting on an amateur basis. The number of drama performances put on for the local community each year.
3450	*Literature and Writing*—Outcomes involving the preservation or development of forms and works in the production of prose, verse, and other writings.	The average number of literary works each year published by students, former students, and/or faculty members. The number of students and faculty each year who have entered a formal state or national writing competition.
3460	*Music*—Outcomes involving the preservation or development of forms, works, and performances in the professional and amateur theatrical arts.	The number of musical productions put on each year by the college that are open to the public. The number of students involved in public music recitals and other performances.
3470	*Painting, Drawing, and Photography*—Outcomes involving the preservation or development of forms or works in the graphic and pictorial arts.	The number of paintings, and their quality in the campus art gallery. The number of awards won over a certain period of time for pictorial works by students, former students, and faculty members.
3480	*Sculpture*—Outcomes involving the preservation or development of forms or works in the carving, chiseling, casting, modeling, or other sculpturing areas.	The number of sculptures that have been commissioned by the college and placed throughout the campus. The forms of sculpture that have been developed on the campus.
3490	*Other Fine Arts*	
3500	*Other Knowledge, Technology, and Art Form Outcomes*	

Category Code Number	4000 RESOURCE AND SERVICE PROVISION OUTCOMES	
4100	**Provision of Facilities and Events**—The availability, use, and participation in campus happenings, buildings, equipment, and other resources by students, other individuals, and particular groups or communities.	
	(Categories)	(Examples of Outcome Measures or Indicators)
4110	**Provision of Facilities**—Availability and use of campus grounds, buildings, rooms, equipment, etc.	Number of facilities made available to the students during a particular period of time. Total number of hours each facility was used by people in the community, and the number of people-hours of use over a specific period of time.
4120	**Provision or Sponsorship of Events**—Availability and participation in happenings on the campus or off that are provided or stimulated by the college or one of its components.	The number of people who attended athletic events, cultural events, or other events provided and/or sponsored by the college in any one year. The number of column inches of newspaper coverage received by specific events in local, regional, and national newspapers.
4200	**Provision of Direct Services**—The availability, use, and receipt by students, other individuals, and particular groups or communities of assistance, care, or other service.	
	(Categories)	(Examples of Outcome Measures or Indicators)
4210	**Teaching***—Activities and programs designed to instruct and to impart knowledge, skills, attitudes, etc.	Average number of courses taught and number of contact hours per semester in the regular program. Extension courses provided in any one calendar year.
4220	**Advisory and Analytic Assistance**—Activities and programs designed for the purpose of (upon request) offering suggestions, recommendations, counsel, information, calculations, and studies.	Number of advisory and analytic assistance services offered to students, staff, and/or to the public. Number of person-hours spent by staff in providing this assistance over a specific period of time.
4230	**Treatment, Care, and Referral Services**—Helping and direct assistance services, other than those above, provided by the institution, institutional units, and/or institutional staff.	The treatment, care, and referral services offered by the institution and its staff, and health services, day care for children of working mothers, counseling, crisis referral, and drug treatment and the amount these services are used. The reported satisfaction of users of these services with the treatment and care received.
4240	**Provision of Other Services**—An example would be direct civic leadership provided to the community. Another example would be offering keypunching service.	
4300	**Other Resource and Service Provision Outcomes**—An example would be the attention and good will the college draws to the local community because it is located there.	
	*Some people would consider teaching to always be a producer/facilitator activity that leads to outcomes. Others would, however, consider teaching to be an output that results from the interaction of faculty, equipment, students, and other educational resources. Those who hold the first viewpoint should just ignore this category.	

Category Code Number	5000 OTHER MAINTENANCE AND CHANGE OUTCOMES
5100	**Aesthetic-Cultural Conditions**—Preserving or bringing about changes in tastes, level and kinds of aesthetic-cultural emphasis, aesthetic-cultural availability and opportunities, aesthetic-cultural activity and participation, etc.
5200	**Organizational Format, Activity, and Operations**—For organizations, groups, and systems (and their components), maintenance or change in organizational communications, operational methods and interaction, operational effectiveness, organizational relationships, organizational arrangement and configuration, organizational activities and programs, and other such organizational characteristic outcomes.
5300	**Other Maintenance and Change**—Outcomes not covered by any of the other subcategories of "Maintenance" and "Change" in this dimension of the Outcomes Structure. An example might be "destruction of life support in the environment."

APPENDIX B

Major Sources of Information

Major Sources	Information, Instruments, or General Services Available
1. The American College Testing Program 2201 North Dodge St. PO Box 168 Iowa City, IA 52240 (319) 356-3711 Contact: Dr. Aubrey Forrest Director, Instructional Design and Assessment	College *Outcomes* Measures Project. Measures of general education and intellectual skills. An activity inventory, a measurement battery, and an objective test. (See Forrest, 1977.) Also follow-up questionnaires.
2. Association of Governing Boards One Dupont Circle Washington, DC 20036 (202) 296-8400	Self-study guide and criteria for *governing boards*.
3. Association of Research Libraries 1527 New Hampshire Ave., NW Washington, DC 20036 (202) 232-2466	A developing battery of self-study and evaluation tools for *academic libraries*.
4. Webster, Duane E. "The Management Review and Analysis Program: An Assisted Self-Study to Secure Constructive Change in the Management of Research Libraries." *College and Research Libraries*, March 1974, pp. 114–125.	A review of early efforts at *self-study in academic libraries*. ARL has sponsored several other efforts since this report was written.
5. Johnson, Edward R., and Mann, Stuart A. *Organization Development for Academic Libraries*. Westport, CT: Greenwood Press, 1980.	A compendium of methods to improve *academic libraries*.

6. Johnson, Edward. "Academic Library Planning, Self-Study and Management Review." *Journal of Library Administration*, vol. 2, nos. 2–4, 1982.

   A current review of methods for improving *academic libraries.*

7. Kania, Antoinette. *Development of a Model Set of Regional Accreditation Standards for an Academic Library.* Ed.D. Dissertation, Rutgers University, 1983.

   A valuable source of standards and methods to use for *analysis of academic libraries.*

8. Casserly, Mary. *Self-Study and Planned Change in Academic Libraries.* Ph.D. Dissertation, Rutgers University, 1983.

   Theoretical and practical analysis of *self-study and planning in academic libraries.*

9. Educational Testing Service
   Box 2813
   Princeton, NJ 08540
   (609) 921-9000
   Contact: Nancy Beck, Director
   Institutional Research
   Program for Higher Education

   Institutional Goals Inventory; Institutional Functioning Inventory; Student Reactions to College, Undergraduate Assessment Program; Student Instructional Report; Graduate Program Assessment; Global (International) Understanding.

10. Higher Education Management Institute
    c/o American Council on Education
    One Dupont Circle
    Washington, DC 20036
    (202) 833-4727
    Contact: Dr. Richard Webster

    A battery of *management analysis and development* instruments and training elements. *Also,* the ACE Office of Self-Regulation publishes *guidelines for practice in several administrative areas.*

11. Kansas State University,
    Center for Faculty Evaluation
    and Development
    1627 Anderson Ave.
    Box 3000
    Manhattan, KS 66502
    (913) 532-5970

    IDEA instrument for *instructional development and effectiveness assessment*; and department chairperson effectiveness assessment instrument.

12. McBer Company
    137 Newbury St.
    Boston, MA 02116
    (617) 261-5570

    Management analysis instruments; learning style inventory; student self-definition and thematic analysis (general education outcomes).

13. National Center for Higher Education
    Management Systems
    PO Drawer P
    Boulder, CO 80302
    (303) 447-1980

    A whole battery of data collection schemes and *information system constructs*: facilities, students, finances, course information, staff, and goal achievement measures.

14. UCLA Center for Research on Higher
    Education
    320 Moore Hall
    405 Hilgard Ave.
    Los Angeles, CA 90032
    (213) 825-8331
    Contact: Dr. Robert Pace

    Higher Education Measurement and Evaluation Kit and other items.

15. National Association of College and
    University Business Officers
    One Dupont Circle
    Washington, DC 20036
    (202) 296-2346

    Data sheets associated with the NACUBO planning system; standard procedures for reporting and using *financial information.*

16. National Association for Foreign
Student Affairs
1860 19th St., NW
Washington, DC 20009
(202) 462-4811
Attention: Mary Peterson

Self-regulation program and self-study guide for *foreign student and overseas programs*.

17. Council for the Advancement of Standards for
Student Services/Development Programs
c/o Secretary: William L. Thomas
Vice Chancellor for Student Affairs
University of Maryland
College Park, MD 27402

Principles and *guidelines for student services functions* as formulated by representatives of eighteen cooperating professional associations.

Reference Sources

18. Harpel, R. L. "Planning, Budgeting, and
Evaluation in Student Affairs Programs: A
Manual for Administrators." *NASPA
Journal*, Summer 1976, pp. i–xx.

Information on *student services and student affairs instruments*.

19. State University of New York. *Student Affairs
Planning and Evaluation Guidelines*. Albany:
SUNY, 1977.

20. Washington State Student Services
Commission. *A Manual for Student Services*.
Seattle: Washington State Board for
Community College Education, 1977.

21. Griffin, G., and Burks, D. R. *Appraising
Administrative Operations: A Guide for
Universities and Colleges*. Berkeley:
University of California, 1976.

Information on *general administrative services*.

22. Frances, Carol, and Coldren, Sharon I., eds.
Assessing Financial Health. New Directions
for Higher Education Series, no. 26. San
Francisco: Jossey-Bass, 1979.

Information on the *planning system* of the National Association of College and University Business Officers.

23. Jung, Stephen M. "Accreditation: Improving
its Role in Student Consumer Protection in
Postsecondary Education." *North Central
Association Quarterly*, Spring 1977,
pp. 363–373.

A self-study guide regarding *consumer protection*.

24. American Institute for Research in the
Behavioral Sciences. "Institutional Self-
Study Guide for Postsecondary Education."
Washington, DC, 1981 (1818 R St., NW, 20009,
c/o Project on the Status and Education of
Women, Association of American Colleges).

Reference and assessment tool for sex equity—*the status of women on campus*.

APPENDIX C

Sample Alumni Follow-up Questionnaires

A Program Follow-up Survey
An Institutional Follow-up Survey

RUTGERS, THE STATE UNIVERSITY OF NEW JERSEY
GRADUATE SCHOOL OF EDUCATION
DEPARTMENT OF EDUCATIONAL ADMINISTRATION
SUPERVISION AND ADULT EDUCATION

DIRECTIONS: Circle the appropriate response or complete as indicated.

For Coding Purposes Do Not Mark

	Col.

1. In which year did you begin your graduate work in the *Department of Educational Administration, Supervision and Adult Education?* _____   1–2 ___

2. In which year did you graduate? _____   2–3 ___

3. What degree were you awarded?   4 ___
   1) Ed.M.   2) Ed.S.   3) Ed.D.   4) None

4. Please indicate your sex.   1) Male   2) Female   5 ___

5. What is your age?   1) Less than 25   2) 25–30   3) 31–35   6 ___
   4) 36–40   5) 41–45   6) 46–50   7) Over 50

6. How do you describe your race?   7 ___

   1) American Indian or Alaskan Native   4) Hispanic
   2) Asian or Pacific Islander   5) White, Non-Hispanic
   3) Black, Non-Hispanic   6) Other

IF YOU ARE EMPLOYED FULL TIME, PLEASE ANSWER QUESTIONS 7–13.
IF NOT, SKIP TO QUESTION 14.

7. What is the title of your full-time job? _____   8–9 ___

8. Who is your employer? _____

9. Where is your employer located?   State _____   9–10 ___
   County, if N.J. _____   10–11 ___

10. Prior to graduation, what was your long-range occupational goal?   12–13 ___
    List job title: _____

11. What is your current full time salary to nearest $100? $_____   14 ___

12. How related is your present employment to your course of study at GSL?   15 ___
    1) Closely related   2) Somewhat related   3) Not related

13. Which factor was most important in finding first job after graduation from R.U.?   16 ___

    1) Employed at this job while at RU   5) Employment Agency
    2) Faculty member assistance   6) Newspaper
    3) RU Placement Office   7) Direct application to employer
    4) Announcement in professional   8) Friends or relatives
       publication   9) Other

		For Coding Purposes Do Not Mark

14. In how many professional organizations do you hold membership?

15. How many professional articles/books have you had published since graduating from Rutgers? 1) Books _____
     2) Articles _____

16. How satisfied were you with each of the following college services listed below? (Circle one response per item):

	Very Satis- fied	Satisfied	Dissatisfied	Very Dis- satisfied	No Experi- ence With	Col.
1) Admission Procedures	1	2	3	4	5	22 ___
2) Registration Procedures	1	2	3	4	5	23 ___
3) General availability of department faculty for out of class discussion/ assistance	1	2	3	4	5	24 ___
4) Availability of faculty advisers	1	2	3	4	5	25 ___
5) Effectiveness of faculty advisement	1	2	3	4	5	26 ___
6) Grading System	1	2	3	4	5	27 ___
7) Professors' competency in major field	1	2	3	4	5	28 ___
8) Departmental faculty quality of instruction	1	2	3	4	5	29 ___
9) Variety of course offerings	1	2	3	4	5	30 ___
10) Library facilities	1	2	3	4	5	31 ___
11) Time when courses are scheduled	1	2	3	4	5	32 ___
12) Course content in major	1	2	3	4	5	33 ___
13) Innovative modes of instruction	1	2	3	4	5	34 ___
14) Other, please specify	1	2	3	4	5	35 ___

Col. 17 (for questions 14)
18–19, 20–21 (for question 15)

_____

_____

Col.

36 ___

17. If you had the opportunity to select a graduate institution again,
all things being equal, would you choose Rutgers University?
(Circle one)
1) Yes   2) No   3) Undecided

18. How helpful were your experiences in the Department of Administration, Supervision
and Adult Education in reaching each of the goals listed below? (Circle one response
for each item.)

	Very Helpful	Helpful	Little Help	No Help	Not a Goal of Mine		
1) To prepare for a new career	1	2	3	4	5	37	___
2) To increase my knowledge in Administration and/or Adult Education	1	2	3	4	5	38	___
3) To improve my leadership skills	1	2	3	4	5	39	___
4) To improve my technical skills required in my present job	1	2	3	4	5	40	___
5) To increase my chances for a possible raise and/or promotion in my present job	1	2	3	4	5	41	___
6) To increase my research skills	1	2	3	4	5	42	___
7) To increase my understanding of organizations	1	2	3	4	5	43	___
8) To increase my human relations skills	1	2	3	4	5	44	___
9) To increase my concept skills	1	2	3	4	5	45	___
10) To increase my understanding of utilizing theory in practice	1	2	3	4	5	46	___

	For Coding Purposes Do Not Mark
	Col.

19. Courses taken within the Department of Educational Administration, Supervision and Adult Education that you consider *Most valuable.*

1) _____ 47–49 ___
2) _____ 50–52 ___
3) _____ 53–55 ___

20. Courses taken with the Department of Educational Administration, Supervision and Adult Education that you consider *Least valuable.*

1) _____ 56–58 ___
2) _____ 59–61 ___
3) _____ 62–64 ___

21. Should a supervised internship in a practice setting be required of degree candidates in:

Adult Education?   1) Yes   2) No   3) Undecided   65   ___
Administration and Supervision?   1) Yes   2) No   3) Undecided   66   ___

22. Viewing my whole experiences at the Graduate School of Education, it was: (Circle one)

1) An integrated, coherent, logically cohesive program   67   ___
2) A series of courses with most integrated into a program
3) A series of courses with little integration
4) A series of courses with *no* integration

23. Do you feel there was duplication in departmental course content? (Circle one)

1) Much duplication   2) Some   3) Little   4) None   68   ___
If you circled 1 or 2 please explain where the duplication is occurring. _____

_____

24. How much theoretical emphasis should be included in departmental courses?   69   ___

   1   2   3   4   5   6   7
Much less   About right   Much more

25. How much practical emphasis should be included in departmental courses?   70   ___

   1   2   3   4   5   6   7
Much less   About   Much more
practical   right   practical
emphasis   emphasis

26. What are the department's greatest strengths?

27. What are the department's greatest weaknesses?

28. General comments (Use back if necessary)
    About Rutgers:

    About this survey form:

THANK YOU FOR YOUR COOPERATION

MERCY COLLEGE Office of the President · 555 Broadway, Dobbs Ferry, New York 10522 · 914 693-4500

MIDDLE STATES STEERING COMMITTEE

ADMA D'HEURLE, Ph.D.
Professor, Psychology

ANN E. GROW, Ph.D.
Professor, Philosophy
and Social Sciences

EILEEN KAPPY, B.S.
Secretary of the Corporation

MARY KRAETZER, Ph.D.
Associate Professor, Sociology

WILLIAM LINDSEY, M.A.
Assistant Dean for College
Opportunity Programs

JAMES F. MELVILLE, JR., Ph.D.
Dean for Academic Affairs

ANDREW G. NELSON, M.A.
Dean for Admissions
and Records

January, 1977

Dear Mercy College Graduate, Class of '74:

Mercy College is conducting a study of the effectiveness of
its academic programs and student services. This study is
an integral part of the College's self-evaluation in
preparation for a visit by the Middle States Association
Commission on Higher Education which accredits the College.
The enclosed questionnaire is a most important, serious
and useful part of the over-all self study process.

Please take a few minutes to complete the questionnaire and
return it by February 1, 1977, in the stamped, self-addressed
envelope which has been provided.

Please do respond. We are using a limited sample for our
study and every response is important. This is an anonymous
questionnaire. The results will not be identified with you
in any way. All data will be compiled and used solely for
the purpose of institutional improvement.

Thank you for your assistance and your continued interest
in your alma mater.

Sincerely,

Dr. Donald Grunewald
President

MERCY COLLEGE SELF-STUDY QUESTIONNAIRE

I. BACKGROUND INFORMATION:
(Please check the appropriate box)

Year of graduation: 1971 (   )   1974 (   )

Sex: Male (   )   Female (   )

Degree received: Bachelor of Arts (   )   Bachelor of Science (   )

Were you a transfer student from another college or university?   Yes (   )   No (   )

I attended most semesters as a: Full-time Student (   )   Part-time Student (   )

Were you a HEOP or CLP student at Mercy College?   Yes (   )   No (   )

Final cumulative grade point average at Mercy College:

   3.51 - 4.00 (   )   3.01 - 3.50 (   )   2.51 - 3.00 (   )   2.00 - 2.50 (   )

Major concentration at Mercy College:

Behavioral Sciences........... ( )	History.................... ( )	Social Sciences............... ( )
Biology.................... ( )	Interdisciplinary Studies....... ( )	Social Work.................. ( )
Business Administration....... ( )	Italian.................... ( )	Sociology................... ( )
Criminal Justice.............. ( )	Mathematics................. ( )	Spanish.................... ( )
English.................... ( )	Modern Foreign Languages..... ( )	Speech.................... ( )
French.................... ( )	Music.................... ( )	Speech Pathology............. ( )
	Psychology................. ( )	

II. GENERAL ACTIVITIES AND ACCOMPLISHMENTS SINCE LEAVING MERCY COLLEGE:
(Please check any and all appropriate items)

A. Since leaving Mercy College, I have . . .

1. been employed in an area related to my major concentration at Mercy .... (   )

2. been employed in an area related to my teacher education program at Mercy .... (   )

3. attended graduate or professional school .... (   )

4. received my master's degree................... (   )

5. received my doctorate .... (   )

6. been married .... (   )

7. had children............................ (   )

8. served in the armed forces.................... (   )

9. been active in politics....................... (   )

10. been active in a professional organization or other agency .... (   )

11. been an active volunteer for a social service or other agency .... (   )

12. been an active member of a service organization (Rotary, Lions, League of Women Voters, etc.) ... (   )

13. started or assumed ownership of my own business .... (   )

14. held an elective office in city, regional, state or national government .... (   )

15. served as a local school board member.......... (   )

16. held a military appointment at the rank of captain (or the equivalent) or above .... (   )

17. published a newspaper, journal or magazine article .... (   )

18. written a book which has been published .... (   )

19. exhibited my art work in a show .... (   )

20. served as a middle level manager in a corporation .... (   )

21. served as an executive officer of a corporation .... (   )

22. travelled extensively outside the continental United States .... (   )

B. My present primary vocation or job category is . . .

1. owner/entrepreneur of a business.............. (   )

2. manager/executive of a business or in a corporation .... (   )

3. government official .... (   )

4. teacher/research/artist/writer .... (   )

5. doctor, lawyer or similar professional .... (   )

6. skilled craftsman......................... (   )

7. service worker .... (   )

8. military service .... (   )

9. civil service employee .... (   )

10. other (please specify) ——————————

11. not employed by choice.................... (   )

12. not employed, not by choice................. (   )

C. In the last twelve months
I have:

	Often or Most of the Time	Occasionally or Part of the Time	Never or None of the Time
1. regularly read a major newspaper or news magazine...	( )	( )	( )
2. read books for enjoyment	( )	( )	( )
3. visited a museum	( )	( )	( )
4. attended a concert	( )	( )	( )
5. written a piece for the purpose of publication	( )	( )	( )
6. volunteered my services to a political, social or charitable cause	( )	( )	( )
7. created a work of art for the purpose of display	( )	( )	( )
8. travelled outside the continental U.S.	( )	( )	( )
9. "run" for an elective office of some kind	( )	( )	( )
10. taken a course of some kind	( )	( )	( )

III. OPINIONS ABOUT THE FULFILLMENT OF COLLEGE GOALS

A. The goals of Mercy College are listed below. Based on your personal experience at Mercy and on your experiences since graduation, please check the box which indicates the extent to which you feel the college has fulfilled its goals:

	Completely	Largely	Slightly	Not at All	Don't Know
1. Mercy College (provides) education *reflective of traditional values*	( )	( )	( )	( )	( )
2. (and) *reflective of contemporary trends*	( )	( )	( )	( )	( )
3. (to enable) *students to fulfill their potential*	( )	( )	( )	( )	( )
4. (and to) *serve society*	( )	( )	( )	( )	( )
5. (Mercy makes) a special commitment to those students returning to academic life	( )	( )	( )	( )	( )
6. (Mercy makes) a special commitment to the culturally deprived	( )	( )	( )	( )	( )
7. (Mercy makes) a special commitment to students with physical handicaps	( )	( )	( )	( )	( )

B. With respect to you personally, has your Mercy College Education:

	Completely	Largely	Slightly	Not at All	Don't Know
1. prepared you to become a functioning citizen of the community?	( )	( )	( )	( )	( )
2. stimulated your intellectual growth?	( )	( )	( )	( )	( )
3. stimulated your intellectual maturity?	( )	( )	( )	( )	( )
4. provided you with the tools needed to communicate effectively and helped you to interpret intelligently the communication of others?	( )	( )	( )	( )	( )
5. given you a sense of literary and artistic form?	( )	( )	( )	( )	( )
6. given you an awareness of history, behavioral science and natural science?	( )	( )	( )	( )	( )
7. given you a concentrated, in-depth and detailed knowledge of one discipline or professional field?	( )	( )	( )	( )	( )

C. Do you feel that Mercy College:

	Completely	Largely	Slightly	Not at All	Don't Know
1. has remained committed to the liberal arts and sciences?	( )	( )	( )	( )	( )
2. employs diversity, flexibility, and novel methods and approaches in its academic programs?	( )	( )	( )	( )	( )
3. employs diversity, flexibility, and novel methods and approaches in its services to students?	( )	( )	( )	( )	( )

	Completely	Largely	Slightly	Not at All	Don't Know
D. Are the goals of Mercy College as specified or implied in items (1) through (3) above appropriate?	( )	( )	( )	( )	( )
E. Has Mercy College helped you to achieve *your* personal goals?	( )	( )	( )	( )	( )
F. With respect to preparing me for my present job or type of career, my education experience at Mercy College was beneficial.	( )	( )	( )	( )	( )

G. Specifically and based on my personal experiece, I would rate Mercy College preparation in the following areas as:

	Excellent	Above Average	Average	Below Average	Poor
1. writing skills	( )	( )	( )	( )	( )
2. critical thinking/problem solving	( )	( )	( )	( )	( )
3. technical skills in my discipline	( )	( )	( )	( )	( )
4. public speaking	( )	( )	( )	( )	( )
5. general liberal arts	( )	( )	( )	( )	( )
6. understanding of myself	( )	( )	( )	( )	( )
7. development of my continued interest in self development	( )	( )	( )	( )	( )
8. development of my interest in leadership and service to others	( )	( )	( )	( )	( )

H. If I had it to do again, I would attend Mercy College ..... Yes ( )   No ( )   Don't Know ( )

I. I would recommend that others attend Mercy College .... Yes ( )   No ( )   Don't Know ( )

J. Here are suggestions I have for improving Mercy College:

1. _____

_____

2. _____

_____

3. _____

_____

K. General Comments:_____

_____

_____

_____

_____

_____

_____

_____

_____

Thank You!

APPENDIX D

Sample Tables of Contents and Other Organizational Descriptions of Self-Study Reports

Brookdale Community College—Organized
  According to Goals Statements
John F. Kennedy University—Organized
  According to Accreditation Standards
University of Southern California—
  Comprehensive Self-Study Report
University of California, Riverside—A Current
  Special-Studies Approach Report
North Country Community College—
  Comprehensive with Special-Emphasis Report

BROOKDALE COMMUNITY COLLEGE, LINCROFT, N.J.
INSTITUTIONAL SELF-STUDY REPORT 1979

Table of Contents

BROOKDALE COMMUNITY COLLEGE

Preliminary Outline of The Self-Study Process

I. Introduction

The purpose of the self-study is to analyze the educational resources and effectiveness of Brookdale Community College in light of its Philosophy, Mission, and Goals as revised and approved by the Board of Trustees on February 26, 1976.

The Commission on Higher Education of the Middle States Association accredited the College in June of 1972, with a review for reaffirmation due in 1977–78. At the request of the College, the Commission on Higher Education granted a delay in the evaluation visit until the Spring of 1979.

In view of the fact that the College has embarked upon a long-range planning project which has as its first step in the project a self-study, this study will also meet the need for the Middle States Evaluation.

II. The Self-Study Process

A. Goals:

The nine Goals of the College express desired end results. These goals reflect the values and beliefs expressed in the College's statements of philosophy and mission. They accommodate the needs of diverse constituencies while allowing responsiveness to changing societal demands. Taken together, the philosophy, mission and goals comprise the *Philosophical Platform* of the College, which stresses Brookdale's commitment to providing postsecondary educational opportunities for the people of Monmouth County.

During the self-study process, questions such as the following must be answered:

Is the College successfully doing what it says it is doing?
Are there additional services which the College should be providing in order to better implement its goals?
Does it offer programs and services which no longer serve the postsecondary educational needs of the community?
Is the present set of goals still appropriate for Brookdale?
Will resources continue to be available to conduct the necessary programs and services?

In order to answer these questions and others, it is necessary to move beyond the goals to consider more measurable expressions of what the College is currently doing.

B. Objectives:

While its goals provide a general, broad image of what the institution is striving to become, its objectives specify, in measureable terms, desired results for programs and services over shorter periods of time (e.g., one year). Thus, the focus for the institutional self-study must be the objectives.

C. Goals Committees:

The Self-Study will be carried out by five Goals Committees. Each Goals Committee will be responsible for assessing the achievement of the following College Goals:

Goals Committee I—(College Goals 1 and 3)

College Goal 1: Maintain an institution that is open to those who desire to learn.
College Goal 3: Provide an educational environment that facilitates human development.

Goals Committee II—(College Goals 2 and 4)

College Goal 2: Provide an educational program that assists students in formulating realistic career goals and prepares them for achievement of those goals.
College Goal 4: Provide an educational program that accommodates individual differences in learning styles, learning rates, and prior knowledge.

Goals Committee III—(College Goals 5 and 6)

College Goal 5:   Utilize the total resources of the community as a laboratory for learning.

College Goal 6:   Implement or cooperate in programs which contribute to the educational, economic, social and cultural development of the Monmouth County community.

Goals Committee IV—(College Goal 7)

College Goal 7:   Maintain an institution which contributes to the growth and development of the members of the College staff.

Goals Committee V—(College Goals 8 and 9)

College Goal 8:   Implement the concept of accountability by defining outcomes, differentiating processes, and evaluating results for all undertakings.

College Goal 9:   Demonstrate both fiscal responsibility and educational accountability to the community at large.

Each Goals Committee will prepare plans for assessing the College's current achievement of its Goals. A separate plan will be written for each Goal and each plan will include the following:

1. College Units to be studied
2. Information required from each unit
3. Methods to be used for gathering, validating and processing information.

III. Reports

A. Goals Committees' Reports

The Goals Committees' Reports will include the following:
1. 1977–78 objectives relating to Goal and units responsible for those objectives.
2. Strengths—Information describing the achievement of objectives for Goal.
3. Weaknesses—Underlying problems which restricted achievement of objectives for 1977–78.
4. Recommendations based on information obtained.

B. Institutional Report

The final Institutional Self-Study Report will be organized around nine chapters. Each chapter will bear the title of one of the nine College Goals, and will follow the format of the reports from the Goals Committees, as described above.

12/16/77

LIST OF MATERIALS ON FILE FOR MIDDLE STATES EVALUATION TEAM

The following materials are on file in the Conference Room reserved for the Team, or as indicated:

FILE NO. 1 . . . . Self-Study Data for Chapter 1 (Goal No. 1)

FILE NO. 2 . . . . Self-Study Data for Chapter 2 (Goal No. 2)

FILE NO. 3 . . . . Self-Study Data for Chapter 3 (Goal No. 3)

FILE NO. 4 . . . . Self-Study Data for Chapter 4 (Goal No. 4)

FILE NO. 5 . . . . Self-Study Data for Chapter 5 (Goal No. 5)

FILE NO. 6 . . . . Self-Study Data for Chapter 6 (Goal No. 6)

FILE NO. 7 . . . . Self-Study Data for Chapter 7 (Goal No. 7)

FILE NO. 8 . . . . Self-Study Data for Chapter 8 (Goal No. 8)

FILE NO. 9 . . . . Self-Study Data for Chapter 9 (Goal No. 9)

FILE NO. 10 . . . . Institutional Self-Study Report, 1979

FILE NO. 11 . . . . Institutional Self-Study Report, 1972, with Team Chairman Report, and Follow-up Reports to Middle States

FILE NO. 12 . . . . College Catalog, 1978/80

FILE NO. 13 . . . . Student Handbook

FILE NO. 14 . . . . Staff Handbook

FILE NO. 15 . . . . Faculty Agreement

FILE NO. 16 . . . . NASA Agreement

FILE NO. 17 . . . . Administrative Association Agreement

FILE NO. 18 . . . . Police Agreement

FILE NO. 19 . . . . Board of Trustees Policies Manual

FILE NO. 20 . . . . College Regulation Manual

FILE NO. 21 . . . . Faculty Schedules

FILE NO. 22 . . . . Goals and Objectives Manual, 1977–78

FILE NO. 23 . . . . Position Descriptions Book

FILE NO. 24 . . . . General Learning Corporation Reports—Master Plans

FILE NO. 25 . . . . Book of Program Cost Reports

FILE NO. 26 . . . . List of Memberships

FILE NO. 27 . . . . Sample Learning Programs from each Institute

FILE NO. 28 . . . . Student Government Constitution

FILE NO. 60 . . . . Annual Report 1977–78—Educational Services Division

FILE NO. 61 . . . . Annual Report 1977–78—Administrative Services Division

FILE NO. 62 . . . . Career Services Program

On File in Personnel Office . . . . Affirmative Action Plan

On File in President's Office . . . . Board of Trustees Minutes Book

On File in Office of Vice President/Treasurer . . . . Audit Reports

The following Studies and Reports are on File in the Research Office:

Faculty Load Report, Winter Term '79

Opening Enrollment, Winter Term '79

Grades Analysis Report, Fall Term '78

Degrees Awarded, 1971–78

Credits Earned—Credits Enrolled, Fall Term, '78

Cumulative Achievement, Fall Term, '78

Student Progress Report (Possibly)

Students Enrolled in Development Courses (Possibly)

HEGIS Reports

JOHN F. KENNEDY UNIVERSITY, ORINDA, CALIFORNIA, INSTITUTIONAL SELF-STUDY REPORT, APRIL 1979

Table of Contents

---

* Standards of the Accrediting Commission for Senior Colleges and Universities, Western Association of Schools and Colleges.

UNIVERSITY OF SOUTHERN CALIFORNIA REACCREDITATION REPORT SUBMITTED TO THE WESTERN ASSOCIATION OF SCHOOLS AND COLLEGES, MARCH 1976

Contents

UNIVERSITY OF CALIFORNIA, RIVERSIDE, REACCREDITATION REPORT, DECEMBER 1977

Table of Contents

* Recently completed study

NORTH COUNTRY COMMUNITY COLLEGE, SARANAC LAKE, N.Y.
INSTITUTIONAL SELF-STUDY, 1979

Table of Contents